Advances in the Study of

AGGRESSION

Volume 1

Contributors

D. Caroline Blanchard
Robert J. Blanchard
Paul Frédric Brain
Leonard D. Eron
L. Rowell Huesmann
Dan Olweus
Gerald R. Patterson
J. P. Scott

Advances in the Study of

AGGRESSION

Edited by

Robert J. Blanchard

Department of Psychology
University of Hawaii at Manoa
Honolulu, Hawaii

D. Caroline Blanchard

Békésy Laboratory of Neurobiology
University of Hawaii at Manoa
Honolulu, Hawaii

Volume 1

1984

 ACADEMIC PRESS, INC.

(Harcourt Brace Jovanovich, Publishers)

Orlando   San Diego   New York   London

Toronto   Montreal   Sydney   Tokyo

ACADEMIC PRESS, INC.
Orlando, Florida 32887

United Kingdom Edition published by
ACADEMIC PRESS, INC. (LONDON) LTD.
24/28 Oval Road, London NW1 7DX

ISBN 0-12-037701-2

ISSN 0748-6103

PRINTED IN THE UNITED STATES OF AMERICA

84 85 86 87   9 8 7 6 5 4 3 2 1

Contents

Contributors

Numbers in parentheses indicate the pages on which the authors' contributions begin.

D. Caroline Blanchard (1), Békésy Laboratory of Neurobiology, University of Hawaii at Manoa, Honolulu, Hawaii 96822

Robert J. Blanchard (1), Department of Psychology, University of Hawaii at Manoa, Honolulu, Hawaii 96822

Paul Frédric Brain (63), Department of Zoology, University College of Swansea, Swansea SA2 8PP, Wales

Leonard D. Eron (139), Department of Psychology, University of Illinois at Chicago, Chicago, Illinois 60680

L. Rowell Huesmann (139), Department of Psychology, University of Illinois at Chicago, Chicago, Illinois 60680

Dan Olweus (103), Department of Personality Psychology, University of Bergen, Bergen, Norway

Gerald R. Patterson (173), Oregon Social Learning Center, 207 East Fifth Street, Eugene, Oregon 97401

J. P. Scott (217), Department of Psychology, Bowling Green State University, Bowling Green, Ohio 43403 and Department of Psychology, Tufts University, Medford, Massachusetts 02155

Preface

This volume inaugurates the series *Advances in the Study of Aggression*. The preface to the first volume is obviously a good place to explain some of the aims and intentions that went into the setting up of such a series. First, the series is by and, to a considerable degree, for scientists. The fact that such a series is possible is itself reflective of the tremendous upsurge of scientific research on aggression that has occurred over the past decade or two. This research cannot be identified with conventional discipline rubrics such as psychology, sociology, or anthropology. In fact, aggression research is really not identifiable with social sciences exclusively, since many of the factors promoting or controlling aggression (and manipulated in attempts to modify aggression on the human level) are physiological, e.g., endocrines, neurotransmitters, and system-specific brain activity. At the same time, however, aggressive behavior does occur in a social context, accompanied—in people at least—by subjective states that are of greatest interest to the psychologist.

The topic holding together all of these diverse research approaches had better be pretty robust. Fortunately, it is. There have long been debate and disagreement in the scientific community about the origins of aggression and its relative dependence on "innate" versus experiential factors. A more sophisticated version of this "nature–nurture" controversy will probably emerge from time to time as this series progresses, in the form of information and analysis concerning the interaction of biological and social events in the production of aggressive behaviors. However, regardless of whether one views aggression as a natural and normal feature of life, or as a sort of epiphenomenon arising largely as the result of suboptimal social conditions, there is no question whatever that it exists. Aggression is a characteristic behavior pattern in every species of higher animal in which it has been sought through scientific analysis. It is one of a handful of behavior patterns—eating, drinking, sleeping, sexual activity, parental care are some others—that not only occur in all mammals (and frequently in submammalian forms as well) but are also sufficiently similar to human behaviors as to be almost instantly recognizable as they are seen in different species. Mistakes have sometimes even been made with this relatively clear and straightforward behavior system. On the whole, however, aggression is a concept that both scientists and nonscientists can describe, agree on, and identify when it occurs. It is something that exists independently of the efforts that have been made to identify it.

Another factor that makes this series especially timely is that aggression is important. The point has been made elsewhere in this volume. Moreover, it is self-evident: There is no level of human life, from the day-to-day experience of the individual up to the highest levels of social and political organization, at which aggression is not a factor. Aggression is a major force in both the creation and the destruction of human social organizations, as it is in the social organizations of lower animals.

It is this two-headed role of aggression that makes clear analysis especially important. If aggressiveness were purely a "disease," an abnormal manifestation of a system that works quite differently than when it is "well," then scientific research and analysis could be aimed unequivocally toward knowledge leading to the ability to control or eliminate this dysfunctional phenomenon. On the other hand, many biological views (and, increasingly, those for the social sciences as well) stress that it may also be functional and adaptive. We must therefore be able not only to determine those biological, experiential, and social factors that produce aggression, but also to differentiate in some analytically meaningful fashion those instances of aggression that are normal and/or constructive, from those that are abnormal and/or destructive. The ultimate goal is to control the latter while not interfering with the former.

All of this requires an immense body of knowledge, based on a formidable amount of work. Not a volume, but a series. This first volume is seen as an attempt to span some of the variety of aggression research, pinpointing areas in which phenomena or concepts that have arisen or been tested extensively with animal models are now being applied to human aggression. It thus provides a sort of sampler of the problems and rewards to be found in moving from a more simple system, subhuman animals, for which precise controls and experimental manipulations are routinely possible, to the much more complex and difficult-to-manipulate human level. Except for this willingness to try to move between animal-based models and human behavior, the viewpoints represented in this volume have little in common. The approaches with which they are identified range from biological, through sociobiological, to strictly social. On the other hand, these approaches are hardly exclusive, and we would suspect that proponents of each approach might readily admit that the other factors are also greatly influential: Aggression is a complex, multiply determined phenomenon. Some view of the complexity of the system, as it applies to people, may be seen in the article by Olweus. His approach stems, much less directly than do the others, from animal models and theories, but it is especially important in showing how some of the factors emphasized in other approaches can actually combine to predict and explain certain types of human aggression.

This, perhaps, is the final conceptual trigger for the new series. Aggression is an important, and *analyzable* phenomenon in the behavior of higher animals. The history of science has provided a number of examples of topic areas that suddenly coalesced, with questions that had been debated for years being answered, with phenomena formerly regarded as independent being recognized as identical or complementary. We would be foolish indeed to claim that aggression research was on the verge of such closure. However, one can begin to sense that a real movement is underway, that advance in the study of aggression is a fact, not merely the title of a series of books. This progress may be measured in terms of numbers, such as the great increase in aggression papers indexed and cited in relevant bibliographic sources, or in membership of the thriving "International Society for Research on Aggression," founded in 1972. But such numbers are more a reflection of the optimism of scientists than the cause of it. Those of us in any one of the diverse areas of aggression research can now talk meaningfully with our opposite numbers in different disciplines and from different theoretical backgrounds. Not, certainly, with perfect agreement, but at least with assurance that we are discussing the same phenomenon, in a language that is translatable into our own.

Future volumes in this series will each focus on an integrative topic, with different approaches being brought to bear on an important aspect of aggression. For example, Volume 2, which is now in preparation, will involve the control of aggression. This organizational focus will thus foster communication, not only between author and reader, but also between different authors and different approaches to the study of aggression. It is our sincere hope that this series will be an important mechanism in the understanding of a phenomenon with which all of our lives are so intimately involved.

Robert J. Blanchard
D. Caroline Blanchard

Affect and Aggression: An Animal Model Applied to Human Behavior

D. CAROLINE BLANCHARD *and*
ROBERT J. BLANCHARD

University of Hawaii at Manoa, Honolulu, Hawaii

*Advances in the
Study of Aggression, Volume 1*

I. INTRODUCTION

Given our daily bombardment by events reflecting or embodying aggression, it might be thought unnecessary to attempt to illustrate the importance of understanding aggressive phenomena. But too much experience engenders its own protections, and most of us continue to function adequately, indeed cheerfully, in a world in which both the quality and the very continuation of human life are periled by threats of aggression.

Nevertheless, when individuals are touched directly by aggressive acts or their consequences, the potency of this behavior system is immediately apparent: There is nothing like personal experience of anger to make one understand the urge to hurt someone else; nothing like being a victim to illustrate the costs of aggression, in pain, in dollars, in risk to human relationships and social institutions. For perpetrator and victim, and indeed for the societies which must deal with both of them, aggression raises inevitable questions: Why has this happened? How could it have been controlled? Who, and what, is to blame?

It has long been a tenet of science that knowledge is good in and of itself, without need for justification in terms of application of this knowledge to human affairs. In fact, researchers sometimes make a point of indicating that they do not care if their research has any ultimate relevance to important human phenomena. Under some circumstances neither of these is an unreasonable position, and each may be further justified on the basis that "pure" science often does yield information that proves to be very relevant indeed to human life.

On the other hand, if a phenomenon is important, and if it occurs in both humans and lower species, how much better to use the methodological precision and the analytic power of science to create a body of knowledge designed in part to help with human problems! This is an age in which there is widespread skepticism about the ability of science—social science in particular—to provide meaningful insights into important problems. We personally do not share this skepticism, but must admit that the track record is very spotty.

What is required in order to improve this record is for some portions of the schism between basic and applied research to be bridged. The disinterested curiosity and willingness to try new models and new techniques that is typical of much basic research should be combined with the explicit focus on specific phenomena typical of applied work. This combination might, in fact, ultimately produce better science as well as better application, by avoiding the more scattershot research strategies that sometimes typify basic research in underdeveloped fields.

Aggression is a phenomenon that may be particularly amenable to such an approach. It exists, not as a concept invented by scientists or philosophers, but as a characteristic feature in the evolution of higher animal life. As such, there is much reason to believe that the principles that account for, and control, aggression in the highest animals known—ourselves—are based in large part on causal and control factors that operate in rather analogous fashion in somewhat lower animals.

This is not to say that understanding aggression in rats will enable similar prediction and control of human aggression: It is not in question that human behavior is more complex, and more responsive to experience than that of a rat. It is also unquestionable that humans have a richer experience, shaped by cultural and social forces in addition to the rather more "physical" environment of the rat. Finally, humans have greater capacity to use that experience to conceptualize reality and in turn base their behaviors, at least in part, on these conceptions. In short, no one is arguing that an understanding of aggression, or sex, or learning in lower animals can be transferred in any simple and direct fashion to people.

Despite these caveats, it seems to us to be a superior research strategy to begin with the assumption (for which there is considerable evidence) of an evolutionary continuity between animals and people for aggression and fear and the major factors that control them. This assumption suggests that studies of animal aggression and defense may provide valuable insight into similar behavior patterns in people, insofar as good examples of these behaviors on the animal level are selected for analysis. The best example, or model, is likely to be the one that permits the fullest range of behaviors, in a situation as close as possible to the environment in which the subject species has evolved. The only acceptable limitations on these two requirements for a model are those associated with the ability of the experimenter to observe behaviors as fully as possible, and to manipulate major variables in order to reap the substantial benefits of experimental, as well as observational, tests and analyses.

Another caveat is that attempts to make even tentative generalizations from animal behavior to human behavior should be based on analyses that are systematic, thorough, and validated for the original species. Application of theories arising from poorly analyzed or irrelevant animal models to suggest methods for intervention in human affairs has much more potential for damage than for good. People have been in the business of analyzing other people for a million years or more, and the conventional wisdom with reference to common human emotions and actions is probably more accurate than most of the simple causal relationship statements arising from current research on animal behavior.

This chapter is therefore explicitly aimed at clarification of the relevance of animal aggression research to human aggression. We shall first consider an animal model and an analysis based on this model, and then attempt to construct a brief sociobiological view of aggression and its immediate determinants over a number of mammalian species. Finally, we shall describe some features of human aggression and endeavor to link these to the animal model as it was "expanded" in terms of our view of human evolution.

II. AGGRESSION: AN ANALYTIC APPROACH

In the "real world" of animals, as well as that of man, acts that appear to reflect aggressiveness are common: Dogs, cats, and other household pets bite, scratch, or otherwise do injury to children or adults who have frightened, teased, or otherwise annoyed these animals; territorial animals, usually males, drive off intruding males; males of many species fight over females in heat; cats kill birds and eat them, mice kill crickets and eat them (etc.); most adult and juvenile animals of nondomesticated vertebrate species will forcefully resist being approached and handled by humans, in much the same fashion that they forcefully resist approach by potential predators, or attacking members of their own species.

Are all of these activities the products of a single neurobehavioral system? Is there an organization to aggressive behaviors? What criteria should we employ to demonstrate such an organization?

Beginning with the last question first, where should the analysis of an elaborate behavior pattern such as aggression begin? What is the best strategy to approach so complex an issue? One tactic described in an influential paper some years ago (Moyer, 1968) is to categorize ag-

gressive episodes in terms of the sex, or the status of the two combatants, or, in terms of the situation occasioning the encounter (cf. predation, territorial defense, irritable aggression).

This is quite a sophisticated approach, reflecting cognizance of stimulus variables in the form of the target animal, as these may be modified
by situational factors, plus recognizing that different potential aggressors may react with systematically different behaviors to these compound stimuli. This sophistication reflects the acknowledged complexity
of aggression, even on the animal level, and it received and still receives,
much attention by psychologists.

A second dominant approach in the history of recent psychological
treatment of animal aggression consists of attempts to relate aggression
to single causal factors such as pain (cf. Ulrich & Azrin, 1962) or frustration (Dollard, Doob, Miller, Mowrer, & Sears, 1939). Such concepts involve the implicit position that aggression is a unitary phenomenon,
with a specific stimulus configuration or event, or, an internal reaction
of the subject to this configuration or event, as its cause.

Students of behavior traditionally break down the major variables
with which they are concerned into three components: stimulus variables, organismic variables, and response variables. It is readily seen
that the "one-cause" models of aggression are either concerned with the
effects of specific stimuli (including complex stimulus contingencies) or
organismic variables on aggressive behaviors. The specific view depends on the theorist, in that frustration, for example, may be viewed
either as a set of stimulus events or as the normal emotional reaction to
such events.

The Moyer classification system appears to encompass a more complex and wider range of phenomena by acknowledging that events other
than those delineated in the single-cause models may produce aggression, and by suggesting that stimulus and organismic variables may
interact to result in aggressive tendencies. Nevertheless, it is notable
that this analysis remains largely fixed on stimulus and organismic
variables.

The set of variables that both of these approaches neglect is analytically the most important of all. We hold that behavior patterns are best
differentiated in terms of behaviors, not only by the conditions that elicit
or occasion them. The classification and functional analysis of any complex behavior system must begin with, and proceed in the light of, an
adequate description of the full range of the actions composing that
system. The structure and organization of natural behavior must provide the starting point for an analysis.

The problem, in terms of classic "psychological" measures of animal aggression, is that the behavioral choices available to an animal subject have usually been limited by the constraints of the test situation, which often provided no real opponent, and no opportunity to flee. Additionally, experimenters have often tended to ignore behaviors for which the significance was yet not understood, or—worse yet—to assume that one response is as good as another to measure behavior. Thus "biting wood" (for rats) and "crying" (in babies) are among the many dubious "aggression measures" reported in the psychological literature. In fact, regardless of the single measure used if an animal's behavior is only measured as "bite or no bite," or "bar press or no bar press," then most of the information in that animal's behavior is likely to be lost. The only way that the full power of behavioral analysis can be used is to arrange circumstances so as to permit as rich a behavioral expression as is possible, by animals that—in terms of experience as well as sex and age variation—might be expected to show the full range of relevant acts.

Actually, considerable attention has been given to the description of aggressive behavior patterns in lower mammals. In particular one might note the classic work of Grant (1963) on agonistic behaviors in laboratory rats and that of Eibl-Eibesfelt (1960) on wild rats. Ewer (1971) took this rat classification scheme the logical step further, applying it to wild *R. rattus* in conditions described as "semi-domestication" (these animals were wild living but were fed in certain places both to make them easily visible and to induce conflict over food items).

What Grant (1963) and Ewer (1971) did for rats, Leyhausen did for cats. Leyhausen's magnificent treatise, originally published in 1956, was not translated into English (with updating and extensions) until 1979. However, it is not really possible to believe that earlier availability of this classic would have produced an instant shortcut through the methodological morass that characterized much "aggression" work in America during the 1960s and 1970s: After all, Paul Scott's (1958) equally detailed and meticulously analyzed work on mice [and dogs (Scott & Fuller, 1965), with note of other species] and S. A. Barnett's (1963) work combining situational–species variables with behavioral detail to describe social behaviors of rats, were both available, in English, from an early date. Something—the zeitgeist, one supposes, in the form of a science still dominated by mechanistic models and single-measure tests—was not ready to integrate these pioneering efforts into the mainstream of experimental psychology.

Our own efforts in this line began very late, in the early seventies, and involved the combination of a number of important research trends such as an emphasis on rich environments and experience, willingness to measure behaviors by visual inspection rather than through mechanical devices, and measurement of a large number of actions rather than a few preselected acts or "displays."

We wanted to retain the advantages of experimentation (this being somewhat underused in much of the classic work in this area with the exception of Scott's studies). We also had the real advantage of knowing some of the classic ethological literature on "displays" or "signals," without, however, being in any sense committed to the traditional interpretations made of these phenomena. Finally, having spent several years attempting to analyze some of the functional relationships involved in changes in defensive or fear reactions to different classes of stimuli and different stimulus situations, we were ready to view behaviors as strategies with differing probable outcomes under different circumstances.

All of these factors influenced the resulting work. This model was based on behavior but explicitly attempted to link behavior to stimulus and organismic variables with a view to a sort of sociobiological analysis of the functions of individual behaviors in the context of the variables that elicit or suppress each such action. Considerable chunks of this analysis were independently produced at about the same time by several other investigators: David Adams (1971); Klaus Miczek (1974), Dick Lore and our now-collaborator, Kevin Flannelly (Lore & Flannelly, 1977; Luciano & Lore, 1975). The outcome is thus not only richly detailed, but is also an explicitly replicated and corroborated analysis.

A. The Colony Model

The colony model is based on small groups of rats, usually three males and three females with their young, up to about 30 days of age. Each group is kept in an enclosure about 1 m square, with a light wood-chip substrate and freely available food and water. The animals are only disturbed for routine cleaning and by the introduction of intruders at varying intervals.

When the adult rats are first placed in the colonies, there is considerable social interaction. Occasional fights do occur, most of them involving the males of the colony. Work presently underway in our laboratory suggests that the time required for fights to develop is less than we had previously thought, a matter of a few hours rather than days. One male in each colony initiates most of these fights, whereas the subordinate males soon begin to respond by either running away or, especially, by a rather peculiar "boxing" movement in which they rear up to face the initiator, but without making any sort of attack motion toward this rat.

If a strange male rat of the same strain is placed into a newly established colony, it elicits a great deal of sniffing of the anogenital area by the colony males, though these rarely show any attack behaviors. When we placed one intruder every week in each of a number of new colonies, an average of 5 weeks was required before biting attack on the intruder was seen. Once the biting attack pattern develops, however, it is extremely stable, with an attack made on every intruder placed in an established colony (Blanchard, Takahashi, & Blanchard, 1977). The overwhelming majority of attacks at a strange male intruder are made by the same male rat who may also be identified as the initiator of fights within the colony: the dominant colony rat or "alpha."

B. Attack and Defense:
A Description of Conspecific Fighting in Rats

The attack of an experienced alpha male on a stranger in his colony is very sterotyped and usually quite intense. The alpha approaches the stranger and sniffs at its perianal area. If the stranger is subadult (Thor & Flannelly, 1976), or castrated (Christie & Barfield, 1979; Flannelly & Thor, 1979), or if the alpha has been rendered anosmic, unable to smell (Alberts & Galef, 1973; Flannelly & Thor, 1976), attack usually does not ensue. If the intruder is an adult male, the alpha's sniff leads to piloerection. In over 500 observations of alpha–stranger interactions in established colonies we have never seen piloerection of an intruder, nor has an attacking alpha failed more than a handful of times to piloerect although this may occur more often in single resident situations (Fass, Gutterman, & Stevens, 1979). Piloerection, like most of the behaviors making up the attack and defense patterns, thus provides an absolute, rather than a statistical, separation of the colony alpha and the stranger. It is generally assumed that the function of piloerection is to increase the apparent size of the dominant animal: Whether this is its primary function or not, it certainly does make the alpha seem larger.

Shortly after piloerecting, the alpha rat usually bites the intruder, and the intruder runs away. The alpha chases after it, and after one or two additional bites, the intruder stops running and turns to face its attacker. It rears up on its hindlegs, using its forelimbs to push off the alpha. This distinctive "boxing" response is an active series of movements that keep the defender's face in opposition to that of the attacker. However, rather than standing nose to nose with the boxing intruder, the attacking rat abruptly moves to a lateral orientation, with the long axis of its body perpendicular to the front of the defending rat, and with its head and posterior ends curved in somewhat toward this animal. It moves sideways toward the intruder, crowding and sometimes pushing it off balance. If the defending rat stands solid against this "lateral attack" movement, the alpha may make a quick lunge forward and around the defender's body to bite at its back. In response to such a lunge, the defender usually pivots on its hindfeet, in the same direction as the attacker is moving, continuing its frontal orientation to the attacker. If the defending rat moves quickly enough, no bite will be made.

However, after a number of instances of the lateral attack, and especially if the attacker has succeeded in biting the intruder, the stranger rat may roll backward slowly from the boxing position, to lie on its back. The attacker then takes up a position on top of the supine animal, digging with its forepaws at the intruder's sides. If the attacker can turn the other animal over, or expose some portion of its back and dorsal sides, it bites. In response to these efforts, the defender usually moves in the direction of the attacker's head, rolling slightly on its back to continue to orient its ventrum toward the alpha, and continuing to push off with both forelimbs and hindlimbs. Although all four legs and abdomen of the defending rat are exposed, the attacker does not bite them. This sequence of bites, flight, chasing, boxing, lateral attack, lying on the back, and standing on top, is repeated in a rather variable sequence until the stranger rat is removed. Sequential analyses of the behavior patterns have been provided by Grant (1963), whereas Koolhaus, Schuurman, and Wiepkema (1980) and Olivier (1981) have done flow charts of these sequences. Much research indicates that these patterns are the same in wild and laboratory rats (Takahashi & Blanchard, 1982).

These behaviors, repeated consistently by hundreds of different pairs of rats in colony tests, make it very clear that there is an internal organization of offensive or alpha attack in rats, and of defense as well. Our initial task was therefore to analyze these patterns, in order to determine if some type of principle or generalization might account for many or all of the specific behaviors that constitute offense, and many or all of the specific behaviors that constitute the defensive pattern.

C. Attack and Defense: A Functional Analysis

One of the first conclusions to be drawn from watching many, many instances of attack by colony males on intruders is that the actual behaviors involved are stereotyped. The lateral attack, for example, varies very little from rat to rat, and the same is true for piloerection, or for the specific movements involved in standing on top of a supine intruder, and so on. Similarly, the intruders' boxing and lying on the back behaviors are quite consistent across rats: In a way this is even more remarkable than the stereotypy of attack, because the intruders in these studies were naive animals, often housed individually since weaning. It thus strains credulity to assert that these rats had all acquired these behaviors as a result of individual experience. In fact, Eibl-Eibesfeldt (1961) presented limited evidence of the preprogrammed nature of these patterns in rats years ago.

The second, and equally remarkable impression one has of these fights, is that the actions of attacker and defender—neither of which has ever encountered the other—are beautifully coordinated. Certain attack behaviors seem to go with certain defensive acts, to form dyads such as flee–chase, box–lateral attack, and on the back–on top. The first of these, flee–chase, conveys the flavor of such interactions very well: Alpha chasing does not always occur when the intruder is in flight; sometimes the alpha seems indifferent or distracted, or flops down for a brief rest. But certainly chasing occurs only during flight, and the time spent in alpha chasing is directly proportional to the time that the intruder spends in flight (Blanchard & Blanchard, 1981).

In the case of flight, the goal seems simple: to get away from danger. For the corresponding attack behavior—and here we get a first clue that aggression may be a bit more complex than is defense—two rather different functional outcomes are apparent. First, the attacking rat may chase an intruder in order to drive it off. In fact, in real-life situations of rats in stable populations and environments, encounters often do end in just this fashion, with one animal being driven out of the vicinity of the other, with little contact between the two (Robitaille & Bovet, 1976; Telle, 1966).

On the other hand, if successful flight is prevented, as in the colony situation and many natural situations, the attacking rat does not hesitate to bite the fleeing intruder. Indeed, in colony tests, the most dangerous defense for the intruder is flight, as it so often results in a bite by the attacker. Viewed in this light, the goal of chasing is to permit the attacker to gain access to the intruder in order to bite it.

As flight and chasing are also universal human behaviors, at least during childhood, and as most of us can very well remember our thoughts and emotions while doing these things, it is tempting to add that the goals of (for example) chasing are not only to be defined in terms of adaptive significance (as the possible dispersal effects of chasing away a conspecific) or of sequential behavior analysis (that chasing frequently terminates in an attacker bite or blow): The perceived goal of chasing an opponent is usually to hurt that opponent or to force it to do something that the chaser wishes it to do. Thus our ordinary perception of our goal in chasing another person fits very well with what rats actually do when chasing another rat in an agonistic encounter.

But what of the other attack–defense dyads? Both the lateral attack–boxing dyad, and the on top–on-the-back dyad involve close contact of attacker and defender. If access in order to bite is a goal of the attack behavior, why doesn't the attacker simply go ahead and bite? Why spend so much effort in these rather stereotyped behaviors? Conversely, why does the defending rat display the boxing posture, often for long periods of time, or lie on its back?

Initial observations suggested that bites made by attacking rats on intruders were by no means randomly distributed on the body of the victim. In fight after fight we observed that the vast majority of bites, and the resulting wounds, involved the back of the defending rat. We therefore began to look more closely at the attacker's behaviors that immediately preceded these bites, and we were astonished to discover that the attackers appeared to be actively trying to attain access to their opponents' backs in order to effect a bite.

We therefore ran a series of studies to experimentally test whether the complex actions of the attacker were an effort to direct attack at specific target sites (Blanchard, Blanchard, Takahashi, & Kelley, 1977). For these studies we used terminally anesthetized rats that were placed into the colonies, with all colony rats except the alpha removed. These intruders were tied to a platform so as to expose only the back, or, only the ventrum (thorax, abdomen, genitals) as targets. The alphas attacked these targets readily and bit them freely on the back. Bites to the ventral areas were almost nonexistent, even when these sites were easily accessible and the back was hard to reach. In fact, when a box was placed over the anesthetized target's head and shoulders, making it hard for the attacker to burrow under and reach the back, some attackers stopped biting altogether.

These studies strongly indicated that the back is a specific target for bites by an attacking rat. Moreover, this distribution of attacker bites is not the result of evasive actions by the defender rat, because it appears even when the defender has been terminally anesthetized and is not "behaving" at all.

Put back into the context of colony encounters, this factor of bite targets suddenly makes good sense of both of the remaining attack–defense behavior dyads. In fact, these dyads turn out to have exactly the same functional relationship to each other as do chasing and flight: The defensive component is an act that removes the vulnerable (back) target from the reach of the attacker. In turn, the attack component is a strategy that counteracts the defensive behavior, giving the attacker access to the defender's back.

Thus, in boxing, the defender juxtaposes its own ventrum and its own head, to the head of the attacker. The ventrum is invulnerable, as the attacker will not bite it, and the head is protected by two additional mechanisms: First, the defending rat can, and sometimes does, show retaliatory biting. Second, the rat's head is to some extent protected by the vibrissae, long snout hairs that function as sensitive tactile receptors. These are erected by the defending rat to form a sort of tactile field around its snout. If the vibrissae are removed, or if the defender is anesthetized, the head becomes an additional target for attacker bites (Blanchard, Takahashi, Fukunaga, & Blanchard, 1977).

As these auxiliary mechanisms protect the head, the boxing rat is well protected as long as it can maintain a frontal orientation to its attacker. The lateral attack can counter this defense in two ways. First, by crowding against the defender the attacker can sometimes push it over or make it turn and flee, both of which provide access to the back. Second, even if the defender holds firm, the attacker can lunge in a tight circle around to the back, grabbing a quick bite. The defender's response to this sort of lunge is to pivot along with the attacker's movement, in an attempt to continue its frontal orientation to the attacker and thereby thwart attack. Recent work in our lab and by others suggest that experience helps to improve an intruder's ability to defend itself by such maneuvering (Blanchard & Blanchard, 1980a).

Lying on the back and standing on top are the other such pair of functionally intertwined acts. Lying on the back obviously protects the back very effectively against a direct assault. However, the attacker may still attempt to roll the defender over to expose its back. If an attacker tries to do this, the defender rolls in the direction of the attacker's snout. In this context the attacker behavior of standing on top of the supine defender is probably effective because it provides more flexibility to the attacker's efforts: The attacker may push the defender in one direction and then abruptly switch its attack to a back site exposed by the defender's own efforts to counter the initial direction of movement.

Further research indicates that these acts actually do function together as we have suggested, with a very close relationship between the occurrence of a given defender behavior and the occurrence of the corresponding attacker behavior. Our data indicate that between 70 and 100% of the time that a defending rat shows one of these two defensive strategies, the attacker will show the corresponding attack strategy (Blanchard & Blanchard, 1981). There is no crossover of attack behaviors: In hundreds of hours of observations we have never seen a lateral attack made to an intruder lying on the back or an alpha attempting to stand on top of a boxing intruder.

The lack of this crossover suggests that the alpha behaviors do not serve as signals to the intruder, but instead as strategies aimed at the infliction of a bite on a specific area of the intruder's body. Confirmation for this interpretation may be found in the observation that attacking animals never show lateral attack and almost never stand on top of an anesthetized intruder. They do piloerect, and they bite, but as the intruder is not utilizing a back defense strategy, there is no need for the alpha rat to utilize the attack strategies aimed at countering these back defenses (Blanchard, Blanchard, Takahashi, & Kelley, 1977).

The relationship between specific defensive behaviors and the attack behaviors with which they are functionally linked is thus consistent in time within individual fights. The functional linkage for each dyad, consisting of a defensive behavior and its associated attack behavior, is related to the targeting of bites to the defender's back, and the lack of bites to the ventrum. The strategic attack behaviors have no meaning except in the context of this target-site preference of attacking rats.

This back-attack: back-defense model is a complex hypothesis tying together a number of phenomena: the target site for alpha attack; the form of conspecific alpha attack behaviors; and the form of conspecific defensive activity. The core of this analysis is a view that conspecific attack in rats is targeted toward the back of the younger or subordinate opponent. This targeting is preprogrammed, and not dependent on the behavior of the other animal.

We have interpreted (Blanchard & Blanchard, 1981) this specific targeting as a strategy that enhances the dominant animal's inclusive fitness: By hurting, but not killing or castrating, subordinate males, the alpha rat may drive these animals harmlessly out of its territory. As the alpha frequently has sired most of the younger animals in its territory, their future reproductive success enhances the alpha's inclusive fitness. Another possible mechanism, which may exert greater influence in more experienced alphas, is that a ventral bite puts the alpha's head within biting range of the victim, thus enabling a retaliatory bite. As offensive targeting away from the ventrum may be seen even in naive males, this learning mechanism appears not to be crucial. It may, however, act to sharpen offensive attack in experienced alphas. Regardless of its origin, the target-site preference is a consistent and unequivocal phenomenon of behavior by the attacking rat, and not an artifact occasioned by defensive maneuvering of the attacked animal.

D. Fear-Based Aggression

Although the colony situation provides excellent examples of intraspecies offensive attack in rats, and good examples of intraspecies defensive behaviors, there is more to defense then shows up in this task. For one thing, defensiveness is necessary, not only in dealing with other animals of the same species, but also in reacting to a number of life-threatening situations in which conspecifics are not involved. Thus rats, like most other animals, react defensively to predators (Edmunds, 1975) and also to situations that involve danger even when no other animate stimulus is present (Blanchard, Mast, & Blanchard, 1974). Moreover, the evolutionary necessity for defense is broader than that for aggression, as any totally nondefensive animal living in the real world is virtually guaranteed to come to a quick end. Defensive behaviors are therefore more basic, and broader based (in terms of eliciting stimuli) than are aggressive behaviors. This suggests, first, that there should be less variation in defensive tendencies from animal to animal within a species than in aggression, and, second, that there may be a greater range of defensive acts than aggressive acts in terms of responses that are appropriate to widely different (threat) situations. For example, though many defensive behaviors such as flight and perhaps freezing are seen in a variety of threat situations, other defensive acts are more common with animate threats, such as attacking predators or conspecifics. Some, such as lying on the back, are only effective in the context of a rigidly aimed attack, which is probably why lying on the back is seen more to an attacking conspecific than to an attacking predator. The dependence of the form of defense on features of threat stimuli and situations ensures that the range and relative magnitudes of defensive acts seen in the colony situation will be somewhat different from those given to other threatening situations.

The other and perhaps more pressing reason that the colony tests described do not provide an adequate description of defense in rats is that these tests were usually run with laboratory rats. Laboratory rats have lived and bred in laboratory situations for many, many generations, and during this recent evolutionary history of the species, they have been subject to selection pressures very different from those in the natural habitats of rats.

That this selection has occurred during domestication of the laboratory rat is more than speculation. We have seen brochures from suppliers of laboratory animals that describe the docility and ease of handling of their rat strains. Moreover, some of these suppliers have described to us in conversation their selection against biting and defensive threat behaviors in rats used as breeding stock. However, human selection is merely one of the factors involved. Barnett and Stoddart (1969) have chronicled changes in defensiveness of rats over succeeding generations bred from wild-trapped ancestors. In this case, no caretaker selection was involved and the operant mechanism appears to have been the relative reproductive incapacity of the more fearful rats.

An important way of assessing the effects of genetic, as opposed to environmental, mechanisms mediating defensiveness in wild rats is through cross-fostering studies, but such studies are rarely done. One such mini experiment was made possible in our laboratory through the escape of several wild rats who then took up residence in our rather delapidated laboratory complex. One of the females, finding this new life-style to her liking, bred and produced a litter in an unused drawer where they were found when the pups were about 2 days of age. We trapped the mother and substituted a like number of 2-day-old laboratory rat babies, cross-fostering the wild pups to the laboratory rat mother. Both mothers accepted the new litters without difficulty, and, when adult, both litters were tested by a confrontation with an "approaching" conspecific (actually a terminally anesthetized rat brought up by hand to the subject). Table I shows the reactions of the cross-fostered animals in comparison with those of wild-trapped rats and regular laboratory rats under similar circumstances.

As these data indicate, wild and laboratory rats differ strikingly with respect to defense and defensive attack behaviors. When confronted by a terminally anesthetized conspecific, wild rats scream and jump at the animal. The same, including the bite, is true for the approach of an experimenter.

The bites that occur in this situation are real bites. (Ours may be the only laboratory on the University of Hawaii campus where everybody doing research wears real shoes rather than sandals or thongs.) The wild rats may also bite through the leather gloves we sometimes use to handle them, providing a nice illustration of the reason why so much selection by caretakers was necessary in the domestication of the laboratory rat. If these animals have access to only one portion of an experimenter's body, such as the feet, then they will bite that. However, given a choice, they aim their bites at two types of stimuli: either the thing that is

Table I. Defensive Attack by Normally Reared
or Cross-Fostered Wild and Laboratory Rats

	Screams	Jump attack	Bites
Wild-trapped rats	4.5	5.0	5.3
Cross-fostered wilds	4.5	4.7	3.9
Laboratory rats	.0	.0	.0
Cross-fostered labs	.0	.0	.0

hurting them at that instant (for example, a hand), or, before any contact has been made, the face and eyes of the oncoming predator. This holds for normal predators such as cat, dog, or mongoose, and for attacking conspecifics as well.

If one brings a terminally anesthetized conspecific, a wild rat, up toward another wild rat, then the threatened animal leaps toward the other's head, delivering a bite on the snout. Precisely the same is true of a laboratory rat, although this animal is disinclined to show any fear or fear-based attack unless it receives a simultaneous shock or pinch. And, most meaningfully for us, precisely these same types of bites also occur in the colony tests, made by intruders on the attacking alpha.

When these defensive bites occur in the colony situation they may be distinguished from an offensive attack bite in almost every attribute. They are given only by the defensive (intruder) rat; they occur in the context of defensive rather than offensive behaviors (that is, the biting defender does not preface or follow its bite by a sudden appearance of offensive behaviors); they occur very rarely, in contrast to the great frequency of offensive bites; they occur almost exclusively (around 99% of them) while the defender itself is being bitten or within a second or so after a bite has been received; and they are aimed at the snout of the opponent, the precise organ that has just delivered a hurt to the defensive animal, rather than the back target characteristic of offensive bites.

These differences therefore delineate two types of bites, one of which is the central feature of the rat offensive-attack pattern, whereas the other is an important component of the rats defensive repertory. Except for the fact that each pattern includes biting as a prominant feature, the offensive and defensive behavior patterns of the rat are quite dissimilar, so much so that it might be wondered how they could have been confused for so long.

One reason for this is that they occur together. In fact, the adaptive significance of many conspecific defensive behaviors is based on their "fit" with relevant attack behaviors, whereas other attack behaviors are adaptive in advancing one step further, to enable a bite even though an appropriate defense has been made. Conspecific attack and conspecific defense have thus evolved together, and they are each adaptive only in the context of the other pattern. Thus, under relatively natural conditions it would be almost impossible to obtain one without the other in a conspecific encounter.

In addition to this tendency for conspecific attack and defense to occur together—each in a different animal—in highly polarized situations, there is the even more confusing situation in which both attack and defense occur in each animal. This is perhaps even more common in real-world situations, and it reflects the high degree of overlap between the conditions that produce attack and those that produce defense in which a small shift in relevant conditions, notably the level of pain or fear experienced by an animal, can shift the balance from attack to defense or vice versa.

III. EMOTIONAL CONCOMITANTS OF OFFENSE AND DEFENSE: FEAR AND ANGER

Defensive attack, and indeed the entire pattern of defensive behavior reflects fear. And offensive attack, we maintain, similarly reflects an underlying emotional state, constituting at least a primitive analogue of what we call in humans "anger."

It is clear that the designation of fear as the emotional basis of defensive behavior will be, to most psychologists at least, less controversial and more easily accepted than a similar stipulation for anger and offense. In large part, however, this is simply because so much more is known of defensive or fear-related behaviors (due to an enormous literature on aversive learning in animals) than of anger. Let us outline the case for fear, then, and use this outline as a model on which to base a case for anger.

Why is the construct "fear" needed to supplement or explain or characterize defensive behavior? There are a number of reasons that in the aggregate strongly indicate that the system of defense is much more than a straightforward reflex system.

First, even in rats there is an enormous amount of intrasubject variability in defensive behaviors, depending on features of the eliciting stimulus and on the circumstances in which the stimulus is encountered. Further, both the general and the specific learning experience of the individual animal can influence both the magnitude and the type of defense given to a particular stimulus. To describe each of these sources of variability very briefly, important stimulus parameters include the discreteness or discriminability of the threatening stimulus and whether it moves or not, etc. (Blanchard & Blanchard, 1969; Blanchard, Mast, & Blanchard, 1974). Moreover, if threat is encountered in a familiar as opposed to a novel situation, or one affording an easy escape route as opposed to one that is inescapable, very different components of the defensive repertory may occur (Blanchard & Blanchard, 1969, 1970a,b). Organismic factors influencing defense include a general history of trauma, in which the success or failure of previous defensive behaviors to reduce threat is also greatly influential (Blanchard & Blanchard, 1968;

Seligman, 1972). Finally, specific learning, which is important in determining subsequent defensive behavior, includes habituation of previous
fearful responses to a particular neutral stimulus or conspecific stimulus,
and learning about the outcome of particular behaviors in the presence
of specific stimuli and situations (Sluckin, 1979).

This list seems complicated enough, but it must also be realized that
all of these sources of variability may combine in the same instance to
produce a situation of such complexity than it cannot possibly be described as a straightforward simple reflex situation. The more that defense is examined, the more it becomes certain that there is some underlying element that provides order in the chaotic jumble of input and
output factors. As one example of the complexities of this process, it can
easily be demonstrated that a rat will react to a certain threatening stimulus in a specific situation on the basis of the features of the stimulus
(discriminability, movement, etc.) and those of the situation (familiarity,
availability of escape, etc.). If a neutral stimulus is experimentally paired
with this noxious stimulus, the animal usually begins very quickly to
treat the neutral stimulus as a threat. However, rather than reacting to
the now-conditioned threat source as it did to the threat with which it
was formerly paired, the animal will give defensive responses that are
appropriate to the relevant characteristics of the conditioned stimulus
and that of any situation in which it is encountered (Blanchard &
Blanchard, 1969, 1972). Thus, what is learned is not a defensive response per se, but the emotional reaction to the stimulus. This emotional reaction, in conjunction with stimulus and situational characteristics, then determines the precise response to be made.

This analysis strongly implies that emotions are capable of developing
very rapidly and of manifesting their effects very quickly. This is, of
course, contrary to the common psychological view of emotions as slow-
developing responses. This traditional view holds that emotions represent awareness of slow-developing bodily changes such as adrenalin
secretion with this awareness modified by (i.e., emotions labeled in
terms of) relevant situational events (Schachter, 1964). Fortunately for the
present analysis of emotions as preprogrammed neural events, there is
not a shred of evidence that fear or anger requires any sort of slow-
developing peripheral change in order to develop and function. If a
situation is ambiguous (and human anger-eliciting situations often are),
then a certain amount of time and effort may be required to straighten
out the cognitive complexities involved. This, in turn, usually provides a
clearer subjective motivation, by pointing out who we are angry at and
just how angry we are. Unclear or not, however, the anger is quickly
there: It serves, in fact, as the stimulus that prompts the clarifying—

cognitive—analysis. This brief excursion to human anger is, however, getting ahead of the argument. Suffice it that there is no data-based necessity for regarding either fear or anger in rats (or indeed in people) as events requiring a period of incubation or slow onset in response to appropriate eliciting stimuli.

In a nutshell, then, emotions provide a flexibility that is especially crucial in dealing with reactions to threat stimuli, or in fact to any class of stimuli to which quantitatively different responses must be made in different situations. In evolutionary terms, fear and defensive behaviors constitute an excellent example of such a flexible yet precise system because the selection pressures involved were so strong. Making the wrong defensive response for a given threat stimulus or situation or failing to acquire a fear response to a stimulus that was in fact dangerous may both involve immediate and dire consequences. Within a given species, defensive behaviors appear to be very systematic and predictable, once the variations in stimuli, situations, and subject history have been taken into account. This lack of variability is testimony to the precision of selection against animals who did not do it all just right.

Finally, fear is a very potent motivator. This may be seen in the context of learning tasks where the motivational aspects of fear are transferred, through association, from one stimulus to another, or where a reduction in fear may be used to strengthen some originally irrelevant behavior pattern (Miller, 1948). However, it is not at all necessary to resort to learning situations to demonstrate the motivating effects of fear: The behaviors that make up defense vary in magnitude with the degree of threat, and a high level of fear will virtually obliterate any nondefensive behavior with which it is competing.

These same characteristics of flexibility, conditionability, motivation, etc. may also be applied to anger as an emotional concomitant of offense. It must be recognized at the outset that studies of what we here call "anger" have represented only a minute fraction of the number of studies devoted to fear, so there is no point in expecting the sort of detailed case that could be made for fear. However, the evidence available, sparse and often fragmentary or informal as it is, is in agreement with a view that the relationship between anger and offense is quite similar to that of fear and defense.

First, like defense, offense may be elicited by a variety of stimuli. In the colony model the eliciting stimulus may appear to be rather precise: a postpubescent male stranger in the attacker's colony. However, that interpretation is too specific. Colony males do fight among themselves, so the stranger feature is unnecessary, and they will, if attacked by a female or a smaller male, often retaliate with an offensive attack pattern

(Takahashi & Blanchard, 1982). Social disorganization and some specific instances of resource competition may produce alpha-type attack against conspecifics of virtually any age or sex. Thus, it is simply not true that offense is elicted only by a very specific stimulus in the sense that simple reflexes are elicited by specific stimuli. In fact, the stimuli and situations that combine to produce offensive attack in rats are even more complicated than those that elicit defense in these same animals.

Like defense, offense consists of a number of different behaviors, and these behaviors vary with features of the eliciting stimulus. In a particular encounter, offense may include piloerection, chasing, biting, the lateral attack, standing on top of the opponent, and so on. The determinant of which of these behaviors will be made at a given instant is the behavior of the target animal—the eliciting stimulus. When this animal flees, the alpha chases; when it boxes, the alpha makes a lateral attack; when its back is available, the alpha bites. Similarly, offense may be rather different depending on situational variables such as familiarity with the area in which the encounter takes place, the presence of territorial boundaries, the relative confinement of the situation—for example a burrow as opposed to open space—and so on.

A third parallel may be found in the effects of general and specific experience on offense, as compared to similar effects on defensive behaviors. Offense is promoted or strengthened by a general history of victory in intraspecies fights, even when the opponent is naive. This effect must therefore work through the experienced animal and not rely on greater fearfulness of the opponent. When the two combatants have been paired previously, with one defeating the other, then changes in both animals appear to contribute to the resulting alterations of agonistic behavior.

To continue with the parallels, if we accept that an emotional response of anger underlies each example of offense, just as fear underlies defense, what about the conditionability of anger? Fear is readily conditioned through association and a demonstration of the conditionability of offense would certainly bolster the case for anger. There are factors, however, suggesting that anger conditioning and fear conditioning may not be strictly parallel processes. For one thing, the ability to learn to be afraid of previously neutral stimuli when they turn out to be dangerous (i.e., when they have actually hurt the subject) is a very crucial adaptive behavior. There seems to be no equivalent necessity to associate anger with previously neutral stimuli, on the basis of experience. In evolutionary terms, such an association would be much less adaptive than the association of fear with neutral stimuli under similar circumstances. Additionally, fear is a very unidirectional emotion: It is extremely unpleasant. Anger, on the other hand, appears to be a great deal less unpleasant, and it may even represent a positive affective state, at least for animals with a previous history of victory. Reduction of anger motivation as the incentive for learning should therefore be a much less potent factor in reward behavior.

Despite all these disclaimers, some examples of anger conditioning do seem to occur in rats. For instance, highly experienced attacking colony males often show a conditioned reaction to opening the top that covers the colony. These top covers are opened whenever an intruder is introduced, with the intruder being placed each time in the center of the enclosure. If the cover is opened but no intruder provided, the alpha will run to the center and look up with what can only be described as a "hopeful" expression! A rather similar phenomenon appears to be occurring right now in one of our "burrowing" colonies, in which the animals have dug burrows into the deep soil substrate. The alpha often is sleeping below in a burrow, but when a much subordinate male dares to emerge from its own burrow to grab a bite or drink water, the alpha immediately shoots up to chase this unfortunate individual back down. The alpha has evidently learned to associate certain stimuli with an anger-eliciting event, the presence of the subordinate male above ground, and then reacts by seeking out the event in order to display an offensive pattern.

The final criterion of fear is that it serves as a motivator that energizes or strengthens behaviors leading to a reduction in the level of the motivation. As anger is not—at least in rats—a purely unpleasant emotion, and as the status of attack as an anger-reducing behavior has not been investigated in rats, perhaps it would be better to rephrase this question: Will an angry rat show motivated behaviors enabling it to reach its goal and carry out an offensive attack? This question has been answered in the affirmative by Lagerspetz (1969) who demonstrated that mice will do work, such as crossing obtacles or pressing a bar, in order to be allowed the opportunity to attack another mouse. The behaviors leading up to the alpha bite seem also very relevant in this context. Offensive bites are targeted specifically toward the opponent's back, and our analysis indicates that the strategic behaviors—those tending to make this goal possible—are the flexible units in the system. The question then becomes this: To what extent will rats persist in their efforts to reach this back target if it is hidden? To what extent will they utilize new or different techniques to make this access possible?

Our studies of deeply anesthetized target rats who were presented with their backs concealed provide some evidence (Blanchard, Blanchard, Takahashi, & Kelley, 1977). The dominant rats were extraordinarily persistent, burrowing around the tied-down targets, biting at the attaching cords, and chewing at the platform to which the target was attached or to its cover. It may be argued that none of these was a new behavior to the rat, but there is no question that the circumstances of life for these animals had never before placed a platform and a Plexiglas cover between themselves and the back of an animal they were in the process of attacking. The fact that they so readily attacked these barriers in aid of reaching the goal of a back to bite seems to us to suggest—as do the earlier examples cited of alphas searching in places in which they were accustomed to find males to attack, and the Lagerspetz studies of motivated attack—that anger is as much a motivating state or condition as is fear.

These briefly outlined parallels suggest that fear and anger serve as the common bonds or mechanisms linking the diverse phenomena of defense or offense, respectively. Needless to say, neither fear nor anger in rats is assumed to involve a subjective experience identical to that of humans. However, when the term *fear* is used in psychology, it is usually treated as a basic analogue to the emotion of the same name, as it functions in human life. We propose that anger be used in a very similar fashion. It is the motivation or tendency to hurt a conspecific under conditions that have not yet been specified in detail but that will be extensively treated later.

IV. THE QUESTION OF GENERALITY: ATTACK AND DEFENSE IN OTHER SPECIES

With the two patterns so clearly established in rats, the next issue is that of generality. How well do these specific attack and defense patterns characterize the fighting behaviors of other animals? To what extent does this system—that attack and defense are different, with attack behaviors organized around a goal of permitting access to certain attack sites and defense organized around protection of these same sites— describe the fighting behaviors of other species?

A. Mice

It is actually stretching the truth a bit to describe application of the distinction between attack and defense to the behavior of mice or cats as an extension. The importance of the difference between the two behavior patterns appears to have been recognized, at about the same time, perhaps 30 years ago, by two individuals working in very different species, J. P. Scott, working with mice, and Paul Leyhausen, working with cats. So it might be more reasonable to say that both of these species served as pioneers and more recent work has extended the distinction to rats as well as to a host of other species. At any rate, it is becoming more and more evident that attack and defense are fundamentally different, though interrelated modes of response, in every higher species studied.

The separation of attack and defense behaviors is as clear in mice as in rats when attack and defensive tendencies have been polarized through appropriate experiential manipulations. Moreover, the attack and defense patterns of mice are similar, though not identical, to those of rats. The attack components that are similar for mice and rats include chasing and lateral attack behaviors, plus a circling action which appears to be functionally similar to the lateral attack in permitting access to the defender's back. The corresponding defender behaviors are flight, boxing, and a "checking" motion of turning to maintain frontal orientation to the attacker. These behaviors are just as polarized as in the rat, with virtually no overlap between attacker and defender actions (Blanchard, O'Donnell, & Blanchard, 1979). Attacking mice do show some preference for biting the back, but have much less reluctance to bite the ventrum, especially if this is the only site available for biting: When a ventrally presented anesthetized target mouse was given, 10% or so of bites were made on the stomach and thorax (Blanchard, O'Donnell, & Blanchard, 1979). This difference between mice and rats may perhaps reflect the less colonial life-style of most mouse species, or, alternatively, a reduced mortality accompanying ventral biting as mice make small punctate bite wounds in comparison to the larger wounds made by rats.

Regardless of the reason for the difference, it is associated with the corresponding change in the mouse attack–defense pattern. Mice show little or no tendency to lie on the back, nor do they show any prolonged on-top behavior. This is quite consistent with the view that lying on the back is effective only because it does afford superior protection to the back. If the attacker is willing to bite the ventrum, as is the case in mice, then the dangers involved in this defensive strategy would outweigh its benefits.

The boxing defense, on the other hand, involves protection of the back through not only the relative invulnerability of the ventrum, but also through the possibility of retaliatory biting: The defender is fully maneuverable in this position and its own head and teeth are in close proximity to the attacker. This combination appears to be sufficient for boxing to continue to be an adaptive defense for the mouse, despite reduced constraints on bites to the ventrum. The lateral attack and a related mouse variant attack, circling, are the major mouse attack strategies against a boxing defender.

Adams (1980) has reviewed offense and defense pattern in a variety of other muroid rodents and presents strong confirmatory evidence for differential patterns in these animals.

B. Cats

In cats, the distinction between offense and defense involves the difference, now familiar in rat analyses, between target sites for offensive attack and defensive attack (Leyhausen, 1979). An attacking cat that shows no defensive tendencies walks slowly, on extended limbs, with straight back and erect, sideways-turned ears, toward its target. Its vocalizations are low and gruff. When it bites, the target is the nape of the conspecific opponent's neck. The "pure" defender—one who has no reason to stay and fight and can leave the situation—will do so. If cornered, however, it shows a variety of postures that have the unequivocal effect of making the nape of the neck inaccessible to the attacker. These include twisting the head sideways and even upside down from a crouching or supine position, and the use of both hind- and forepaws to strike at or push off the attacker. The stereotypy of some of these actions, notably those that involve lying on the back, may suggest a "submission" gesture but this interpretation is explicitly disallowed by Leyhausen (1979), who states:

> From all this it is clear that the defensive posture is not a submissive gesture in Lorenz's sense. . . . It does not offer up to the superior attacker the object of its attack—the nape of the neck—but seeks to protect it. Also, it does not necessarily inhibit the attacker, and the attacked animal does not remain passive in the face of further threats but defends itself and, in certain circumstances, proceeds to counterattack. The attacker is inhibited only by the removal of its target and the danger involved in continuing to attack, i.e., the threat being expressed in the defensive behavior—in other words, precisely the opposite effect to that of a genuine submissive posture. [pp. 186–187]

In cats, as in other animals, these two patterns are frequently intermixed in actual fights in real-life situations. This is because a totally polarized situation, such as is afforded by the colony, would lead to only the briefest of encounters if it occurred where the defender could leave: Those fights that actually do occur, and which leave a lasting impression on those human observers whose homes are located in the midst of the battleground, must necessarily involve combatants who both have considerable offensive motivations. In turn, if one's opponent is making an offensive attack, it is clearly likely that one will show some defense as well; hence the mixture of offense and defense in real-world fights.

The results of field studies provide further hints that target sites of bites, blows, and structural adaptations in these sites are integral factors in intraspecies competition in cats. For example, Schaller (1972) has remarked on the violence of intraspecies fighting in free-roaming lions. Lions live in groups, a striking departure from the usual solitary habits of other members of the cat family, and one which may make it especially adaptive for male lions to have some relatively protected target site for intraspecies bites or blows.

Male lions do have a uniquely developed structural adaptation, a thick mane covering the back of the head and the neck. In describing a male lion mortally wounded in a fight with males of another pride, Schaller noted that tatters of its mane were scattered over an area of 3 × 10 m. While hardly conclusive, such observations do suggest that the head–neck–shoulder area of a male lion is a prime target for blows during intraspecies combat, and that this targeting is so specific as to make the relevant structural characteristic—the thick mane—adaptive.

C. Ungulates

Geist (1978) presented a mass of evidence on target sites for intraspecies attack and defense in ungulates. For example, mountain sheep, like Norway rats, are group-living animals with dominant males having priority of access to breeding females. Fighting among the males is even more oriented toward specific body sites than in the rat: Male mountain sheep fight by pacing off a distance from each other and coming together head-on in a spectacular clash of horns. Despite the violence of this fighting technique, the males are seldom badly injured, as their massive horns distribute the force of the blows onto an abnormally thick skull, both horns and skull having presumably evolved to facilitate this intraspecies fighting pattern.

Such fights are clearly offensive; both combatants must participate in order for the very stereotyped battle to occur, and a bout is terminated when one of the animals turns or runs away. This removes the target for the offensive blow—the horns—as well as taking the retreating animal out of position in terms of delivering an offensive blow itself.

This very specific offensive fighting technique, with the horns serving as both the major weapon system in offensive fights, and as the target for offensive blows, is not restricted to mountain sheep. Other ungulate species also tend to live in large herds that share a common area for grazing, a situation that brings the males into constant contact: At the same time, breeding access tends to be the prerogative of the dominant male, a factor clearly promoting fighting. These factors may put a premium on a fighting technique that enables the opponents to assess strength and endurance without serious risk of damage. The use of specialized horns as both weapons and targets for these weapons fits this need very well indeed, and it is notable that prominant horns or antlers tend to be developed and used in this fashion in many other ungulates. It is becoming increasingly clear that these specialized weapon systems are used almost exclusively in intraspecies fighting, rather than as a defense against predation. The sharp hooves are the primary defensive weapon in ungulates.

The fact that offensive fights can be so easily terminated by removal of the target site—the horns or antlers—also suggests that defensive intraspecies attack may be unnecessary. In fact, the ease with which attack is terminated by removal of the target site by lifting the head or turning it aside has led to interpretation of these defensive movements as submission gestures (Koutnik, 1980).

D. Primates

Adams and Shoel (1981) have undertaken an analysis of fighting in adult male stumptail macaques (*Macaca arctoides*), focusing on specific behaviors, facial expression, and target sites for bites. The fights observed were between dominant monkeys and monkeys that were clearly subordinate or between two dominant monkeys. Logically, the former type of encounter might be expected to produce relatively "pure" offensive and defensive behaviors, whereas the latter seems likely to elicit some mixture of attack and defense from each combatant.

To briefly summarize their results, in these encounters dominant animals aimed their bites toward the backs of subordinate animals; the subordinate animals paired with dominant males made no bites at all. In terms of this omission of any biting for the clearly subordinate monkeys, it may be relevant that these animals' canine teeth had been filed down to reduce tissue damage from bites. It is possible that if the bites had hurt more, some retaliatory bites might have occurred. During dominant–dominant male encounters, where both might be expected to show high levels of defense as well as offense, bites to the face of the opponent were common, though some back biting or shoulder biting was also seen.

This separation by target site for bites obviously corresponds well to the offensive bite–defensive bite distinction made in rats, and it is remarkable that the specific targets seen in macaque fights are so similar to those of rodents. Moreover, the fighting sequences illustrated in the Adams and Shoel report appear to suggest that the behavioral precursors of these bites were grasping, and manipulative head and body movements that facilitated access to the desired bite target, at least for the bites by dominant monkeys on subordinates. The nonbiting subordinates did not, apparently, offer much strategic resistance to these bites, although they did crouch, scream, and try to run away. In addition to these behaviors, which are also seen in the rat, the agonistic repertory of the macaque consists of a number of sexual or dominance-display behaviors. These were much more intense in encounters between dominant males.

E. Across-Species Generality: A Summary

The species for which a distinction between attack and defense—and in particular between offensive and defensive attack—have here been outlined only represent a small sample of mammals. Still, they are a very diverse set of mammalian species, ranging from mice that are small, relatively solitary, altricial, and omnivorous through ungulates which are large, usually very gregarious, precocial, and herbivorous. In addition to this diversity, the total number of species for which a clear attack–defense distinction has been demonstrated could be much expanded by consideration of other muroid rodents (Adams, 1980). Also, even for species in which the analyses necessary to make this distinction have not yet been made, there may be evidence of a difference for offensive and defensive bites or blows. Target sites, weapon use, etc. may suggest this distinction.

In bears, for example, offensive attack consists of a lot of wrestling combined with bites at the neck–ruff area, which (in consequence?) is heavily furred. Paw blows, without claw use, were also directed at this site. A more defensive type of attack consists of clawing at the opponent, and these raking slashes were more often directed at the back and sides, although we did see some slashes at the face–snout area (Blanchard, Blanchard, Takahashi, & Suzuki, 1977).

More recently, we have been very interested to see groups of piglets maintained in close quarters: Their offensive biting attack is directed to the ears, and in consequence low-ranking piglets may have their ears virtually shredded. These, like the back of the rat, are not protected by a special structure such as the lions' mane or the deer's antlers, but they may sustain great damage without real risk of death for the attacked animal. Similarly, fish tend to target offensive attack toward their opponent's fins, also a noncrucial structure.

What is important here is not that the precise pattern of behavior or the precise target site for an offensive bite or blow should be the same from one species to the next. In fact, it is not crucial that target sites specifically should be different in offensive as opposed to defensive attack, although this does provide welcome confirmatory evidence when it is found. What is crucial is that a pattern be detailed for one animal species that can then be recognized on the basis of clear functional similarities in other species. The pattern seems to be, at its most basic, that there is some form of offensive, intraspecific attack pattern for each mammalian species investigated, and that on investigation the form of such offensive attack may be seen as functionally related to the form of defense offered in intraspecies fighting. Usually, but not always, there is a clear defensive attack component to the intraspecies defense pattern (in mammals there is always an interspecies defensive attack component to the defense pattern) and this defensive attack component is distinguishable from the intraspecies offensive attack component.

V. AGGRESSION AND DEFENSE: A SOCIOBIOLOGICAL ANALYSIS

The animal species described in the preceding section—those for which we have a sufficiently fine-grained analysis to indicate differences between offensive and defensive attack—each yield data in support of the view that offense and defense are very different systems, with the latter emerging in the context of body threat or extreme fear. The circumstances under which the former emerges are somewhat different from species to species, but a common thread linking these circumstances is that resources important to the attacking animals are usually at stake.

The view that aggression is an adaptive behavior pattern leading to a greater degree of reproductive success for the aggressive animal is a very old one, originating with Darwin and carried through decades of ethological treatment of fighting in animals. It has most recently been elaborated by sociobiologists who have conceptualized the "cost–benefit analysis" embedded in each instance of aggression, along with a much more explicit consideration of some of the important factors in such an analysis. For example, Maynard-Smith and Price (1973) in their classic treatment of outcomes of different aggression modes suggest energy expenditure, probability of injury, and, above all, the likelihood of success as possible factors in this cost–benefit analysis.

An adequate sociobiological treatment of aggression as it has been detailed in the colony model must consider a number of phenomena, the most important of which is the distinction between offensive and defensive attack. Secondary considerations, such as the aiming of offensive bites or blows toward relatively invulnerable target sites, are also amenable to such an analysis. Finally—perhaps going beyond sociobiology as it is usually conceptualized—these considerations lead impellingly to the question of the mechanism by which cost–benefit analyses of aggressive phenomena are made.

A. The Distinction between Attack and Defense

The first question, that of the evolutionary significance of the distinction between offense and defense, is almost too obvious to be discussed. In sociobiological terms these are entirely different systems that have arisen in response to very different selection pressures during the course of evolution of higher animals. In fact, the only area in which there is any excuse for confusing the two systems—on the basis that one bite means the same as any other—is that of defensive attack: All defensive adaptations, whether structural (cf. cryptic coloration, or hard shell, etc.) or behavioral (cf. flight, concealment, etc.), have in common that they are adaptive in either preventing, reducing, or stopping life-threatening attacks. The utility of defensive attack aimed at an attacker's head is obvious in this context. The threat of defensive attack aimed at vulnerable sites may serve to prevent predatory attack or offensive attack by a conspecific, while the actuality of defensive bites may serve to stop offense from either source. Thus not only the difference in the circumstances of defensive and offensive attack, but their form and target site distinction as well, make excellent sociobiological sense.

B. The Adaptive Significance of Offense

In terms of a more explicit focus on the adaptive significance of offense, sociobiologists are consistent in describing the centrality of resource control as an adaptive consequence of intraspecies fighting. The specific resources for which disputes are adaptive, and those for which fighting would be maladaptive, depend on the ecology—including the social ecology—of the group. For example, when food is hard to obtain and comes in large bits then it may be adaptive for members of a species to fight over it; when it is easier to obtain and comes in smaller bits then the disadvantages of fighting over food tend to outweigh the advantages. Similarly, when control of a breeding territory is crucial to reproductive success, then it is adaptive to fight over control of such a territory; otherwise not. When conception is very likely the result of sexual activity, then it is adaptive for males to fight in order to gain access to the ovulating female; otherwise—and perhaps even a few hours before and after the main event—not.

Rather than viewing resource competition as the immediate cause of aggression, many ethologists and sociobiologists have focused on the establishment of dominance relationships which then act to control access to important resources without the need for fighting over each resource as it arises. It is difficult with the data available to come to any final conclusion on the issue of whether the urge to develop dominance relationships is an important factor even in the total absence of disputable resources or whether dominance relationships develop as a side-effect of fights over resources. In rats, however, it seems to us that the latter is perhaps a more accurate statement. Certainly, fights within a rat group do appear to increase as more resources, such as females in estrus, soil for digging burrows, etc. become available. In mice, too, attack toward certain targets goes up sharply when females are available (O'Donnell, Blanchard, & Blanchard, 1981).

Regardless of whether dominance relationships are seen as primary, or as a consequence of attack and defense, sociobiological analyses of the circumstances in which attack should be adaptive suggest that a challenging conspecific should be an extraordinarily potent stimulus in eliciting attack. That is, insofar as the motivation to establish dominance is the major consideration for a particular animal, a challenging opponent—one who behaves offensively—is the most direct and specific eliciting stimulus imaginable. On the other hand, even in a pure resource competition situation, if such a thing exists, the main reason to attack another animal is that there is an important resource at stake. Thus, to the animal who is itself challenged by a conspecific, the very fact of being challenged implies the presence of a desirable resource, even when such a resource is not readily apparent. That is, the original challenger must be acting in aid of something that is important to its species, for example an estrous female, a food source, suitable territory or nest site, or whatever. Thus a successful aggressive response to being challenged is likely to result in some advantage to the aggressive animal, the one that was itself originally challenged. The important point here is that a challenging conspecific should logically elicit some motivation or tendency toward offensive attack, either in a species that establishes dominance relationships in advance of resource competition or in species that fight only over resources, or, indeed, in species in which fighting involves some mixture of these situations. This is not to say that the only thing to elicit offensive attack is a challenging conspecific: If, for example, an animal is in possession of a desirable and limited resource, then the very presence of a potential competitor may elicit offense. However, in all species that show intraspecific offensive attack, a challenging conspecific should be capable of eliciting some motivation to offense.

C. The Cost–Benefit Analysis:
   An Emotional Calculus

Although a challenging conspecific should logically elicit tendencies toward offensive attack, the key issue determining whether such offense will actually occur is the likelihood of success, vis-à-vis the magnitude of contrary factors; in sum, a cost–benefit analysis occurs, not only in evolutionary terms, but also as a real component of the immediate situation leading to—or away from—each instance of possible offensive attack. Alcock (1979) expressed this important factor very succinctly: "Fighting a long series of losing battles is no way to maximize fitness. Instead, a subordinate should (and does) conserve his energy resources and bide his time. He and his genes are gambling (unconsciously), that he will live to grow larger, older, or more experienced."

Cost–benefit analyses are not, of course, limited to offense situations. A predator confronting potential prey must analyze the costs (cf. probability of injury, energy expenditure, etc.) against the benefit of food for itself and its congeners; sexual decisions involve somewhat similar analyses, as do other important strategic questions. The particular cost–benefit analysis involved in offense, is, however, one of the most complex. One of its complexities may be seen in the fact that offense almost always involves conspecifics. For animals living in small related groups, the alpha male is likely to be directly related to—indeed to have fathered—many of the younger animals in the group. We have elsewhere suggested (Blanchard & Blanchard, 1981) that this relationship is very important in the evolution of the back-attack–back-defense system of conspecific fighting in rats.

Another consideration is that, given the cost of attack even if such attack is successful, the benefits of success should be rather clear. Thus dominant males of many species permit subordinates to copulate freely with females in estrus, except for the point at which conception is most likely to occur. Similarly, we have noticed in our colonies (D. C. Blanchard and R. J. Blanchard, unpublished observations) that rats are more inclined to fight over high-quality food items than over standard rat chow even when moderately deprived. These are considerations that weigh heavily on the benefit side of the analysis.

The crucial issue, though, is success. No matter what benefits may accrue, they are as nothing if defeat is certain. This suggests that cost–benefit analysis may involve something of a two-stage procedure, with probability of success vis-à-vis a given opponent weighed first, and then, if this seems fairly reasonable, a further refinement in the equation is realized through adjustments to reflect the strength of extraneous motivations toward consummation of the particular resource that is at stake.

This particular conception may seem a bit arbitrary, but it explains well a phenomenon that we have just seen in our laboratory, a minor drama that was almost over the time that we noticed it. In order to simulate more natural conditions of life for our animals, and to give them greater possibilities for formation of defensible individual territories in a colony, we are now using earth-floored enclosures into which burrows may be dug. Subordinate animals usually dig or claim a burrow, and are free from harrassment from the colony alpha as long as they remain there. Despite the spaciousness of the enclosure, one very subordinate male of such a colony became so fearful of the alpha that he simply stayed in his burrow, nearly starving to death before we noticed his plight. There was nothing physically wrong with this animal, and it was very familiar to the alpha and vice versa: They had been placed together in the colony at the same time before any burrows had been dug. Nevertheless this animal appeared to base its "decision" not to come out of the burrow for food and water almost exclusively on the high probability of defeat, seemingly giving little weight to its urgent need for food and water. Flannelly and Lore (1977) noted the same thing in strangers introduced into a colony and attacked by the colony alpha. It might be noted that our unfortunate subordinate male had not, in fact, been severely bitten by the alpha. The deciding factor in its cost–benefit analysis was not pain, but fear, and the fear was based on an experientially determined overwhelming probability of defeat.

The other side of the initial equation, that is, that component which is most directly concerned with the success or failure of an offensive attack before modification by extraneous motivations, is anger. This formulation is by no means self-evident, so a bit of a digression is called for. We have suggested that anger is the emotional component of an offensive attack, the tendency to make an attack under certain circumstances. It is now time to consider what those circumstances may be.

We have noted that most sociobiologists pinpoint either direct or indirect resource control as the major mechanism by which conspecific aggression in animals leads to enhanced reproductive success for some individuals. The specific resources that are adaptively defensible may vary from one species to another, although the available choices center around space, females in estrus, and food (Wilson, 1975). The crucial factor determining which resources will be fought over for a particular species is whether (given that all these are crucial for extended fitness) it is worth the risk of fighting to try to control that particular resource. Thus for one bird species, a nest site may be the occasion for fights while food items (which are abundant, or, in small bits) elicit no competition. In another species, the opposite may be true. In evolutionary terms, those animals who have had reactions of anger—the motivation to hurt challenging conspecifics—in situations involving direct or indirect competition over crucial and defensible resources have had greater reproductive success insofar as this anger was elicited in specific situations when success of any actual offense was likely.

Anger, like fear, is a link between the evolutionary cost–benefit analysis that produces specific fighting strategies in each species and the individual cost–benefit analysis that must be undertaken each time a potential combat situation is faced. The ability to feel and respond to fear is based on evolution. The amount of fear experienced in a particular situation is based on preprogrammed reactions to stimuli and situations relatively specific to that species, *and on the individual history of that animal.* In absolutely parallel fashion, the ability to feel and respond to anger is based on evolution. The amount of anger experienced in a particular situation is based on preprogrammed reactions to stimuli and situations relatively specific to that species, *and on the individual history of that animal.*

The major difference between these two systems comes in the relative contributions of preprogramming and individual experience. Fear is a more conservative system, which makes perfectly good sense in terms of the lack of subtlety of danger. Anger, based on threats or challenges to resources that have been defensible in the history of a particular species, is determined by a more complex set of circumstances and is thus from the beginning a less primitive emotion. If the evolutionary history of an animal says that a particular stimulus is dangerous, it takes an awful lot of experience to convince that animal of the contrary. If the evolutionary history of an animal tells it that this is a defensible resource, but it gets beaten up every time it tries to defend it, then experience may have a more immediate effect.

It is in this context that the final value of emotions as the substrate for attack and defense becomes clear. Each emotion, fear or anger, sums or pools the values of a number of diverse factors to result in a particular intensity at a given time. Thus the level of anger may reflect the presence of a challenging conspecific, modified by the importance to the subject of any resources at stake in the situation. Each of these determinants may have both preprogrammed and experiential elements: The challenge of a conspecific may be, in lower animals, a very reflexive, built-in reaction, but in higher animals even the form of a challenge has learning components. With reference to the latter factor, importance of the resource to the individual, this involves both the evolutionary significance of the resource plus whether or not it is defensible for that species, and the magnitude of that individual's need or motivation for that particular resource based on his or her own experience, physiology, hormonal levels, etc. Finally, the specific history of control of this particular resource may be a factor in determining what an individual interprets as a challenge, and this may even influence his or her motivation toward that resource. Thus an animal in possession of a territory treats strangers as challengers even when they are not displaying any signs of offense (for example, when they are totally anesthetized; see Blanchard, Blanchard, Takahashi, & Kelley, 1977). Similarly, a mother mouse's experience with pups—specifically the experience of being suckled—may alter her hormonal status and lead to attacks on strangers in protection of the pups (Svare & Gandleman, 1973).

The point here is that an enormous amount of effort would be necessary to cognitively calculate the values and the sums of each of these interacting factors. Does a rat—indeed do people—perform such calculations? Could they possibly do so in the time span involved in many encounters, such as 5 to 10 seconds or so between the introduction of a stranger into a rat colony and the first alpha bite on this intruder?

The answer to this problem is emotion. Rats no more calculate such factors cognitively than they calculate their blood sugar levels (along with other relevant factors) to determine how hungry they may be. Anger may be a bit different from hunger, in that some of the factors that promote anger involve more cognitive mechanisms (and these, as we shall see, are of greater relative importance in higher animals), but any cognitions involved feed into and operate through the emotion. Anger sums and integrates stimulus input with organismic factors: It is the one value rather than independent lines of eliciting stimuli and situations that powers the offensive attack pattern.

Fear is also a major component of the analysis that determines whether a particular anger-eliciting situation will lead to actual attack. In brief, anger draws from all its diverse sources in a particular incident, and fear similarly summates its own inputs. The next and final step in this emotional calculus is the comparison of the relative magnitude of anger and fear. When anger is greater, offensive attack happens; when fear is greater, offensive attack does not occur. When the two are relatively equal but both are low, there is no agonistic encounter. If they are even and high, one might expect to see components of both offensive and defensive patterns. This is basically the situation in most real-life encounters involving relatively prolonged fighting.

It is close to impossible to measure anger or fear in animals independently of their expression through some aspect of offense or defense, respectively. As will be detailed later, however, anger and fear can be elicited by the same situation and perceived as simultaneous but independent emotional states in people. This suggests that fear does not directly inhibit anger and vice versa or, at any rate, that such inhibition is only partial. Fear does, however, inhibit offense in situations in which offense would clearly have otherwise occurred.

One clear demonstration of this may be seen in the colony situation in which alpha males, who would normally attack intruders with only the shortest of latencies, showed a virtual abolition of attack tendencies when a strong threat stimulus (a nonattacking cat) was placed into the colony along with the rat intruder. In fact, the cat could be briefly presented, and then removed prior to introduction of the strange rat. Offense toward the stranger was still nearly wiped out: Fear inhibits offense. Other less direct but nevertheless consistent demonstrations of this include an inhibition of offense toward intruders who were emitting distress cries, if and only if the attacking rats were themselves inexperienced and thus more fearful (Blanchard & Blanchard, 1980a). One might also regard territoriality itself as constituting an especially potent example of the relationship between fear and offense: The attacker on its own territory is more inclined to attack—and win—because it is unafraid. Repeated successful experience of intruders also provides a very specific reduction in fear to strange rats.

For at least some of these demonstrations it might be argued that the fear involved, although effective in reducing offense, was not really related to the offensive pattern it influenced. That is, there was no reason for the rat to believe that it would encounter further danger as a result of making an offensive attack toward a given animal. People, one might expect, should have much better developed abilities to separate a situational threat from one which will occur as the consequence of one's own actions.

This point contains an important truth but is in equal measure misleading. With reference to the latter, rats as well as people can make the distinction between fear contingent on a specific behavior and fear not contingent in this fashion. The avoidance conditioning literature is replete with examples (cf. Mast, Blanchard, & Blanchard, 1982). However, this cognition of the rat takes a long time and a lot of shocks to develop,

and in the real world the animal would probably have left such an
unpromising situation long before it was likely to arrive at an understanding of it. In other words, its emotional reaction to the situation
would have resulted in an adaptive response even if the animal's cognitive or conceptual capacities were relatively underdeveloped.

However, the system not only continues to work but is actually improved, in terms of adaptive functioning, in species in which these
cognitive abilities are better developed and provide more precise input
and direction to the emotions. People are a great deal better than rats
(though hardly perfect, as a glance at the daily newspaper will attest) at
conscious analysis of the causes of their emotions and in determining
the probability of good or bad outcomes of behaviors they may be con-
templating. These conscious and rational considerations do not, however, serve as the sole decision-making element. Even in people, the effective cost–benefit analyzer, the emotional calculus, continues to serve as
the immediate determinant of the overwhelming majority of aggressive
acts.

More of this, later, in the context of human aggression.

VI. THE ATTACK–DEFENSE DISTINCTION: PHYSIOLOGICAL CONSIDERATIONS

Substantial support for the view that attack and defense are independent neurobehavioral patterns comes from a comparison of the physiological systems that influence each of these. Several reviews, most
notably those of Adams (1979) and Ursin (1981), have summarized what
is presently known of the neural systems underlying attack or defensive
behaviors, whereas the investigation of the relationship between hormones and these two behavior patterns has become one of the scientific
growth areas of the past decade.

A. Neural Systems

Although each of these areas is important, interesting, and complex,
no more than a brief summary is necessary here. Beginning with the
neural elements underlying attack or defense, it is very clear that these
represent virtually nonoverlapping systems. The amygdala, for example, which was for many years considered to be a major component of
the circuit or system underlying aggression, is now seen as a portion of a
defense system. This change came about largely through reanalysis of
the behavioral measures that show differences after amygdala damage.

Such tasks—for example reactions to being handled by a human experimenter—turn out to involve defense and defensive attack, rather than offense. Studies explicitly aimed at determining the effects of amygdala damage on offensive attack (cf. Busch & Barfield, 1974; Takahashi, 1981) strongly indicate that damage to the area of the amygdala has no effect whatever on offense, while at the same time producing a striking decrement in reactivity to nonpainful threat stimuli. There is some indication that animals can learn to behave defensively after actually having been hurt (Blanchard & Blanchard, 1972), but there is no question that large lesions in the area of the amygdala do produce a drop in defensiveness to a wide range of stimuli to which normal rats and wild rats ordinarily respond. The further qualification concerning this particular portion of the brain is that it is not clear exactly what portion of the amygdala is responsible for these effects, and indeed it may be that the crucial site involves only a small part of the amygdala, or even structures that are dorsal to the amygdala proper (Blanchard, Blanchard, Lee, & Williams, 1981). Nevertheless, it is clear that the relevant area is involved with defense and defensive attack and not with offense.

The hypothalamus is another area in which lesions or other manipulations have long been regarded as altering aggression. As the hypothalamus is an enormously complex area through which run many of the neurotransmitter systems originating in old brain areas and passing anteriorly to the forebrain, lesions here often produce a range of nonspecific effects. However, offensive attack behaviors seem to be differentially associated with the lateral hypothalamus, increasing with stimulation and decreasing following lesions of the area. Defense and defensive attack, on the other hand, appear to be more involved in manipulations of medial hypothalamus. There have also been a number of recent investigations of a site in the posterior hypothalamus in which lesions increase offensive attack (Koolhaas, Venderbe, & Terhorst, 1980).

The midbrain central gray is another area in which lesions produce dramatic changes in aggression, which, however, turn out to represent decreases in defense. Here, unlike the amygdala–temporal lobe lesions they otherwise resemble, the deficits appear to be relatively unresponsive to painful experience (Blanchard, Williams, Lee, & Blanchard, 1981). One explanation for this phenomenon may be the abundantly documented (Hasobuchi, Adams, & Linchitz, 1977; Nashold, Wilson, & Slaughter, 1969) involvement of the central gray in the perception of painful events, but there are also suggestions that the endogenous opiate mechanisms that presumably underlie such effects may be as much involved with fear as with pain (Panksepp, Vilberg, Bean, Coy, & Kastin, 1978) so the final story on this intriguing area is also not yet told.

At any rate, however, it is a defense–defensive attack system, rather than an offense system, that is implicated in these effects.

Finally, there also appears to exist a potent fear-inhibitory system with one major component located in an area ventral to the anterior portions of the septum. Lesions here produce startling hyperdefensiveness in rats, including exaggerated defensive attack to handling or other non-painful as well as painful threat stimuli. This system, much investigated in work by Albert and his colleagues (cf. Albert & Richmond, 1977) was—predictably—interpreted as influencing aggressiveness until a clear distinction was made between attack and defensive attack. At that point, it was easily demonstrated that defensive rather than offensive attack was potentiated in rats with lesions in this site (Blanchard, Blanchard, Lee, & Nakamura, 1979). In fact, offensive attack is strikingly reduced in these animals (Blanchard, Blanchard, Takahashi, & Takahashi, 1977; Lau and Miczek, 1977).

This brief outline has suggested that more is known of the neural control of defense and defensive attack than of offensive attack. This is absolutely correct. One reason for this is possibly that defense, a more primitive and basic behavior system, is more widely represented in the brain than is offense. Another consideration is that the measurement of changes in offensive attack are much more difficult and require more specific procedural attention than do changes in defense: Alterations of defensive attack are thus more readily noted than are changes in offense. A description of the neural systems underlying offensive attack will require behavioral procedures designed explicitly to detect these behaviors, a program only just beginning with the realization that the more easily detected defensive attack behaviors are not analytically interchangeable with intraspecies offensive attack.

B. Endocrines and Aggression

As Paul Brain presents in this volume a treatment of hormonal aspects of aggression, it is hardly necessary here to do more than mention the main lines of evidence that the hormonal control of offensive and defensive behaviors are clearly separable and distinct.

The model of hormone–behavior relationships that guides much thinking in this area is that of Leshner (1978), who proposed a two-way relationship between hormones and agonistic behaviors; certain hormones promote or inhibit fighting; the experience of fighting, and especially of victory or defeat, in turn, may change the levels of these same hormones.

Extensive work by Leshner (1978) very nicely illustrates the operation of these systems as does a dissertation by Schuurman (1981). By using rats with indwelling jugular catheters, Schuurman was able to take repeated and nontraumatizing blood samples from male rats before and after attack on a home cage intruder, or placement in a cage already (but briefly) occupied by another animal. These samples were assayed for plasma testosterone, a gonadal hormone consistently linked to aggressiveness in rats and mice. As predicted, rats with higher testosterone levels were more aggressive in their own home cage, and also in confrontation with a strange rat in an unfamiliar area. In the latter situation, the correlation between baseline plasma testosterone and a summed attack measure was $r = .75$, which was highly reliable.

In an additional set of experiments, Schuurman found that rats defeated in a conspecific fight are subsequently less aggressive and more defensive behaviorally, while their baseline plasma testosterone level drops dramatically. In contrast, victors are slightly more aggressive (these were experienced rats so this encounter did not dramatically increase their aggressiveness), while their testosterone levels showed a slight nonsignificant increase. Perhaps the most interesting feature of this experiment was that it also involved blood samples taken during the fight that resulted in victory or defeat. Assays of these samples indicated a rise in testosterone during the fight for both winning and losing animals (the rise was, however, greater for the former group), followed by a drop to baseline for the winners and a decrease to well below baseline for the losers, at about 3 hours after the encounter. Rats with a history of defeat may show no elevation in testosterone levels during fights.

Whereas gross manipulation of testosterone has long been known to alter offensive behaviors in rats and other rodents, from Schuurman's work it now appears that baseline testosterone levels are both good predictors of aggressiveness and responsive on a long-term basis to the animal's history of victory or defeat.

In contrast to this long-term variability, a feature of the individual and its history, corticosterone, a pituitary–adrenal hormone, tends to show short-term changes to stress in all animals, but chronic changes only in a few. (There are hormones other than corticosterone that are much involved in fear and defensiveness, but the subtleties of these are beyond the scope of this brief treatment.) In a procedure identical to the one just described, Schuurman measured corticosterone in male rats before, during, and after fights in their home cages or in unfamiliar cages. Plasma corticosterone rose on placement of rats into the unfamiliar area and during fights in both locales, with a higher rise in the unfamiliar cage. In a longer fight (1-hour duration), in which some experimental rats were losers and others winners, corticosterone rose much more dramatically

for the losers and was still elevated 5 hours later. In contrast, corticosterone for the winners dropped to baseline very quickly. The defeated rats later showed a corticosterone surge in response to the sight of
a strange male conspecific or on being placed in a cage in which they had
previously encountered such a male. Moreover, some defeated rats had
chronically elevated levels. An interesting finding here is that the rats
that showed the pronounced chronic corticosterone elevation after defeat tended also to show a wild drop in blood sugar level during defeat,
which persisted for hours. Victors, and those losers not showing an
exaggerated corticosterone level, subsequently tended to show much
less modification of blood glucose either during or after the fight.

The emerging literature on hormone control of aggression and defense thus suggests that some hormones (notably testosterone) exert a
long-term and modulating influence on the tendency to show offensive
attack, whereas others are more transient and situation bound at least
for the majority of individuals. Moreover, it seems clear that testosterone primarily influences the tendency to show alpha attack, without a
direct influence on fearfulness or defensiveness. However, corticosterone, which is apparently a correlate of stress or fearfulness, can suppress testosterone synthesis (DesJardins & Ewing, 1971), providing an
elegant mechanism for at least some portion of the effect of fear on
aggressiveness.

A final physiological differentiator of attack and defense, for which
the precise mechanism is not yet known, is DU 27725, a compound that
appears to exert a relatively selective suppressing or inhibitory effect on
offensive attack behavior but not defense (Olivier, 1981). As behavioral
work with this compound has only recently begun, it is certainly pre-
mature to conclude that DU 27725 only influences attack behavior. However, there is no question that defense behavior is not altered by a range
of dosages that clearly reduce offense, and that the mechanisms involved are central, rather than motoric.

VII. HUMAN AGGRESSION

The foregoing descriptions of aggression in rats and other animal
species provide an extremely detailed outline of the structure of attack
and defense, including defensive attack, in these animals. It is notable
that this structure, which provides an absolute separation of attack and
defensive patterns in terms of eliciting stimuli and situations, organismic influences, and the actual behaviors involved, is quite consistent
from one species to the next. A more theoretical examination of these

two behavior patterns in terms of the emotions that underlie each of them, and in terms of their adaptive significance, provides still further reason to view these as distinct and to some degree antagonistic patterns.

In attempting to link this model to aggression in people, the logical starting point is behavior. Are there differences in human behavior that correspond to the offense–defense distinction in lower animals? There is an immediate problem in this area in that no one has seriously attempted to analyze possible differences in actual behaviors of combatants in fights that polarize offense versus defensive tendencies. In fact, given the current ethical and legal constraints on human research, it would be virtually impossible to do such a study.

A. Facial Expression

However, there is relevant evidence for such a difference from a number of indirect sources. There is, for example, the well-established and easily identified difference in facial expression for anger as opposed to fearfulness. Izard (1971) reported that subjects from a number of different cultures are capable of identifying posed photographs of individuals expressing fear or terror versus those showing anger or rage. Earlier studies by Tompkins and McCarter and by Woodworth (both reported in Izard, 1971) indicated that there are distinct facial expressions associated with these emotions.

The fearful expression described by Izard (1971) involves transverse (horizontal) wrinkling of the forehead with eyebrows raised and eyes wide open and staring. The pupils are dilated, the mouth open and rigid, and the nostrils flared.

In anger, the eyebrows are drawn down and together, the forehead is wrinkled vertically, and the eyes are opened wide but with pupils contracted. The teeth are usually clenched together tightly and the lips may either be clenched together or drawn back to expose the teeth. The nostrils may be distended.

It might also be noted that children from about 3–4 years of age can recognize these posed expressions as typical of fearful or of angry persons (Izard, 1971). This does not, of course, mean that these two expressions are necessarily an unconditioned and innate response to the emotions with which they are associated, but it certainly attests that the children making these discriminations have experienced consistency between these expressions and verbal or behavioral indications of anger or fear by the expressing subjects.

The possibility that these expressions may have been originally learned through observation and imitation is counterindicated by Eibl-Eibesfelt's (1979) report that the facial expressions of persons born deaf and blind share many features with the relevant angry or fearful expressions of nonhandicapped people. As learning of these expressions would be quite difficult for deaf–blind persons, it seems reasonable that at least some components of these expressions are in fact unlearned, and reflect an inherent difference in the human expression of anger as opposed to fear. This should not be taken to suggest that learning plays no role in human emotional expression—in fact, even in rats, practice results in a smoother and more coordinated offense or defensive behavior pattern—but it does suggest preprogramming of some elements of these.

B. Emotions and Behaviors

A related matter, that of the subjective differences between the emotions of fear and anger, has been summarized by Plutchik (1980). He, and other emotion theorists, have constructed schemas that relate and differentiate various emotion states. In these schemas, based on a variety of scaling techniques, fear and anger are classified as separate emotions, frequently occurring as opposite or near-opposite, rather than similar, subjective experiences. Of the two, fear is regarded as much more unpleasant than is anger: In fact, anger is regarded as the "least unpleasant" of all the negative emotions (Plutchik, 1980).

The first attempt from our laboratory (C. Fukunaga-Stinson, 1978, unpublished study) to investigate human emotions and behaviors that might correspond to an offensive or defensive pattern involved a questionnaire given to 119 students at the University of Hawaii at Manoa. The questionnaire involved two vignettes, one of which described a situation in which the respondent had been given a badly needed work area and then found that it had been taken over by another person who refused to give it up and was rude to boot. The other vignette involved an attack by a stranger in an isolated spot. These vignettes obviously were chosen to tap, in the first case, reactions to disputes over property plus the insult value of having one's books thrown on the floor (as the usurper is described as doing), whereas the second involves physical attack (the stranger is described as grabbing your collar).

After reading each vignette, respondents were asked to list their immediate reaction to the situation, then to indicate, in terms of a line scale, how angry, fearful, determined (as opposed to uncertain), or aggressive they would feel. The final task for each vignette was to indicate the likelihood (on a scale from 1 to 5) of their doing each of a number of actions, such as leaving the scene, hitting the other person, etc.

It does not require a vast amount of clinical judgment to predict that the desk dispute would produce a predominant emotion of anger, whereas being grabbed by a stranger would elicit fear. When anger and fear scores on the line scale were compared, the desk situation elicited a mean score of 74.87 for men and 75.67 for women on the anger scale (minimum = 0, maximum = 100) and 26.85 versus 37.60 (male–female) on the fear scale. In striking contrast, the vignette involving attack by a stranger produced high levels of fear for both men and women (81.74 versus 89.06) and much lower levels of anger (53.39 for women, 37.39 for men). Among the behavioral items ranked, "demand an explanation" was the most likely behavior of those listed for the anger situation. From here, the next most favored choice was to "warn the other person," followed by physical threats such as yelling or scowling, then threatening to involve the authorities, and a desire to hit or kick the other person (but not actually doing it). No actual physical violence appeared among the top six choices, although a desire to attack the other person was a consistent choice.

In reaction to the stranger-attack situation, "I would leave or try to leave as soon as possible" was the most likely action for almost every respondent. However, reactions to the attacking stranger became rather variable after this consistent initial choice. Most of the women selected "look around for something to hit the person with" as the second choice item. The men were somewhat unexpectedly more passive, electing to "cooperate rather than be hurt" or "try to work it out" as second or third choices. For women, these "cooperate" or "work it out" items were generally third and fourth choices, followed by "hit to harm."

The item "I would hit or kick the other person . . . and try to harm him badly" is especially interesting because this behavior was so seldom selected in the desk usurpation vignette. This difference, between wanting to hit but not hitting (for the desk usurper situation) and actually hitting to hurt (for the attacking stranger), strongly suggests some sort of inhibitory influence in the first situation that is not operative in the second.

One final result from this questionnaire is that many respondents added physical symptoms or physiological response patterns to their descriptions. Some of these, such as heart rate changes, were common to both the anger and the fear situations; others, such as "freeze," "stiff," and "nervous breath" were much more common in the context of fear. It is notable that freezing is exclusively associated with defense in infrahuman agonistic behavior. On the other hand, such reactions as "adrenalin surge" and "hot" or "burning" were associated exclusively with anger, as were "clenching fist," "staring at," or "giving stink eye" to the opponent (the latter is a very descriptive Hawaiian phrase indicating an annoyed or mean stare). This pattern of results strongly suggests that fear and anger are differentiable by immediate and low-level reaction patterns, as well as in terms of goals and perceived motivations.

These data, then, present a consistent picture of differences for both emotional reactions and behavior patterns in two situations selected to correspond to either an offensive or a defensive attack model. In the first situation, the protagonist freely elects to stay, but escalates through reason and increasingly potent warnings to a desire to hurt. It is of considerable interest that the desire to hurt was rated as a much more likely event than was an actual attack on the desk usurper. It seems likely that the factor preventing such an attack from actually being carried out was fear of the consequences, either of being hurt by the opponent or of the social or ethical censure that might result. Though speculative, this fits the animal data suggesting that fear is a potent inhibitor of alpha or offensive attack.

In the stranger-attack vignette, subjects wished, above all else, to leave but would either fight or cooperate if escape was not possible. This latter finding strongly suggests that a defensive attack component is included in the defensive repertoire of humans as well as lower animals. In contrast to offensive attack, this defensive attack appears not to be inhibited by fear: It is listed as a highly probable response even for subjects who listed themselves as extremely fearful, with women both more fearful and more likely to attack. It is also notable that this defensive attack is embedded in a situation in which the major goal for all respondents was clearly defensive, to leave the situation as soon as possible. This goal and its allied behavior—flight—provide another parallel to the defense pattern of rats, as do the frequent references to freezing and allied behaviors. In fact, the only behaviors seen in the rat defense pattern that seem to have no direct parallel here are the strategic acts (boxing, lying on the back), which specifically protect the target site for bites in rats. This omission may reflect a lack of appropriate choices in the ranked responses portion of the questionnaire, but it was notable that Adams and Shoel's (1981) study of attack and defensive patterns in macaques failed to suggest a major role of such strategic defense behaviors in these primates, despite clear targeting of offensive bites at the backs of defenders. Perhaps these specific defenses are of less value in facing primate opponents with their uniquely manipulative hands. With this exception, the parallels between the human defense pattern and that of rats are strongly supportive of an evolutionary continuity for both emotional and behavioral aspects of defense.

The Fukunaga–Stinson study, though it provides a wealth of information on emotions and perceived agonistic motivations, is less helpful with reference to possible differences in the actual behaviors that might correspond to an offensive or defensive attack pattern. One—admittedly less than satisfactory—source of such information is found in retrospective reports of fights that people have personally experienced: We have asked a variety of students, colleagues, and acquaintances to describe such fights in terms of the dominant emotions felt at the time and in terms of specific behaviors. These retrospective reports suggest that fear-based attack is, at least under ordinary conditions of life, a much less common event than is attack based on anger. In part this may reflect reluctance of subjects to describe a degrading experience. Another factor is that when a clearly fear-based attack is described, it frequently is lacking in essential detail: The subject remembers the fear, but this memory overshadows what he or she actually did. "I was so scared that when he grabbed me I just went berserk" is a typical description. Despite these limitations, some consistent behavior patterns have begun to emerge from this material. Screaming, as opposed to yelling, is often reported in fear-attack situations; yelling (or no vocalization other than speech) is typical of angry attack. Similarly, biting appears to be largely restricted to defensive attack, as does clawing. These two attack modes are often directed specifically toward the hands of an attacker who has grabbed the fearful individual or toward the attacker's face. These phenomena were exemplified in a very recent episode involving personal acquaintances of one of the authors: One of these individuals, with a history of emotional instability involving paranoia and anxiety, was in the process of having a very vocal anxiety attack in a public place. The other participant was merely a passer-by who attempted to calm the anxious one by putting an arm around his shoulder. Unfortunately this well-meaning individual was a very large person of an ethnicity that, in Hawaii, is popularly associated with high levels of violence. The predictable—and obtained—result was that the anxious party screamed and bit his would-be comforter on the forearm that had been placed around his shoulders.

As fear increases, so does the extent to which the fearful attacker is unmindful of the possibility of damage done to the opponent. At the extreme of fearful attack, the attacker may be so out of control, so reflexive as opposed to calculating, that serious injury to the opponent is a distinct possibility. Reports of abused wives or children turning on their tormenters and killing them may reflect this phenomenon.

Offensive attack in children has been described (Margaret Manning, personal communication; see also Scott, this volume) in terms of an overhand blow to the opponent's head or shoulders. In adults, virtually any blow with the open hand (slap) or with the fist is more likely to reflect anger than fear. One polarized situation, involving anger but usually no fear, is the attack of an adult on a child. This, of course, is to some degree culturally determined, but it is notable how precisely the same rules as in offensive attack in rats may apply: Hurt is accomplished without inflicting serious injury by delivering slaps aimed largely at the heavily muscled posterior (as in many western cultures), or by pinching or pulling sensitive but noncrucial areas such as the earlobe or nose (Latin cultures). It is interesting that, when the attacked party becomes more able to effectively retaliate (cf. during adolescence), this noninjurious offense mode gives way to closed-fist blows aimed at more vulnerable areas such as the head or thorax.

C. Causes of Fear-Based Attack

The Fukunaga–Stinson study just described suggests that fear-based attack is a quite different phenomenon than is angry aggression. Although the use of only two situations in that study makes it difficult to conclude that systematically different types of situations produce fear as opposed to anger, other evidence does support such a conclusion. For example, we have given students a number of brief vignettes describing common aversive events. Subjects were asked to rate their emotional reactions to these events and also to describe both what they would *want* to do in the situation and what they would *actually* do.

The results of this study (D. C. Blanchard and R. J. Blanchard, unpublished observations) strongly suggest that the situations that produce fear-based attack are very specific. High-fear ratings occurred only in the context of an immediate threat to one's own body, or to the person of a loved one such as one's own child. When fear (without anger) did occur in one of these aversive situations, it still did not produce any overt attack unless the situation was described as relatively inescapable, with imminent danger to the person's body.

Attention to the precise events that produce fear-based attack is important because so many of the phenomena interpreted as pain aggression in people seem to us to represent anger aggression instead. This can be true, with anger more influential than fear, even when there is a certain objective danger involved. For example, one of the vignettes we used describes a situation in which an automobile passes too closely and forces the respondent to swerve. Although this situation does involve some possibility of physical harm, students nevertheless responded with high levels of anger and only low levels of fear. It was as if the "insult" value of the situation were more potent than its fear-eliciting properties, despite the real danger involved. Almost all subjects reported that they would want to chase the offending car and ram or otherwise molest it or its driver—but only a few, virtually all of these male, indicated that they would actually do this in such a situation. In fact, they probably would have done it. We selected this situation because college-age men so often gave us retrospective descriptions of fights begun in this fashion. As men were less likely than women to list fear as a response to this event, it seems likely that anger rather than fear was the emotion most directly responsible for any attack tendencies in this situation. Anger may therefore be the more direct determinant of attack even in some situations that offer the possibility of physical harm.

In fact, it may be virtually impossible to elicit a pure human defensive attack reaction in laboratory studies because so many restrictions are necessarily placed on human research. Even if some noxious stimulus is to be delivered, it is usually delivered through nonnatural means such as attached electrodes. Even more importantly, subjects must be informed that no actual danger to themselves is involved.

It was not always so. Some 15 years ago, we attempted to examine the effects of an unexpected and somewhat painful attack against people by giving quite low levels of shock (.3–.4 mA) to college-age volunteer subjects without warning through a shock prod. (We had informed them that shock was involved, but they did not expect it from the prod.) The level of shock used, when given through an attached electrode to the typical "reassured" subject, was quite tolerable and produced little reaction except flinching. In contrast, our first prod-shock subject reported great fear and quit the experiment. The second subject began to scream and attacked the experimenter. There was no third subject.

When we abandoned this project due to the extreme reactions it elicited, we had no idea that these two subjects had actually given us a rather comprehensive sample of defensive behaviors, from withdrawal to defensive attack. Because of higher standards for informed consent, etc. for human subjects, this experiment is not likely to be repeated. Our best examples of human fear-based attack appear destined to come from retrospective reports.

D. The Causes of Angry Aggression

As fear-based attack is so rare, at least under relatively normal conditions, it follows that the applicability of the rat-based colony model depends largely on the extent to which offensive attack can be related to human angry aggression.

Perhaps the central question in this context is the extent to which the emotion of anger can be tied to a specific set of eliciting conditions that resemble those analyzed earlier as the occasions for offense in a range of mammals. Another consideration is the extent to which the same set of external factors—notably fear—which inhibit offensive attack in animals, will play a similar role in human angry aggression.

The first of these questions is by far the most complicated: What do the situations or events that make people angry have in common? How are these related to the events that elicit offensive attack in lower animals? In this context it may be useful to recall that our analysis of offensive attack in subhuman mammals suggested three major types of offense-eliciting situations. First was a dispute over control of important resources. Second, or perhaps an alternative to the first, was the establishment or maintenance of within-species dominance relationships. We suggested that the relative importance of these two factors, both of which might well be embedded in the same confrontation situations, might vary from species to species, with the degree of social cohesiveness of the particular species a major variable influencing the evolution of resource control as opposed to dominance as the more important aggression elicitor. In either of these cases, however, a challenging conspecific should tend to elicit high-level attack tendencies that would then be expressed unless the same animal (or situation) also produced considerable fearfulness.

It is something of a paradox that the literature on events causing aggression—or at any rate anger—in the real world is rather sparse. It is not necessarily the case that few studies have been done; however, the causes thus obtained through interview or questionnaire material are often grouped in such a fashion that they become rather difficult to compare. Averill (1978) has done a service in compiling some of these materials in a manner that, although it certainly does not permit any direct or quantitative comparison with the view just outlined, certainly suggests that most episodes of anger in people are triggered by either resource competition (i.e., disputes over prerogatives), dominance, or perhaps both.

For example, analysis of answers to a questionnaire involving the latest instance of anger for the respondents yielded a list that consisted of "frustration of ongoing activities," "violation of expectations and wishes," "loss of pride, esteem, worth," "violation of socially accepted ways of doing things," "property damage," and "injury and pain." The first two of these categories could and probably did include instances involving both resources or rights and dominance. Both "frustration of ongoing activities" or "violation of expectations and wishes" implies that some object or event that the respondent felt he or she should be able to control was disputed. Such disputations, of course, constitute a challenge to the person's dominance over this specific item or event, and perhaps threaten his or her status on a more general level. The relative mixture of the two motives is very difficult to untangle from the category descriptions, and indeed it might be difficult to untangle if one were actually an observer: In people, just as in animals, the two causes are closely intertwined.

Of the remaining categories, two ("loss of pride . . ." and "violation of socially accepted ways of doing things") are more clearly related to the dominance explanation. The second of these may at first seem a little hard to fit, but a moment's reflection suggests that people who become angry with violation of social mores tend to be people who feel themselves as part of the prevailing cultural establishment, and it is the authority of this establishment that is challenged by unorthodox behavior. Ergo a challenge—by extension—to the dominance and authority of the respondent's attitudes. A third category, "property damage" is clearly related to resource competition, leaving only the last, "injury and pain," as unrelated to either of the factors pinpointed in animal studies. Injury and pain, however, are obviously similar to conditions that produce defensive attack in lower animals, and, as the Fukunaga–Stinson study indicated, some anger (though much less anger than fear) can result from the sort of conspecific attack that produces in people a very high probability of retaliatory attack.

Our feeling for the correspondence of the causes of human anger and angry aggression and the results of sociobiological analyses of offense in lower animals is based on more than abstract verbal comparisons. We have now read thousands of aggression questionnaires and conducted scores of in-depth interviews on the aggressive histories of young men and women. In the college-age population, and for the relatively few older people we have interviewed, anger occurs when the angry person perceives a challenge—either implicit or explicit—to something that he or she regards as his or her own prerogative or to the prerogative of another group or party with whom the respondent identifies. In some cases (more so among children, adolescents, and young men), the precise nature of the prerogative itself is not very clear, but the challenging status of the anger-eliciting person is very clear indeed. In fact, every culture known has some form of symbolic challenge in the form of a gesture or verbal taunt. By and large mature individuals can distinguish between meaningful insults (which actually do threaten some valued area of self-esteem) and totally meaningless and rather impersonal insults of the variety that enjoy such popularity among male youth. The existence of culturally defined insults and also their important status as

anger elicitors in college students both suggest that the challenging conspecific is an important cause of anger in people as well as in subhuman
mammals.

Our experience, as well as the results of previous studies in the area,
thus suggest that the causes of human aggression may be very similar to
the factors that elicit offense in animals. There seems to be no question,
though, that in people the relative proportion of agonistic incidents
stemming from disputes over resources is rather less than the number
stemming from challenges to rather more abstract rights or prerogatives.
A few words about this shift, and its meaning in terms of some important differences between people and lower animals, might be in order.

Small children do indeed become angry and fight over material resources. In fact, such resource disputes may constitute the bulk of aggression incidents in early childhood (Hall, Lam, & Perlmutter, 1981).
However, as children grow up, such incidents give way in frequency to
angry aggression not based on disputes over material objects.

There are probably a great number of reasons for this shift. For example, many of the items—toys, candy, and the like—which are so es-
teemed by young children, come soon to be regarded as of lesser importance than the good social relationships with peers that might be
jeopardized by fights. However, increasing maturity inevitably brings a
new host of material items that are as important (to the adolescent or
teenager, for example) as is candy is to the young child.

The major difference between a small child and an older child or adult
is that the latter are much more cognizant of the well-defined rules or
laws concerning ownership in our culture, or indeed in any other
culture. Confrontation over resources is much reduced by a rather clear
understanding of just what items belong to whom. In most cases the
question of ownership never gets anywhere near an official adjudica-
tion, although the law may well be applicable. Instead, disputes over
property come increasingly to be settled through local authorities such
as one's father or mother rather than through fighting. The latter is
usually discouraged as a technique for controlling resources, and for
most people fights over material resources become quite rare by adolescence.

It is not that anger ceases to accompany resource disputes in adults.
Instead, people have created a major cultural mechanism to deal with
such disputes, thus averting much of the anger and even more of the
overt aggression that might be expected to arise from the complex questions of ownership that plague materialistic societies. This mechanism is
the law, viewed in both its formal and informal aspects. It is arguable
that the most elaborate and extensively utilized portion of the law is that

which concerns ownership, property, rights (to control resources), and the like. We maintain that these legal rights, and indeed those that deal with intangible prerogatives as well, represent cultural management of the enduring psychological dispositions of people to claim and defend both resource and status prerogatives.

Although the law covers both material and nonmaterial rights, it seems to be somewhat more effective in handling cases involving the former. Prerogatives of a nontangible sort tend to change somewhat faster than do ownership statutes, and this creates a considerably larger gray area for disagreement. Also, complex human societies with their densely interdependent social and political roles have created an almost unmanageably large number of relationships involving rights or prerogatives. Finally, there is no question that special interest groups and individuals often use the law in a rather opportunistic fashion, creating prerogatives through judicial interpretation rather than legislative intent. For all these reasons and more, resource disputes (within a country, at least; the international situation is quite different) tend to be referred to appropriate authority, whereas interpersonal and non-material prerogatives are more often settled by the individuals, with anger and sometimes aggression as the result. In fact, it might even be argued that the growth and development of a system involving appeal to authority to settle disputes (and this may be seen in some higher primates as well as in man) also served as a spur for the development of symbolic challenges or insults for the specific function of arousing anger, but not providing grounds for authority to intervene. If small boys were absolutely prevented from making the gestures they make now, another set of equally insulting behaviors would probably be developed in short order!

All of this also demonstrates that though the law is a major determinant of what people regard as their prerogatives, legal prerogatives and psychological prerogatives are not identical. A right or prerogative is ultimately whatever an individual believes that he or she can claim with some degree of success. In an important psychological sense, might *does* make right, and the aphorism to the contrary may be seen as only one of many efforts to elevate human motivations above their basic animal origins. For this is very close to the usage of the term in animals, in which experience and biological mechanisms interact to produce a claim on certain resources, and it is equally applicable to the behavior of small children who can recognize a right although they have never heard of a law. In children, as in adults, both material (property) and nonmaterial rights may be claimed and defended, insofar as the claimant has any real expectation of success. Although the child is angry and fights more over

things, and the adult over nontangible prerogatives, the mechanism for
the two types of rights is rather similar. Success in pressing a claim—
even inconsistent success—will produce the belief that this claim is, in
fact, a prerogative. Consistent failure, and especially consistent failure
accompanied by authoritative announcements that the claimed item
does not belong to the claimant, will eventually result in abandonment
of that claim. The child who has been accustomed to success in delaying
bedtime through tantrums will abandon these if and only if bedtime is
strictly and consistently enforced. What is meaningful in this situation is
that the anger as well as the protests will quickly disappear. When the
concept "I can stay up if I want to!" changes to "Bedtime is *always* eight
o'clock" then there is no anger at being put to bed at eight. Regret,
perhaps, but no anger.

E. Anger Control and Aggression Control Mechanisms

This analysis suggests that the factors that elicit aggression in people
are very much analogous to those that produce offense in lower animals.
However the number and variety of events that embody these factors
have been magnified by cultural and technological advancements that
have sharply increased both the material and the social–political prerogatives claimed by individuals or groups. These complex prerogative
systems are managed in part through a specific and relatively successful
network of relevant laws. Nevertheless, legal systems can never be expected to totally control or contain (much less prevent) all challenges to
human prerogatives. Anger is still, and will continue to be, a common
and even normal part of human life.

As anger-eliciting situations are common for people, cultural factors
that act to reduce anger directly, as well as additional mechanisms that
suppress the acting out of aggressive impulses associated with such
anger, are crucial to successful societies.

With reference to the first, the legal and moral codes that are so
involved with the specification of prerogatives are also necessarily (and
perhaps even more importantly) involved with specification of what is
not the prerogative of an individual. Examples of these dicta run as
threads through the fiber of human experience, from elegant and general statements ("Do unto others as you would have them do unto you")
to the most specific and prosaic ("A parent may not claim a casualty loss
deduction for damage to a car registered in his son's name, although the
parent provided funds for the purchase of the car"—*Income Tax Manual*).

The purpose of such statements, at least in part, is to control both
anger and the confrontations to which anger gives rise, through limita-

tion of prerogatives: A commitment to one of these codes will therefore modulate or perhaps even eliminate anger at events that might otherwise result in an aggressive response. If one does not have a prerogative, then anger is not experienced when the prerogative is challenged. Insofar as people can be convinced that their prerogatives are limited, they will endure—without anger—encroachments that would elicit rage from those who perceive their rights as more encompassing. This psychological relationship between rights and anger has long been understood as a fact of political life: Repressive regimes can function without substantial danger of rebellion insofar as the masses can be convinced that they have no right to expect more. In such an atmosphere the concept of human rights can be explosive.

A final consideration in this brief treatment is concerned with the expression of anger in overt aggression. This provides an important parallel between offensive attack in the animal model and anger-based attack in people: Fear inhibits both of these. It may be recalled that fear does not reduce defensive attack in rats, and that very high levels of fear were compatible with high-level defensive attack tendencies in the Fukunaga–Stinson study. However, fear proved a very potent inhibitor of offensive attack in the colony model.

The evidence concerning fear as an inhibitor of offensive attack in people is scattered and sometimes indirect, but consistent. Fear of any of the numerous consequences of nondefensive aggression can reduce the probability of such aggression in people. For example, there is an extensive literature on laboratory studies of human aggression indicating that subjects who believe that their victim will be allowed to retaliate show less aggression than if no retaliation is possible (cf. Donnerstein & Donnerstein, 1973, 1975; Donnerstein, Donnerstein, Simon, & Ditrichs, 1972; Wilson & Rogers, 1975). Several real-life cases illustrating the same point were given in Blanchard and Blanchard (1982), for example, victim selection often involves fine discriminations between those who are likely to retaliate or to have allies capable of retaliation, as opposed to those (foreigners, old people, etc.) who are not. Another source of punishment for aggression is based on disapproval by family and friends: There is a clear negative relationship between the level of disapproval of aggression for particular individuals within a culture and the amount of aggression displayed by those individuals. Thus, in Hawaii, women of Japanese descent are more subject to sanction by their families for violence, and display less, than do women of Chinese, Caucasian, or Hawaiian descent. We have argued that both the informal cultural sanctions (manifest through family and peer disapproval, reduction of employment opportunities, etc.) and certainty of legal sanctions for violence are major factors in the drastically lower level of violence in Japan as opposed to the United States (Blanchard & Blanchard, 1982).

A final area through which punishment reduces aggression is that of guilt. In addition to specification of prerogatives, moral and religious codes almost universally add a proscription of violence except under certain (prerogative-based) conditions. In fact the teaching of guilt (i.e., a code by which the child comes to punish himself for transgressions) is a major task of childrearing in any culture. Such teaching is by no means always effective, especially in cultures without a dominant ethical code, but there is no question that even very angry people can fail to show aggression because they feel that they would be subject to remorse or guilt at their actions.

F. Pathological Aggression

If there exist separate neurobehavior systems of fear-based and anger-based attack, then one might expect different manifestations of pathological violence stemming from the two systems.

Of the two, defensive attack is clearly the more programmed in terms of specific brain systems for which the normal behavioral output is a somewhat stereotyped and stimulus-controlled action pattern. This brain system is strikingly represented in the temporal lobe, and lesions in this area in rats sharply reduce defense (Blanchard, Blanchard, Lee, & Nakamura, 1979; Blanchard, Blanchard, Lee, & Williams, 1981; Woods, 1956). In people, a syndrome of episodic dyscontrol is often associated with abnormal brain functioning in the temporal area. The subjective experience of the dyscontrol patient involves dread, anxiety, tension, and feelings of being pressured by others. When dyscontrol violence does erupt, it may involve screaming, clawing, and biting (V. Mark, personal communication). The patient seems comparatively little affected by the damage he or she is producing even when severe injury to friends or family ensues, nor is the threat of immediate punishment or legal difficulties very effective in controlling such dyscontrol violence. We have interpreted such violence as a pathological manifestation of defensive attack (Blanchard & Blanchard, 1980b).

In contrast, although the emotion of anger and some behavioral manifestations of offensive aggresion also reflect neurobehavioral systems that might be directly influenced by hormonal or neurochemical variation, there is no question that normal human anger is also a response to events that have been processed through complex cognitive mechanisms. Here, learning is a more crucial factor than in defense, and those events that elicit and control anger in an individual may reflect the integration of concepts coming from many sources.

It follows, then, that one source of pathology in angry aggression is an abnormal or defective conceptualization of one's own prerogatives vis-à-vis those of others, or, through susceptibility to an unusual range of insults. Some of these factors may be seen in the very elegant studies of bullies and "whipping boys" reported by Olweus in this volume. Bullies who routinely pick on other boys with minimal provocation tend to be the product of unloving and punitive parents (especially mothers). This experience may be interpreted as having produced in these boys a slanted and defective view of what constitutes their prerogatives and what events challenge these prerogatives (on the elicitation side), and, equally importantly, an alteration in the perceived cognitive consequences (self-respect versus shame) of aggression.

With reference to the first, a straightforward role-modeling interpretation (with cognitive overtones) appears justified: Punitive treatment reinforces the attitude that "might makes right." Moreover, to be the recipient of harsh or undeserved punishment is disagreeable and demeaning; a habitually punished child may recognize more than others that to *give* punishment can sometimes involve personal satisfaction, a sense of power, enhancement of a sense of self-worth. This last is especially important when one's own sense of self-worth is fragile—and a history of having been abused is often associated with feelings of humiliation and worthlessness. The unloved and abused child thus feels anger at events that pose no challenge to the prerogatives of normally reared individuals. They also may receive greater satisfaction from humiliating others. Note that a somewhat similar mechanism may perhaps be involved in the motivations of certain rapists (Groth & Loredo, 1981).

Variation in control factors may also be involved in pathological aggression. Fear of the consequences of aggression is a major control element for normal people. For example, we have recently analyzed data indicating that the least aggressive people are those whose parents punished them for both justified and unjustified acts of aggression in childhood: A parental distinction between unjustified aggression (which was punished) and justified aggression (not punished) leads to higher levels of violence in adulthood. The mechanism of this effect appears to be that, when one is angry, one almost always feels somewhat justified in this anger and in a desire to hurt the challenger. If justified aggression is all right, then the familial and ethical sanctions for such an act appear (at the moment of anger, at least) to be less likely or less negative. For the individual who has been censured for any aggression, regardless of its justification, this out is not available.

In applying this reasoning to the bully, aggression is perceived more as an ego-enhancing, than as an ego-reducing, act. Whereas the social and perhaps familial consequences of aggression may still be negative, these are less important as the bully has less to lose in them anyway; his or her home and school relationships are less satisfying to begin with. (It might be noted that a potentially important technique for reducing violence in such an individual is to give him or her a meaningful—emotional—stake in society. Of course this is easier said than done.)

It is also possible that there is a class of pathologically aggressive individuals for whom none of these background–learning factors apply, who may have had a relatively normal upbringing and family affection, etc., but who simply do not respond by entering into meaningful emotional relationships which then act to promote respect for the rights and welfare of other people. This sociopathic personality may not be overtly violent—he or she still responds to fear of punishment—but the lack of reluctance to do harm frequently results in harm done. Such people do not necessarily feel more angry, but a major factor controlling angry aggression is lacking in them. Although traditional explanations for the appearance of such personality traits have concentrated on learning factors, it is possible that biological variation is involved also.

Finally, biological variation appears to be definitely involved in some instances of—if not pathological—at least heightened offensive aggressiveness. Testosterone levels, long known to influence aggression in lower animals, also act in a rather similar fashion in people. For example, Olweus (this volume) reports that in normal boys—not bullies—the tendency to react forcefully to violation of perceived rights is significantly correlated with testosterone levels. Women being treated for episodes of violence at a neuropsychiatric institute (Hovey & Rickler, 1980) also have significantly elevated testosterone levels. Thus both biological and cognitive–experiential factors are involved in the elicitation and in the control of angry aggression. Variation in either biological or learning factors may result in heightened aggression through enhanced elicitation or through reduced control. The model is complicated, but if it were not, it could not hope to cover the complexities of human aggressive behavior.

VIII. AGGRESSION IN ANIMALS AND HUMANS: A SUMMARY

The major thrust of this treatment—and indeed of the series of which this volume is the first—is that aggression is a phenomenon that will ultimately be understood. There is no question that it needs to be understood, but the enormous gap between human manifestations of aggression and the far simpler behaviors of lower animals has made it difficult to use the latter as a model for the purpose of experimental analysis.

What we have specifically addressed here is this question: Is there sufficient correspondence between aggression in animals and humans to make such modeling scientifically productive? Can an animal model illuminate some of the mysteries of human aggression? And our answer—hardly in doubt at this point—is yes. Starting from a model of offensive and defensive attack in rats, which extends without major difficulty to other subhuman animals, we believe that we can find similarly differentiable behavior patterns in people. Moreover, these patterns of fear-based attack and angry aggression have clearly different antecedents, different subjective (emotional) concomitants, and are influenced by different organic factors. Finally, those factors that elicit and control the two types of attack in the animal model appear to act in an almost identical fashion in human aggression.

Have we tried to build a complex edifice with very few bricks? Certainly it would be nice to have more evidence. On the other hand, evidence relative to a very specific hypothesis, such as this one, is not likely to be forthcoming until the hypothesis is explicitly stated. Moreover, though still rather sparse, what evidence is available is very much in agreement with the model. It is, for example, instructive to go over the experimental literature on human aggression (cf. Baron, 1977) and to attempt to reinterpret each study in terms of the distinction between fear- and anger-based attack, and in light of the factors (here briefly outlined) that influence angry aggression. Just as contradictions in the animal aggression literature began to disappear when the attack–defense distinction is applied to that literature, so does this model seem capable of illuminating some of the complexities of the human aggression literature.

The concept of a prerogative or right as an important event the individual feels he or she should be able to control and the allied concept of the challenging conspecific as an immediate eliciting stimulus constitute the lynchpins of the connection we have tried to draw between offensive attack in animals and human angry aggression. To the methodologically more precise reader these concepts may appear rather vague. On the other hand, rights have a real meaning in human life, both in terms of abstractions (as in the law, or philosophy, or religion) and in terms of the values illustrated in the everyday behaviors of individuals. The universal preoccupation with what is "mine" and what is not and the ubiquity of culturally determined insults or challenges suggest concepts that have evolved hand in hand with the increasing complexity of behavior and cognition in the transition from subhuman animals to man. With all due respect to those distinguished thinkers who have tried to explain the cause of human aggression solely by concepts such as frustration or pain, we think it cannot be done. The causal and control factors for human aggression are linked to both biology and to some of the most elegant of human conceptual faculties. To understand aggression is not only to see better ways of controlling it, but also to appreciate better its normal functioning in the regulation of human affairs.

In fact, one of the major benefits of the model we are here proposing is that it directs attention specifically toward analysis of the normal, functional aspects of aggression, as compared to those that are pathological and/or deleterious to human life and social institutions. For defensive attack especially, it is obvious that attempts to totally eliminate aggression might produce greater harm than good, more injustice than justice. If psychology has any role to play in the construction of guidelines for the management of defensive attack, it seems likely that this role will involve identification and treatment of individuals who react with defensive attack to nonthreatening situations, or whose reactions are grossly out of proportion to the magnitude of the occasioning stimulus.

For offensive attack, the situation is much more complicated. Although the capacity to feel and respond aggressively to anger is largely biological, the specific causes of anger—the insults, the challenges to prerogatives, the prerogatives themselves—are in large part based on cultural models. In this context, management of aggression should involve very careful analysis of just what constitutes, either within a culture or in the context of law, unwarranted or excessive aggression. Only for such instances is control appropriate. When it is, however, the model of which we have here given a preliminary sketch should suggest not one but many ways in which constructive control is possible.

References

Adams, D. B. Defense and territorial behavior dissociated by hypothalamic lesions in the rat. *Nature,* 1971, **232,** 573–574.

Adams, D. B. Brain mechanisms for offense, defense, and submission. *The Behavioral and Brain Sciences,* 1979, **2,** 201–241.

Adams, D. B. Motivational systems of agonistic behavior in muroid rodents: A comparative review and neural model. *Aggressive Behavior,* 1980,**6,** 295–346.

Adams, D. B., & Shoel, W. M. Motor patterns and motivational systems of social behavior in male rats and stumptail macaques—Are they homologous? *Aggressive Behavior,* 1981, **6,** 267–280.

Albert, D. J., & Richmond, S. E. Reactivity and aggression in the rat-induction by alpha-adrenergic blocking agents injected ventral to anterior septum but not into lateral septum. *Journal of Comparative and Physiological Psychology,* 1977, **91,** 886–896.

Alberts, J. R., & Galef, B. G. Olfactory cues and movement: Stimuli mediating intraspecific aggression in wild Norway rat. *Journal of Comparative and Physiological Psychology*, 1973, **85**, 233–242.

Alcock, J. *Animal behavior: An evolutionary approach*, Sunderland: Sinauer Associates, 1979.

Averill, J. R. Anger: A Review. In R. A. Dienstbier (ed.), *Nebraska Symposium on Motivation: Human Emotion*, Lincoln, Nebraska: University of Nebraska Press, 1978.

Barnett, S. A. *The rat: A study in behavior*, London: Metheun, 1963.

Barnett, S. A., & Stoddart, R. C. Effects of breeding in captivity on conflict among wild rats. *Journal of Mammology*, 1969, **50**, 321–325.

Baron, R. *Human aggression*, New York: Plenum Press, 1977.

Blanchard, D. C., & Blanchard, R. J. Violence in hawaii: A preliminary analysis. In A. Goldstein and M. Segal, (eds.), *Global perspectives on aggression*, New York: Pergamon Press, 1982.

Blanchard, D. C., Blanchard, R. J., Lee, E. M. C., & Nakamura, S. Defensive behaviors in rats following septal and septal-amygdala lesions. *Journal of Comparative and Physiological Psychology*, 1979, **93**, 378–390.

Blanchard, D. C., Blanchard, R. J., Lee, E. M. C., & Williams, G. Taming in the wild Norway rat following lesions in the basal ganglia. *Physiology and Behavior*, 1981, **27**, 995–1000.

Blanchard, D. C., Williams, G., Lee, E., & Blanchard, R. J. Taming in the wild rat following lesions of the mesencephalic central gray. *Physiological Psychology*, 1981, **9**, 157–163.

Blanchard, R. J., & Blanchard, D. C. Escape and avoidance responses to a fear-eliciting situation. *Psychonomic Science*, 1968, **13**, 19–20.

Blanchard, R. J., & Blanchard, D. C. Passive and active reactions to fear-eliciting stimuli. *Journal of Comparative and Physiological Psychology*, 1969, **68**, 129–135.

Blanchard, R. J., & Blanchard, D. C. Dual mechanisms in passive avoidance I. *Psychonomic Science*, 1970, **19**, 1–2. (a)

Blanchard, R. J., & Blanchard, D. C. Dual mechanisms in passive avoidance II. *Psychonomic Science*, 1970, **19**, 3–4. (b)

Blanchard, R. J., & Blanchard, D. C. Innate and conditioned reactions to threat in rats with amygdaloid lesions. *Journal of Comparative and Physiological Psychology*, 1972, **81**, 281–290.

Blanchard, R. J., & Blanchard, D. C. The colony model: Experience counts. *Behavioral and Neural Biology*, 1980, **30**, 109–112. (a)

Blanchard, R. J., & Blanchard, D. C. Animal aggression and the dyscontrol syndrome. In M. Girgis, (ed.), *Progress in biological psychiatry* (Vol. 2), *Limbic epilepsy and the dyscontrol syndrome*, New York: Elsevier, 1980. (b)

Blanchard, R. J., & Blanchard, D. C. The organization and modelling of aggressive behavior. In P. F. Brain and D. Benton, (eds.), *The biology of aggression*, Noordhoof/Sijthoff: Alphen aan den Rijn, 1981.

Blanchard, R. J., Blanchard, D. C., Takahashi, T., & Kelley, M. Attack and defensive behavior in the albino rat. *Animal Behavior*, 1977, **25**, 622–634.

Blanchard, D. C., Blanchard, R. J., Takahashi, T., & Suzuki, N. Aggressive behaviors of the Japanese Brown Bear. *Aggressive Behavior*, 1978, **4**, 31–41.

Blanchard, D. C., Blanchard, R. J., Takahashi, L. K., & Takahashi, T. Septal lesions and aggressive behavior. *Behavioral Biology*, 1977, **21**, 157–161.

Blanchard, R. J., Mast, M., & Blanchard, D. C. Stimulus control of defensive reactions in the albino rat. *Journal of Comparative and Physiological Psychology*, 1974, **88**, 81–88.

Blanchard, R. J., O'Donnell, V., & Blanchard, D. C. Attack and defensive behaviors in the albino mouse (*Mus musculus*). *Aggressive Behavior*, 1979, **5**, 341–352.

Blanchard, R. J., Takahashi, L. K., & Blanchard, D. C. The development of intruder attack in colonies of laboratory rates. *Animal Learning and Behavior*, 1977, **5**, 365–369.

Blanchard, R. J., Takahashi, L. K., Fukunaga, K. K., & Blanchard, D. C. Functions of the vibrissae in the defensive and aggressive behavior of the rat. *Aggressive Behavior*, 1977, **3**, 231–240.

Busch, D. E., & Barfield, R. J. A failure of amygdaloid lesions to alter agonistic behavior in the laboratory rat. *Physiology and Behavior*, 1974, **12**, 887–892.

Christie, M. H., & Barfield, R. J. Effects of castration and home cage residency on aggressive behavior in rats. *Hormones and Behavior*, 1979, **13**, 85–91.

Dollard, J., Doob, L. W., Miller, N. E., Mowrer, O. H., & Sears, R. R. *Frustration and aggression*, New Haven: Yale University Press, 1939.

Donnerstein, E., & Donnerstein, M. Variables in interracial aggression: Potential ingroup censure. *Journal of Personality and Social Psychology*, 1973, **27**, 143–150.

Donnerstein, E., & Donnerstein, M. The effect of attitudinal similarity on interracial aggression. *Journal of Personality*, 1975, **43**, 485–502.

Donnerstein, E., Donnerstein, M., Simon, S., & Ditrichs, R. Variables in interracial aggression: Anonymity, expected retaliation, and a riot. *Journal of Personality and Social Psychology*, 1972, **22**, 236–245.

Edmunds, M. *Defense in animals*. London: Longmans, 1975.

Eibl-Eibesfelt, I. The fighting behavior of animals. *Scientific American*, 1961, **205**, 112–122.

Eibl-Eibesfelt, I. Human ethology: Concepts and implications for the sciences of man. *The Behavioral and Brain Sciences*, 1979, **2**, 1–57.

Ewer, R. F. The biology and behavior of a free-living population of black rats (*Rattus rattus*). *Animal Behaviour Monographs*, 1971, **4**, 127–174.

Fass, B., Gutterman, P. E., & Stevens, D. A. Evidence that resident male albino rats are not immune to attack by conspecific intruders. *Aggressive Behavior*, 1979, **5**, 135–141.

Flannelly, K., & Lore, R. Observations of the subterranean activity of domesticated and wild rats (*Rattus norvegicus*): A descriptive study. *Psychological Record*, 1977, **21**, 315–329.

Flannelly, K. J., & Thor, D. H. Social experience and territorial aggression in rats: A replication with selected aggressive males. *Journal of General Psychology*, 1976, **95**, 321–322.

Flannelly, K. J., & Thor, D. H. Territorial aggression of the rat to males castrated at various ages. *Physiology and Behavior*, 1978, **20**, 785–789.

Geist, V. On weapons, combat and ecology. In L. Kramer, P. Plimer, & T. Alloway (eds.), *Advances in the study of communication and affect*, New York: Plenum, 1978.

Grant, E. C. An analysis of the social behavior of the male laboratory rat. *Behavior*, 1963, **21**, 260–281.

Groth, A., & Loredo, C. M. Rape: The sexual expression of aggression. In P. F. Brain and D. Benton, (eds.), *Multidisciplinary approaches to aggression research*, Amsterdam: Elsevier/North Holland, 1981.

Hall, E., Lamb, M. E., & Perlmutter, M. *Child psychology today*, New York: Random House, 1981.

Hasobuchi, Y., Adams, J. E., & Linchitz, R. Pain relief by electrical stimulation of the central gray matter in humans and its reversal by naloxone. *Science*, 1977, **197**, 183–186.

Hovey, J. E., & Rickler, K. C. Characteristics of aggressive patients in a neuro-behavioral outpatient clinic. *Aggressive Behavior*, 1980, **6**, 276.

Izard, C. E. *The face of emotion*, New York: Appleton-Century-Crofts, 1971.

Koolhaas, J. M., Schuurman, T., & Wiepkema, P. R. The organization of intraspecific agonistic behaviour in the rat. *Progress in Neurobiology,* 1980, **15,** 247–268.

Koolhaas, J. M., Vanderbe, M., & Terhorst, G. J. The nucleus premammilaris ventralis (pmv) and aggressive behavior in the rat. *Aggressive Behavior,* 1980, **6,** 250.

Koutnik, D. L. Submissive signalling in the male deer. *Animal Behavior,* 1980, **28,** 312–313.

Kruk, M. R. *Origins of hypothalamic aggression in the rat.* Ph.D. Thesis, University of Leiden, Leiden, 1981.

Lagerspetz, K. M. J. Aggression and aggressiveness in laboratory mice. In S. Garattini & E. B. Sigg (eds.), *Aggressive behavior,* New York: Wiley, 1969.

Lau, P., & Miczek, K. A. Differential effects of septal lesions on attack and defensive-submissive reactions during intraspecies aggression in rats. *Physiology and Behavior,* 1977, **19,** 479–485.

Leshner, A. I. *An introduction to behavioral endocrinology,* New York: Oxford University Press, 1978.

Leyhausen, P. *Cat behavior: The predatory and social behavior of domestic and wild cats,* New York: Garland STPM Press, 1979.

Lore, R., & Flannelly, K. Rat societies. *Scientific American,* 1977, **236,** 106–116.

Luciano, D., & Lore, R. Aggression and social experience in domesticated rats. *Journal of Comparative and Physiological Psychology,* 1975, **88,** 917–923.

Mast, M., Blanchard, R. J., & Blanchard, D. C. The relationship of freezing and response suppression in a CER situation. *The Psychological Record,* 1982, **32,** 151–167.

Maynard-Smith, J., & Price, G. R. The logic of animal conflict. *Nature,* 1973, **246,** 15–18.

Miczek, K. A. Intraspecies aggression in rats. Effects of *d*-amphetamine and chlordiazepoxide. *Psychopharmacologia,* 1974, **39,** 275–301.

Miller, N. E. Studies of fear as an aquireable drive. *Journal of Experimental Psychology,* 1948, **38,** 89–101.

Moyer, K. E. Kinds of aggression and their physiological basis. *Communications in Behavioral Biology,* 1968, **2,** 65–87.

Nashold, B. S., Wilson, W. P., & Slaughter, D. G. Sensations evoked by stimulation in the midbrain of man. *Journal of Neurosurgery,* 1969, **30,** 14–24.

O'Donnell, V., Blanchard, R. J., & Blanchard, D. C. Mouse aggression increases after 24 hours of isolation or housing with females. *Behavioral and Neural Biology,* 1981, **32,** 89–103.

Olivier, B. Selective anti-aggression properties of DU-27725—Ethological analyses of inter-male and territorial aggression in the male rat. *Pharmacology, Biochemistry, and Behavior,* 1981, **14,** 61–77.

Panksepp, J., Vilberg, T., Bean, N. J., Coy, D. H., & Kastin, A. J. Reduction of distress vocalizations in chicks by opiate-like peptides. *Brain Research Bulletin,* 1978, **3,** 663–667.

Plutchik, R. *Emotion: A psychoevolutionary synthesis,* New York: Harper and Row, 1980.

Robitaille, J. A., & Bovet, J. Field observations on the social behavior of the Norway rat *Rattus norvegicus* (Berkenhout). *Biology of Behavior,* 1976, **1,** 289–308.

Schachter, S. S. The interaction of cognitive and physiological determinants of emotional state. In L. Berkowitz (ed.), *Advances in experimental social Psychology* (Vol. 1). New York: Academic Press, 1964.

Schaller, G. *The Serengeti Lion.* Chicago: University of Chicago Press, 1972.

Schuurman, T. *Endocrine processes underlying victory and defeat in the male rat.* Ph.D. Dissertation, University of Groningen, Haren, 1981.

Scott, J. P. *Aggression,* Chicago: University of Chicago Press, 1958.

Scott, J. P., & Fuller, J. L. *Genetics and the social behavior of the dog,* Chicago: University of Chicago Press, 1965.

Seligman, M. E. Learned helplessness. *Annual Review of Medicine,* 1972, **23,** 407.

Sluckin, W. (Ed.), *Fear in animals and man.* New York: Van Nostrand, 1979.

Svare, B. B., & Gandleman, R. Postpartum aggression in mice: Experimental and environmental factors. *Hormones and Behavior,* 1973, **4,** 323–334.

Takahashi, L. K., & Blanchard, R. J. Attack and defense in laboratory and wild Norway and black rats. *Behavioral Processes,* 1982, **7,** 49–63.

Takahashi, S. *The effects of amygdala and hippocampal lesions on aggressive behavior of rats.* M. A. Thesis, Department of Psychology, University of Hawaii, Honolulu, Hawaii, 1981.

Telle, H. J. Beitrag zur Kenntnis der verhaltensweise bei ratten, vergleich end dargestellt bei *Rattus norvegicus* and *Rattus rattus. Zeitschrift fuer Angewandt Zoologie,* 1966, **9,** 129–196.

Thor, D. H., & Flannelly, K. J. Intruder gonadectomy and elicitation of territorial aggression in the rat. *Physiology and Behavior,* 1976, **17,** 725–727.

Ulrich, R. E., & Azrin, N. H. Reflexive fighting in response to aversive stimulation. *Journal of Experimental Analysis of Behavior,* 1962, **5,** 515–520.

Ursin, H. Neuroanatomical Basis of Aggression. In P. F. Brain & D. Benton (eds.), *Multidisciplinary approaches to aggression research,* Amsterdam: Elsevier/North Holland, 1981.

Wilson, E. O. *Sociobiology: The new synthesis,* Cambridge: Harvard University Press, 1975.

Wilson, L., & Rogers, R. W. The fire this time: Effects of race of target, insult, and potential retaliation on black aggression. *Journal of Personality and Social Psychology,* 1975, **32,** 857–864.

Woods, J. W. Taming of the wild Norway rat by rhinencephalic lesions. *Nature,* 1956, **178,** 869.

Biological Explanations of Human Aggression and the Resulting Therapies Offered by Such Approaches: A Critical Evaluation

PAUL FRÉDRIC BRAIN

University College of Swansea, Swansea, Wales

Advances in the
Study of Aggression, Volume 1

I. THE PROBLEMS

It seems pointless to review yet again material on the presumed biological correlates of aggression—much of these data are available in a plethora of books (e.g., Brain & Benton, 1981a,b; Eleftheriou & Scott, 1971; Feshbach & Fraczek, 1979; Hamburg & Trudeau, 1981; Hartup & de Wit, 1978; Kutash, Kutash, Schlesinger, *et al.*, 1978; Singer, 1971; Valzelli & Morgese, 1981). Accounts from a biological perspective have often presented an oversimplified view of aggression and have been the subject of extravagent claims concerning the utility of the findings to social and clinical therapy. Indeed, in some quarters such approaches are viewed as dangerous and elitist. One may also suggest that much of the earlier work tends to be partisan with different specialties vying for preferment. It consequently seems more useful to collect together material examining the pros and cons of the data underlying biologically oriented treatments for human aggression in order to evaluate their current status and to consider the ethical problems they generate. This aim may be advanced by initially examining, in the light of recent studies on animals and man, several statements that have been formerly regarded as truisms.

A. Aggression Is an Easily Identifiable Behavior

Workers with animals often acknowledge that aggression is not a unitary concept (Moyer, 1968). Data on rats (Adams, 1979; Blanchard & Blanchard, 1977) and mice (Brain, 1979a, 1981a; Brain, Kamis, Haug, Mandel, & Simler, 1982a; Brain, Parmigiani, & Childs, 1982b) suggest that attack may serve a number of different functions including defense, offense, and predation. Indeed, aggression in infrahumans may be usefully classified as being concerned with social conflict (offense), self-defensive behavior, or with parental defence. Ursin (1980) suggests that aggression is only one strategy of dealing with threatening stimuli (the other being fear).

Brain (1984) has listed some of the enormous range of human situations in which aggression is perceived as an appropriate intervening variable. Defining aggression in humans is at least as difficult as in infrahumans (see Van der Dennen, 1980 for a review of attempts to define aggression and violence). Suffice it to say that aggression and violence are value-laden terms and used perhaps rather too freely. For example, Madden and Lion (1981) noted that "despite the fact that 50,000 automobile fatalities occur a year in the United States, American Society has not yet seen fit to label this group of potentially identifiable individuals as 'violent'." Kiloh (1977) suggested that some psycho-surgical failures may be consequences of poor patient selection "by the assumption that violence, self-mutilation, destructiveness and hyper-kinesis are aspects of the same phenomenon."

B. Aggression Is a Uniformly Negative Attribute

In some studies, aggression is equated with pathology—a condition to be cured. For example, Madden and Lion (1978) claimed that "the goal of therapy with the aggressive patient is to help him effectively control his own aggression to the point where he can be personally and socially, a useful member of society." Midgley (1979) noted that "when people object particularly to *aggression* as innate, they are commonly doing so on the assumption that human nature is good and therefore that if slaughter is bad, it must be brought about by something other than human nature." The trouble is that the labels "good" and "bad" are applied (not always uniformly) by segments of society. One must note that exclusively negative views of aggression run counter to the ethological claim that the behaviors falling under this heading can serve necessary functions, e.g., mate selection and spacing (Brain, 1979a).

C. Aggression Is "Caused" by Biological Factors

An innate (e.g., Lorenzian) view of human aggression seems currently less tenable than was formerly maintained (see discussion in Brain, 1981b). Most workers recognize that behaviors receiving this label are a consequence of subtle interactions between biological, situational, and experiential factors. A reliance on biology as a sole "control" seems crude as the factors are not easily separable. For example, Brain (1984) reviews the importance of the physical environment in human aggression, noting that pain, heat, light, odors, noise, density (number), social stress, social status, and sexual arousal may exert complex actions on a diverse range of activity in man. Simeon (1978) provided another example, suggesting that violent behavior in children is a result of a complex interplay between biological and nonbiological factors. Of course, one can underplay the importance of biological factors. Olweus (1979) suggested that "relatively stable, internal reaction tendencies are important determinants of behavior in the aggressive–motive area and should be given considerably greater weight than has been done recently."

One of the problems in aggression research is that different specialists often seem advocates of their particular means of modifying behavior rather than stressing a balanced viewpoint. Hinton (1981a) noted a distressing polarization between sociological and biological schools in studies on prison populations—with debate often exhibiting political overtones. Advocates of the view that violent crime may have biological correlates are often accused of a rightist bias. One could equally argue that demonstration of an association between a disease state and socially unacceptable behavior is perfectly ethical if it is used to protect an individual. A compassionate society should be prepared to consider both biological and sociological sources of mitigation *and* should be aware of the fears generated in segments of the community by particular viewpoints. It is not the case, however, that demonstrating an association between aggression and a biological factor shows that the biological factor *causes* the behavior. Some associations may be quite rare.

D. Biological Methodologies Will "Cure" Society of Aggression

This view stems from the two prior oversimplifications. Although, for example, Robinson (1971) noted that many types of aggression are potentially treatable by physiological manipulations, one can argue that such methodologies may not be appropriate (for a variety of technical and ethical reasons—see Section VII). Most workers, like Robinson would be prepared to "admit quickly that aggressive behavior due to obvious brain pathology such as seizure disorders, mass lesions and temporal lobe scars should be treated." Madden and Lion (1981) recorded that "violence which appears as the chief complaint is often associated with impulsivity and is described as a rage attack; temper outburst or state of so-called pathological intoxication." One will note that the vast majority of examples of human aggression cannot be simply related to a physical disorder, and do not have the characteristics of the responses recorded by Madden and Lion.

Some workers worry about a concentration on clinical therapies even when the advocates specify them only for a small subpopulation. Earls (1978) noted that "it is conceivable to me that within 10 or 15 years chemical, surgical and behavioral conditioning techniques will be the mainstays of our therapeutic armamentarium for violent offenders and that adolescents will represent a majority of persons so-treated." Earls suggested that biological explanations of violence in youth are minimally important and may be counterproductive. Krebs (1980) suggested that Earls' argument inappropriately counters the needed interdisciplinary approach to a complex problem and states that "there is no point in arguing about whether one discipline is more important than another." Valenstein (1976), in a similar vein to Earls, argued that "while there will continue to be a few assaultive patients with clear brain pathology who may be significantly improved by surgical intervention, for the foreseeable future we should increase rather than decrease, attempts to find social solutions for what are primarily social problems." This is true in one sense, but this approach has its dangers also. One social solution would be simply to abolish the concept of aggression—if all such behaviors were permissible, the problem would have (in one sense) disappeared. It is highly unlikely that any viable society could support such a move.

In penal institutions, psychosurgery may be appropriate when there is clear evidence of damage to the brain but not in the absence of structural change or mental illness. Whitlock (1977) noted in the latter case that "he [the convicted man] is not a patient and trying to induce such a person to accept a sick role, possibly under some degree of coercion or with a promise of remission of sentence if he accepts surgery is, in my opinion, quite improper." In contrast, Lion and Penna (1976) suggest that "both the evaluation of the process and the treatment of persons afflicted with the illness of aggression deserve recognition in scientific clinical psychiatry."

II. SITUATIONS IN WHICH BIOLOGICAL THERAPIES HAVE BEEN THOUGHT TO BE OF UTILITY IN THE "TREATMENT" OF HUMAN AGGRESSION

We have already noted the controversy surrounding the definition of human aggression. Obviously, few individuals would advocate biological intervention in the case of minor aggressive acts and crime involving premeditated (instrumental) aggression. Biologically based therapies have been proposed in a number of areas discussed in this section.

A. Early Social Aggression

Many workers have attempted biological explanations of aggression in young children (where behavior seems relatively uncontaminated by learning) and in adolescent individuals (see Section I,D). Weisfeld (1979) provided a detailed account of ethological views of the biological and behavioral changes occurring around puberty and felt that they promised "to offer a useful perspective on the problems of U.S. Youth." One should also add that some workers (e.g., Lewis & Shanok, 1977) have suggested that some delinquency may be linked to the schizophrenic spectrum of disorders (see below). Few workers would, however, advocate drastic biologically based therapies in such situations.

B. Clinical Aggression

This is a term applied to hostility (above a normally acceptable level) appearing as part of a clinical syndrome. Sometimes behavior is related to a *somatic* disorder (e.g., a brain tumor, an endocrine dysfunction, or possession of a 47,XYY genotype) and sometimes to a *psychiatric* malfunction (e.g., schizophrenia). We have already suggested that it is a mistake to regard aggression as an illness—the behavior may be a symptom—but the strongest advocacy of biological based therapies is in relation to certain clinical populations. It should be obvious that there is *no* clear distinction between aggression in a clinical situation and that in a criminal context [see Section II,C and note Sosowsky's (1980) comment concerning the difficulties of explaining the increased arrest rate among mental patients].

C. Criminal Aggression

This epithet is applied to examples of hostility where the individual's violence results in criminal proceedings *and* conviction. Obviously, the etiologies of different crimes in different situations by different individuals are not likely to be identical. Indeed, identical acts may or may not be crimes in particular countries or even in different contexts in the same location (e.g., assault and battery and boxing). Distinctions may be made between angry and instrumental, intentional and involuntary (Berkowitz & Frodi, 1977) and between primarily sexually motivated and nonsexually motivated crime. Rape has been the subject of much study. For example, Groth and Birnbaum (1979) maintained that such activities are (a) heterogeneous, and (b) best viewed as aggression–dominance acts rather than products of hypersexuality. One should note that many of the early attempts at biological therapy (e.g., castration) have been applied to sexual offenders. It is difficult to know whether curing or punishing is the major motivation here.

D. Sports Violence

This aspect of modern life is currently an area of great concern. Russell (1981) provided an able review of this area. The recorded violence may afflict the participants (note the difficulty of distinguishing sanctioned violence within the rules from nonsanctioned violence) or the spectators of sport (e.g., football "hooliganism"). Although it has been suggested that biological factors may be implicated here, few would view clinical therapies as appropriate methods of dealing with such problems.

E. Aggression in a Military Context

This term is applied (again with difficult value judgments) to violence studied in a military context. Although some workers (e.g., Eibl-Eibesfeldt, 1977) suggest that war is a human equivalent of spacing strategies (e.g., territoriality), others (e.g., Hinde, 1974) have argued that the motivation of most individuals in these situations is far removed from overt aggressiveness. It seems unlikely that biologically based therapies have much application in such situations. Indeed Moyer (1975) argued that drug therapies intended to reduce emotional aggression may make dissident individuals *more* effective in their opposition to authority.

F. The Rationale behind This Review

It would obviously be impossible to organize the extremely diverse material available on biological approaches to the study of human aggression(s) in any totally logical fashion. Situations receiving the same label (e.g., rape and homicide) are by no means as homogeneous as is the impression of such acts in the minds of many of the scientific and nonscientific commentators on the violence problem. It was consequently decided to accept the heterogeneous nature of the behavioral phenomenon (phenomena?) and simply to look at types of biological manipulation that have been related to one or more kinds of aggression.

One should note that biological manipulation *cannot* be genuinely separated from the experiential input preceeding behavioral assessment or the social context in which the behavior is evaluated. This is to make light of the problem of the inherent subjectiveness surrounding the labeling of the actions as aggression and the difficulty of registering an improvement in behavior. Biological topics are not easily compartmentalized but are selected on the basis of well-accepted specialties, for example, genetics, neurophysiology, and endocrinology, but one should recognize the considerable overlap between these areas. I shall include a brief evaluation of current major views of animal studies, drawing attention to some of the complicating factors revealed by such investigations.

III. GENETIC CORRELATES
OF HUMAN AGGRESSION

There have been repeated suggestions over an extended period that there are genetic predispositions for aggressiveness. For example, some evidence from animal studies (Maxson, 1981), using selective breeding and inbred strains, supports the view that genetic factors play a role in determining aggressiveness. Of course, relating behavioral changes to physiological variables (testosterone secretion, size of the Y chromosome, etc.) is difficult, and many studies do not eliminate the possibility that variations in intrauterine environment or maternal behavior account for differences. One should also note that preliminary studies suggest that different *forms* of aggression differ across strains. It is also obvious that phenotypes differing in aggressiveness can be produced by differential experience.

What then of humans? Christiansen (1978) reviewed a Danish twin study on the genesis of aggressive criminality. He noted that the "combined influence of heredity and environment is greater for crimes of violence than property crimes." Monozygotic twins showed more concordance than dizygotic subjects, and females were more similar than males.

A number of workers have reviewed abnormalities of X and Y chromosomes and their relation to aggression. Razavi (1975) noted that such individuals are often mosaics and may have altered reproductive organs and sexual behavioral centers. Indeed some subjects showed polyendocrine disorders that may "provide a mechanism connecting cytogenetic abnormality, focal somatic variation and social failure."

The 47, XYY syndrome provides the best publicized line of evidence linking genetics and aggression. Possession of an extra Y chromosome was viewed as an interesting, but unimportant, variation until Jacobs, Brunton, and Melville (1965) suggested that this chromosomal abnormality was much more common among individuals imprisoned for violent crimes than among the population at large. This naturally led to fierce debate on relationships between genetic endowment (and associated hormonal imbalance?) and crime. Briefly, 47, XYY subjects were said to be (e.g., Benson & Migeon, 1975; Hunter, 1977; Money, Wiedeking, Walker, & Gain, 1976) characterized by (a) excessive height, (b) a slight mental retardation, and (c) occasional (and unpredictable) outbursts of extreme violence.

Approximately 1 in 1000 newborn male infants show this anomaly, but 15 in 1000 prison inmates have it (Jarvik, Klodin, & Matsuyana, 1973). Some workers conclude that the extra Y chromosome predisposes individuals toward aggression. Indeed, Jarvik *et al.* (1973) and Lloyd and Weisz (1975) suggested that the syndrome implicates the single Y chromosome possessed by normal males in aggression (i.e., they maintain that the Y chromosome is responsible for sex differences in aggression). Conversely, Baron (1977) concluded (following an extensive study by Witkin, Mednick, Schulsinger, Bakkestrom, Christiansen, Goodenough, Hirschhorn, Ludsteen, Owen, Philip, Rubin, & Stocking, 1976) that 47, XYY subjects, far from being "aggressive supermales genetically programmed for violence," are "relatively dull and mild-mannered persons who are no more likely than others to engage in criminal behavior, but who are more likely, when they do, to be apprehended." Mayer-Bahlburg (1981a) suggested that there is no simple association between height and aggressiveness in these individuals. Hinton (1981a) maintained that the majority of XYYs do not fall foul of the law.

Sharma, Meyer-Bahlburg, Boon, Slaunwhite, and Edwards (1975) found that plasma concentration and production rates of testosterone (T) in 47, XYY subjects were significantly lower in these individuals than in matched 46, XY controls. An alternative explanation is that 47, XYY subjects have higher metabolic clearance rates or show increased sensitivity to androgen (in negative feedback and behavioral responses). Later studies suggested to Meyer-Bahlburg (1981a), however, that there was no good evidence that these subjects had gross abnormalities of androgen or gonadotrophin production. There was also no indication that 47, XYY subjects showed a prenatal overproduction of androgens, a factor that might be expected to have a lasting effect on their behavioral potential (Meyer-Bahlburg, 1974). It does, however, appear that individuals with this genotype may be more aggressive than normal before puberty (Meyer-Bahlburg, 1981a).

Meyer-Bahlburg (1981a) suggested that many of the studies on 47, XYY subjects (and other genotypes, e.g., XO; 47, XXX; etc.) have serious methodological problems. He placed more faith in the detailed, longitudinal screening of populations. Theilgaard (1981) described a Danish study along these lines, the net conclusion being that society has little to fear in the 47, XYY genotype. Razavi (1975) noted, however, that "where social hazard appears to provoke the physical problem into self-sustaining progress, longitudinal study of the natural history of criminal ethogenesis allows flexible intervention and preservation of a necessary degree of genetic and social variability."

IV. NEUROPHYSIOLOGICAL APPROACHES TO THE CONTROL OF AGGRESSION IN HUMANS

A. General Introduction

Moyer (1971, 1973, 1975, 1981a,b) provides several general reviews that examine the relationship between neurophysiological function and human aggression. One should note, however, that Kelly (1978) cautions against the simplistic view that neurobiological data support an instinctive view of human aggression.

B. Advances in Animal Studies

It seems appropriate to indicate some of the more striking conceptual and methodological advances made in investigations on infrahuman material. For example, Renfrew (1981) reviewed some of the complexities evident in brain stimulation experiments and Adams (1979) examined evidence implicating specific neural circuitry in the control of intraspecific aggression. The latter's evidence was largely gleaned from stimulation, lesion, and recording studies on cats and rats. Adams suggested that there are three hypothetical motivation systems, namely "offense," "defense," and "submission," and he distinguished between motivating stimuli and releasing–directing stimuli. He claimed that the brain mechanisms controlling aggression in primates are similar to those in cats and rats. The commentaries attached to Adam's paper indicate a degree of disagreement in the postulate concerning the existence of three motivations *and* the distinction between motivating and releasing stimuli, but Adams' review is a welcome attempt to bring order to previous confusion. Often there seems too much tenuously related information in this area of research.

Karli (1981) also explored the conceptual and methodological problems associated with the study of the brain mechanisms underlying aggressive behavior. He used the rat's muricide response as his example and stressed the dramatic (and previously rather neglected) effects of prior experience on the precise behavioral consequences of neural lesions. Karli saw groupings of interacting influences (with individual temporal variation) rather than unidirectional, "chains" of factors. This view is echoed by Delgado's (1981a) claim that aggression is altered by changes in "constellations" of neural units rather than by specific centers. He postulated a fragmental organization of behavior which, he claims, can be identified anatomically and functionally. Delgado (1981a,b) has also emphasized that the effects of particular neurophysiological manipulations differ in their effects on primate aggression when applied to restrained, free-moving or colony-living subjects. One must also remember Kling's (1976) demonstration that the presence of lesioned subjects in a primate group can increase aggressive interactions among *nonoperated members of that group.*

On the basis of animal studies, Delgado (1981b), advocated that "intent" and "motor performance" should be considered separately in aggression research. He claimed that human hostility control will not be carried out by understanding the circuits controlling performance but by characterising the "cerebral traces of hates and ideological conflicts which are the triggers for the harmful use of established patterns of behavior."

What then do improvements in neurophysiological methodology add to our understanding of aggression? Bandler and Tork (1981) reported some success with a modification of the technique of horseradish peroxidase retrograde tracing, enabling one to label the cells of fiber origin terminating and passing through the stimulus zone. Delgado (1981a,b) described the use of: roving electrodes that enable one to test up to 3000 points in a single monkey brain; reliable digitally coded radio stimulators that are waterproof, shockproof, and virtually indestructable; hybrid stimulators that produce constant current with low resistance between pulses; external stimoceivers that are combinations of multichannel radiostimulators with a multichannel telemetric system carried on a light harness; transdermal stimoceivers that are microminiature devices enclosed in epoxy and tissue-compatable silastic, implanted beneath the skin; chemitrodes that enable one to electrically stimulate and deliver and collect chemicals at particular neural locations; dialytrodes that provide two-way electrical and chemical communication with the brain. Some of these devices are currently being made available in clinical trials where they make neurophysiological manipulation easy and unobtrusive.

There have also been great advances in studies assessing the neurochemical correlates of aggression in infrahuman animals (see reviews by Cools, 1981; Daruna, 1978; Mandel, Haug, Puglisi, Kempf, & Mack, 1981; Rodgers, 1979; Valzelli, 1978, 1980, 1981). Suffice it to say that there is considerable evidence of the involvement of a wide range of putative neurotransmitters in the control of aggressive behavior in a diverse group of situations. There appears, however, to be no simple neurochemistry of aggression and many of the simpler ideas in this area have been challenged (see Brain *et al.*, 1982a). Some psychopharmacologists seem convinced of the need to assess behavioral actions in much greater detail and to eliminate nonspecific actions of drugs. One must emphasize that it is well-established that fighting experience modifies local concentrations of neurotransmitters in laboratory animals (e.g., Welch & Welch, 1971).

C. Neuroanatomical Lesions and Human Aggression

There have, of course, been numerous examples of claimed associations between destruction of particular areas of the brain and the incidence and intensity of behavior that can be labeled as aggression. Such relationships are naturally correlational and have tended to be oversimplified in the past. The lesions described fall naturally into two categories.

1. Natural Lesions

These areas of destruction may be the result of brain tumors, accidental damage, senile dementia, Huntington's Chorea, encephalitis, rabies, epileptic foci, etc. Moyer (1971) noted that "tumors with an irritative focus frequently result in increased irritability and rage attacks." Mark and Sweet (1974) recorded that limbic tumors and epilepsy appeared associated with clinical aggression and suggested that parietal epilepsy may serve as a control in such studies. Taylor (1969) had earlier provided a review assessing the association between aggression and epilepsy and concluded that "the consensus of several studies is that those affected (by overt aggressiveness) tend to be of male sex, low class, low intelligence and more frequently disturbed on the left side of the brain." Taylor also suggested that these subjects effectively show a failure to learn that generated aggression is not successful as a social mechanism.

Subjects who show episodic behavior disorders have been reported by some workers to show EEG abnormalities associated with the temporal lobe. Moyer (1971) suggested that early studies implicated temporal lobe, frontal lobe, and hypothalamic and septal epilepsy in human aggression. A more detailed account by Blumer (1976) concluded that angry-irritable behavior was evident during the interictal phase (and was sometimes accentuated preictally), and that, whereas this was common in chronic temporal lobe epileptics and could cause problems, it did not appear to be a threat to public safety. Blumer regarded ictal violence as an unlikely event and suggested that the rare cases of unchecked violence in confusional amnestic postictal states had been decreased in importance by modern seizure control.

Mark (1978a) reviewed his (sometimes) successful experiences of treating abnormally aggressive patients with focal brain disease (see Section IV,B). Conversely, Hinton (1981a) regarded most current studies that attempt to relate neurophysiological factors to human aggression as being superficial with small numbers of subjects and many variables. For example, although Blumer (1976) noted that some nonepileptic individuals had paroxysmal EEG abnormalities and seemed prone to react to situations with violence, this phenomenon needs further investigation. Heath (1981) noted that depth electrode techniques have revealed that extremes of clinical violence are associated with changes in firing records from the ventral hippocampus, the medial amygdala, and sites in the mesencephalic tegmentum. Recording changes are produced in the cerebellum and cingulate gyrus in association with bursts of hippocampal activity during emotionally charged behavioral states. Heath also claimed that "combined recording–stimulation data from patients have helped to identify the neural network for violence and aggression."

Martinius (1978) described a computer tomography study in which a single male murderer had a lesion in the right temporal lobe "lateral to right nucleus amydalae." There was, however, an associated endocrine disorder in this subject. More systematically, Flor-Henry (1974) noted that brain dysfunctions of the dominant hemisphere (usually the left) located within the frontal cortical limbic system can be related to aggressive psychopathy. Yeudall (1977, 1978) made similar claims, recording that 90% of *habitual* (Yeudall feels that the responses are not learned and prefers the term *persistent*) criminal psychopaths in Alberta (Canada) Hospital had dysfunction of the anterior (prefrontal and anterior temporal lobes which normally play a more integrative and higher level executive function in relation to other regions of the brain) neural regions as assessed by neuropsychological techniques. In 70% of the cases, the dysfunction was greater for the left cerebral hemisphere [see Flor-Henry's (1974) hypothesis of dominant hemisphere dysfunction in criminal psychopaths and Taylor's (1969) claim concerning the location of epileptic foci and clinical aggression]. For example, Engelman, Dongier, and Reid (1978) recorded that the duration of changes in event-related slow potentials were longer in psychopaths than in nonpsychopaths. Yeudall (1978) claimed that biogenic factors are of primary importance in these conditions although he recognized the existence of other influences (cf. Baron, 1977, who conversely emphasized the crucial nature of external variables in the elicitation and maintenance of aggressive actions).

It has been claimed that neuropsychological tests are good predictors of subsequent violence in Canadian adolescents (Spellacy, 1977) and adult male prisoners (Spellacy, 1978). These tests are said to be as good as or better than self-report questionnaires (*not* a very large claim!). A similar claim was made by Yeudall and Wardell (1978) who suggested that neuropsychological tests are viable for prediction of recidivism and dangerousness and that one needs to identify subgroups using cluster analysis. (One should note that all these reports have a statistical problem in that they use discriminative analysis with a relatively large number of variables to the size of the sample in each group.)

Perhaps these indications are sufficient for us to go along with Monroe's (1975) claim that the time has come to reanalyze the discredited neuropsychiatric model for criminality? There is, however, a danger of wish-fulfillment in this ethical minefield.

2. Surgical Lesions

The "subject" of psychosurgery is an emotive one. In order to provide a balanced account, I shall initially present the claims of the method and then detail the objections to such techniques.

Moyer (1971, 1973, 1975) reviewed the early temporal lobe-lesioning studies and concluded that some amelioration is evident in a proportion of cases following radical ablation of the temporal lobes. Mark, Sweet, and Ervin (1975) described 50 patients with temporal lobe epilepsy who showed *hyposexuality* and episodic aggressivity in which anterior resection of the temporal lobe and medial temporal structures produced a marked reduction in aggressivity (see comments on epilepsy and aggression). Ervin (1977) was also positive, concluding that although one must distinguish social aggression and defensive behavior that "it is lesions in the medial amygdala and probably around the red nucleus or the striae terminalis that are effective in reducing recurrent attack behavior."

Other locations have also been surgically explored for their "aggression control possibilities." In the 1950s and 1960s, cingulectomy was used to reduce aggression and was said to be reasonably successful. Sanjo (1975) advocated postero-medial hypothalamotomy, which he said causes calming in 94% of cases. This is said by most authorities to be sedative surgery rather than an influence on an aggression circuit. The properties of the dorsomedial thalmic nuclei, the fornix, the upper mesencephalon, and the frontal lobes have also been explored with varied success.

What then of the current pro-psychosurgery lobby? Kiloh (1977) claimed that "it seems indisputable that we have techniques available that permit reduction of pathological anger and aggression." Lion and Penna (1976) maintained that "like it or not, there are severely violent patients who are so disabled by their aggressiveness that they will require more drastic forms of treatment" (i.e., psychosurgery). Mark (1978b) recognized the brain–environment interaction evident in behavior control but maintained that the poorly functioning brain "is much more likely to be triggered into expressing abnormal behavior by a minimal or inappropriate environment stimulus than a normal brain is."

There are many critics of psychosurgery. For example, Breggin (1975) described psychosurgery as "any surgery which mutilates or destroys brain tissue to control the emotions or behavior without treating a known brain disease." This presumably means that the surgery can be appropriate when an epileptic focus is evident but not in other cases. Breggin concluded that "the growth of psychosurgery brings us much closer to a future state of totalitarianism based on technological intimidation." Such fears are common in opposition to these technologies.

Valenstein (1973, 1976) provided some of the best-known general criticisms of psychosurgery and Carroll and O'Callaghan (1981) critiqued the use of amygdaloid surgery for the control of violent and aggressive behavior. Both sources expressed doubts about the relevance of animal studies to man (see also Kling's 1976 findings) and the rationale for choosing particular neural targets. They also state their reservations about the empirical evidence of such studies—Carroll and O'Callaghan noted that "marked improvement" is only evident in about 40% of cases and that the evidence for success is often based on vague "discharge rates" and "improvement rates." Valenstein (1973) suggested that "few people, if any, would seriously maintain that the rapidly increasing crime rate in urban centers can be attributed to brain pathology" (see however, Yeudall, 1977; Spellacy, 1977; and others), but worries that some policymakers may be "seduced into believing that surgical or biochemical interventions can make a significant contribution to the problem" (see the fears concerning treatment of juvenile delinquency in Section I,D.). Mark (1978b) claimed that Valenstein did not grasp the

"sociobiological theory of aggression" that "predicts a synthesis of social and biological factors in each act of violence." The gross oversim-
plifcations on both sides should be obvious.

D. Neural Stimulation and Human Aggression

Valenstein (1973) had strong reservations concerning the efficacy of
brain stimulation in modifying human aggression. Of course, the location of the electrodes determines whether stimulation augments or inhibits attack behavior.

Moyer (1971, 1973, 1975) reviewed the early clinical data in this area.
He noted that the oldest investigations suggested that stimulation of the
ventromedial portion of the frontal lobe or the medial temporal lobe
produced a calming effect. There was also some evidence that septal
stimulation could inhibit aggression as well as blocking pain and induc-
ing subjective positive feelings. Moyer (1981a) also described how amygdaloid stimulation at a particular intensity resulted in increased aggression in a woman patient. He stated that "it was possible to turn this
woman's anger on and off with a simple flick of the switch because the
electrode was located in a part of the neural system for hostility." We
have seen earlier that such statements are rather overly simplistic but
the phenomenon seems real enough.

Heath (1981) recorded that intense rage and violence are consistently
induced when focal sites in the amygdala, hippocampus, and midline
tegmental structures are stimulated by deep electrodes. Stimulation of
the midline cerebellum suppressed excessive unit activity in emotional
states, and continuous stimulation of the rostral cerebellar vermis
proved to be an effective procedure for the treatment of 12 violent patients for periods of up to $4\frac{1}{2}$ years. There was no evidence of a kindling
effect following repeated stimulation.

V. PHARMACOLOGICAL APPROACHES TO THE
CONTROL OF AGGRESSION IN HUMANS

There is an extensive complex literature on the effects of drugs on
fighting behavior in diverse species, various situations, and using a
wide range of measures (see reviews by Brain, 1979b; Karczmar, Richardson, & Kindel, 1978; Malick, 1979; Smith, 1977). Many of the results
are difficult to reconcile but Miczek and Krsiak (1979), as well as review-

ing this area, have provided some pointers to bring order to the infrahuman studies. They note that relationships between pharmacological agents and agonistic behavior are influenced by:

1. Behavioral specificity and selectivity of the drug influences
2. Initial behavioral baseline
3. Prevalent behavioral patterns of the animal being given treatment
4. Drug effects typical to the species
5. Dose and regimen of drug application

There are many drugs that influence aspects of agonistic behavior. Miczek and Krsiak (1979) recorded, for example, that generally amphetamines increase flight; barbiturates reduce flight; alcohol, scopolamine, and chlordiazepoxide reduce defense; and Δ^9-tetrahydrocannabinol and lithium reduce attack behaviors. The effects are not simple as many compounds have diverse behavioral actions, for example, acting as psychomotor stimulants. Many agents (e.g., amphetamines, barbiturates, alcohol, and chlordiazepoxide) apparently have biphasic actions at different dose levels. Different models of aggression employing infrahumans also often generate different results for the effects of particular pharmacological agents (Brain *et al.*, 1982a). There has been an attempt to develop more specific antiaggressive drugs (e.g., Olivier, 1981) but these are relatively nonvalidated.

What then of clinical treatments employing drugs? One cannot hope to adequately review such a diverse area here (see Valzelli, 1981), but one should note that there is a vast array of chemotherapies that have been used in violent patients (see Itil, 1981a,b; Lion & Penna, 1976; Monroe, 1975). Indeed Lion and Penna (1976) noted that "the multiplicity of such agents (drugs) attests to the fact that there is no one drug for aggression." One should note that many of the treatments derive from empirical studies rather than extrapolations from animal data, and it seems currently recognized that there is a considerable range of clinical situations in which aggression and hostility are a factor. Itil (1981a) noted that "without excluding psychological modalities and behavioural intervention, chemical treatment is the first choice in the management of an uncontrollable acute aggressive state."

Monroe (1975) advocated increasing doses of anticonvulsants for episodic behavioral disorders with seizures and chlordiazepoxide for conditions involving elevated anxiety but no seizures. He noted that anticonvulsants "do not decrease self-assertive or aggressive behavior when the individual would feel justified in expressing himself in this manner."

Itil (1981b) noted that major and minor tranquilizers are preferred for patients with acute violent aggressive outbursts, and benperidol (a butyrophenone with properties similar to the major tranquilizers) has been used in treating violent sex offenders in British prisons (reviewed by Whitehead, 1981). Monroe (1975) earlier expressed doubts about such "chemical straight jackets." Itil (1981b) noted that chronic aggressive states with episodic outbursts of violence may be treated by central suppressants, stimulants, anticonvulsants, hormones (see Section VI), and lithium. The fact that multiple drug therapy is often required suggests to Monroe (1975) that "the optimal pharmacologic agent has yet to be discovered." It is, of course, equally likely that there is no single agent that will modify all the features that receive the label of aggression. Despite their problems, such therapies appear to be indispensable in many cases.

Another area that provides evidence concerning the effects of pharmacological agents on human aggression is that of drug abuse. For example, Tinklenberg and Woodrow (1974) noted on the basis of their California study that alcohol is frequently associated with serious assaultive and sexual offenses. Evans (1980) examined some of the interpretative problems of such studies, points amplified in Collins (1981). Brain (1982) emphasized the difficulties of relating ethanol's effects on neurophysiology to its effects on aggression in infrahuman animals and man. Tinklenberg and Woodrow (1974) noted that secobarbital use is generally overrepresented and marijuana underrepresented in studies on criminal populations (cf. animal studies). Repeated or multiple use did not appear to increase the likelihood of finding such an association. There is, of course, a substantial literature on such topics (see, for example, Collins, 1981) which can only be hinted at here. A recurrent problem is that in some cases simple apparent associations between drug intake and behavior change appear on close examination to be a good deal less than clear-cut.

VI. ENDOCRINE APPROACHES TO THE CONTROL OF AGGRESSION IN HUMANS

A. General Introduction

There are a large number of reviews assessing the association between hormones and aggression in a variety of situations in infrahuman animals (e.g., Brain, 1977, 1978, 1979b–e, 1980, 1981a,c, 1983; Brain & Benton, 1983; Brain & Bowden, 1979; Brain *et al.*, 1982a; Gandelman, 1981). Different hormones appear to alter aspects of attack–defense in different species. Actions may involve early programming effects (e.g., androgenization), direct effects (presumably by changing aggressive motivation by altering CNS neurotransmitters or firing), and indirect effects by modifying the production or reception of intraspecific social cues (e.g., pheromones and olfactory perception). Many actions may also be via changed behavior, for example, motor activity or sexual receptivity. It has also been noted that many behavioral experiences in conflict situations change circulating hormones which then predispose the animal to assuming particular roles in subsequent encounters. Benton (1981) discussed, for example, the relevance of animal studies to human aggression, citing the example of testosterone in detail.

B. Correlation of Human Aggression with Endocrine Factors

1. Early Influences

There have been a number of reviews that examine the diverse and inconclusive data concerning the effects of early hormonal variations on subsequent adult aggressive potential (Benton, 1981; Brain, 1977, 1978, 1979b, 1981c; Meyer–Bahlberg, 1981b). One of the problems in this area is that one is essentially relying on accidental data as a result of endocrine disorders or hormonal treatment of pregnant individuals. The adrenogenital syndrome (in which the mother's adrenal cortex exposes the fetus to elevated adrenal androgens) is said to cause changes in the developing brain of genetic females. Although there is no striking increase in aggressiveness in either females (Money & Schwartz, 1976) or males, the condition is said to result in a preference for rough and tumble play in girls (Hamburg & van Lawick–Goodall, 1978). The androgen insensitivity syndrome in which there is defective binding of androgens by proteins results in genetic male offspring having a female appearance. These changes have not been closely related to aggressiveness. Pregnant females may be treated with progestins [progesterone or medroxyprogesterone acetate (MPA)] to prevent miscarriage. Such treatment (especially with progesterone) may masculinize female offspring and decrease aggressiveness in both boys and girls. Treatment with estrogen–progestogen combinations (for diabetic pregnancies) is reported to reduce aggressiveness in male offspring. Other hormones may also exert effects. Although many of the effects are in the direction predicted from animal studies, Meyer-Bahlberg (1981b) noted that many of these studies are unsatisfactory. Problems include the facts that:

1. Gender identity and self-image may be modified by parental rearing that can be much influenced by somatic influences of the hormones on the child's genitals
2. Hormonal changes in muscle development may predispose individuals to indulge in aggressive activities, such as sports (not supported by Olweus, Mattsson, Schalling, & Loow, 1980)
3. The direct organizational effects on the brain may (*a*) alter physical activity levels; and (*b*) change the arousal thresholds for aggression
4. Many prenatal effects extend into adult life
5. Normal variations in androgen concentrations are rarely looked at
6. Many conditions are complicated by additional therapies, for example, adrenogenital syndrome is often treated by cortisone injections

Most recent evidence supports the view that early hormonal exposure (especially by sex steroids) has lasting effects that may alter the likelihood of recording aggressive behavior in adult life.

2. Adult Influences

a. Noncriminal Populations. Repeated clinical attempts have been made to correlate testicular androgens with hostility in noncriminal situations. One should initially note, however, that clinical aggression is certainly not a homogeneous category. For example, psychiatric cases and healthy clinical volunteers are likely to generate very different data in drug treatment assessments. Criminality may be a feature of some populations, but we are not dealing with prison situations. Perhaps one should differentiate between individuals in which disorders are manifestly psychiatric and those in which it is somatic, for example, the recorded malfunction of some endocrine gland or the established presence of a brain tumor?

Persky, Zuckerman, and Curtis (1968) claimed that there was a direct correlation between androgenic production (dubiously quantified by estimating 17-ketosteroid production) and aggressiveness (assessed by ward personnel) in hospitalized psychiatric patients. Kendenberg, Kendenberg, and Kling (1973) correlated plasma T levels (eight determinations per patient) and nonverbal ("ethologically determined" they claim!) aggression in 12 psychiatric patients (both interviews and classification by nursing staff were used here). Highly significant *inverse* relationships between circulating T and agitation and *direct* relationships between T and aggression were evident. Production rate of T and aggression (as estimated by the Buss–Durkee Hostility Inventory) correlated directly in 18 young male volunteers (Persky, Smith, & Basu, 1971). A sample of 15 healthy older men failed to show similar correlation in this study. A carefully attempted replication by Meyer–Bahlburg, Nat, Boon, Sharma, and Edwards (1974) did not reveal differences in blood production rate, plasma levels, or urinary levels of androgens in two groups of young males ranking high (6) or low (5) on the Buss–Durkee Hostility Inventory (BDHI). A well-designed experiment (Doering, Brodie, Kraemer, Becker, & Hamburg, 1974) studied plasma T levels and psychological measures in 20 young (ages 20–38 years) male volunteers. They also failed to find a relationship between any psychological measure of aggression and hormone production. The direct correlation between self-perceived hostility and plasma T level approached significance, and self-perceived depression and mean plasma T level was significant. Analysis of individual data suggested that some individuals had direct and others inverse relationships between T levels and hostility. Monti, Brown and Corriveau (1977) carried out a similar study on 107 normal male volunteers from whom they took two blood samples. BDHI hostility measures were not correlated with plasma T but there was a significant positive correlation between questionnaire-assessed suspicion and anxiety and this hormone. Doering *et al.* (1974) found a clear overall inverse relationship between sexual activity and the mean plasma level of T. Consequently, studies in which sexual activity is not controlled seem fairly meaningless. Meyer-Bahlberg (1981b) noted that the absence of replicable positive findings involving questionnaires does *not* preclude a relationship between testosterone and more direct measures of aggression in man. He suggested that the questionnaire should be used with caution and that all studies to date are essentially preliminary and show a predisposition to find a positive relationship between hostility and circulating T levels. Much more complex behavioral analyses are needed.

One of the better studies in this area is that by Olweus *et al.* (1980). They examined 58 normal Swedish boys at 16 years of age, taking two sets of blood samples for T assays, and applying a number of personality inventories and rating scales for aggression and impulsiveness. In addition, they looked at physical variables, including pubertal stage, height, and physical strength. This study reported a significant association between plasma T and self-reports of physical and verbal aggression—

mainly in terms of responsiveness to provocation and threat. A lack of frustration tolerance (impatience) was related to T levels. Meyer–Bahlberg (1981b) reviewed similar evidence that hockey players show responses to threat that correlate with their T levels. Surprisingly, previous hypotheses relating T to strong body build and antisocial behavior received weak or no support (there was only a nonsignificant positive relationship between T levels and self-report scale of antisocial behavior, for example, petty theft and truancy).

Suggestions of relationships between hormones and clinically assessed aggression are not limited to young males. There have been repeated suggestions (see reviews by Bardwick, 1976; Brain, 1977; Dalton, 1964; Lloyd & Weisz, 1975; Moyer, 1971, 1981a; Steiner and Carroll, 1977; Thiessen, 1976) that the apparently increased hostility and irritability of some females in the premenstrual tension syndrome (PMT) has a hormonal basis. Although the behavioral consequences of PMT seem widespread, they are clearly *not* related only to altered circulating hormones (see variations in PMT suffering in different religious groups), and the precise involvement of hormones (if any) is unclear (prolactin, progesterone, and aldosterone have all been claimed to be *the* causative factor by different workers). Meyer–Bahlberg (1981b) reviewed a single unreplicated study in which T secretion in females over the menstrual cycle was correlated with questionnaire-assessed aggression. One should also note that attempts have been made to implicate electrolyte changes in the presumed hostility changes (which may reflect irritability if anything) occurring over the menstrual cycle, but there is, however, no clear concensus that female hostility is associated with the premenstrual period. It has been argued, for example, that the expectancies of females (concerning premenstrual symptoms) may have a bearing on how they react to these physiological changes.

Other hormones may be involved in clinical aggression. O'Brien, Levell, and Hullin (1979) found that the sera of manic–depressive patients reduced the *in vitro* production of aldosterone from adrenal tissue of rats in response to ACTH, angiotensin II, or serotonin. This may indicate that such patients have abnormalities of aldosterone control. There have also been repeated attempts to find an inverse relationship between blood sugar levels and hostility and crime (reviewed by Moyer, 1971, 1981a). Specifically, Yaryura-Tobias (1973), Yaryura-Tobias and Neziroglu (1975), and Neziroglu (1978) have described a syndrome in aggressive mental patients characterized by glucose disturbance and abnormal EEG patterns (the behavioral gluco-dysrhythmic syndrome). Frequently, aggression was directed at family members. It is interesting to note that Benton, Kumari, and Brain (1982) showed a relationship between hypoglycemia and questionnaire-assessed aggressiveness in a normal population of male undergraduates. The precise hormonal involvement (if any) in the glucose changes is not well-documented.

b. Criminal Populations. A major difficulty in defining criminal aggression is that different cultures view activities as criminal or noncriminal depending on their code of law. However, certain actions such as murder and rape are offences under most circumstances in most countries. Hinton (1981b) described a model that differentiates public and domestic violence and suggests that these may be related to the psychological concepts of anger and apprehension, respectively. Certainly, criminals are no more homogeneous as a group than are other factions.

A majority of studies in this area have been carried out on convicted criminals—generally volunteers from prison populations. The relationship between plasma T levels and sexual behavior has already been noted so it seems important to differentiate between crimes that have a largely sexual component and those in which offences are overtly nonsexual.

i. Nonsex offenders. Attempts to correlate plasma T and aggression in healthy prisoners (reviewed by Hinton, 1981a) have generated variable results. Initial aggression categories are generally derived by examination of court records, but questionnaire techniques subsequently provide support for these distinctions.

Recorded juvenile antisocial behavior and plasma T levels in young adult male prisoners were directly correlated (Kreuz & Rose, 1972) (remarkable considering the time elapsed between the two measures). Correlations between androgen production and concomitant (recorded) fighting within the prison or performance on hostility rating scales were not evident (i.e., only correlations with the most distantly assessed index of aggression were found). Thirty-six male prisoners assessed as "aggressive," "socially dominant but not aggressive," and "neither dominant nor aggressive" (12 in each behavioral category) were constructed on the basis of interview techniques (Ehrenkranz, Bliss, & Sheard, 1974). A series of confirmatory psychological tests was subsequently applied and aggression related to the plasma T levels (assessed over 3 days). *No* significant correlations between plasma T and any of the psychological measures (57 variables) were evident. The preselected categories did, however, reveal differences. Aggressive and dominant categories had significantly higher plasma T titers than their nonaggressive counterparts.

Mattsson, Schalling, Olweus, and Loow (1980) carried out a study on a young Swedish criminal population (using measures described in the Olweus *et al.*, 1980 study). They found only weak correlations between T and measures of questionnaire, self-report, or peer-report aggression. They did find, however, that some aggressive individuals showed an elevated T response to provocation.

Woodman and Hinton (1978) obtained evidence that there was an unusually high proportion of individuals with abnormally inflated urinary and plasma norepinephrine–epinephrine ratios in a Scottish security hospital for abnormal, violent offenders. These ratios were reliable when redetermined 9 months later, and a high correlation was demonstrated in a preliminary study between these properties and crude violence ranking from case records (Hinton, 1981a). Some evidence was also produced in the same sample that the most physically violent offenders failed to show a rise or even exhibited a fall in plasma cortisol levels following mild stressors. Less violent subjects showed a significant rise, suggesting that violent offenders show less psychophysiological responsiveness.

ii. Sex offenders. Data is reviewed by Brain (1981c) but a problem here shows that the hormonal actions may produce changes in libido rather than in aggressive motivation. Note, however, the view that activities such as rape often constitute disorders of "aggression" and "dominance" rather than being expressions of excessive "sex drive" (Groth & Loredo, 1981).

Rada, Laws, and Kellner (1976) estimated plasma T levels and personality in 52 rapists (divided into 5 categories on the basis of the violence of the crime for which they were imprisoned) and 12 child molesters. There were *no* significant correlations between hostility scores on the questionnaires and plasma T levels. The most violent rapists, however, (a) scored significantly higher than controls on the Buss–Durkee Hostility ratings (unremarkable); and (b) had higher plasma T levels than all other groups.

Interestingly, alcoholic rapists had higher plasma T levels than nonalcoholic offenders. Perhaps alcoholism elevates plasma T levels: Does alcohol predispose violent people to rape or are violent rapists likely to drink? Clarifying studies are needed in this area.

It is suggested that the introduction of enzyme immunoassays of steroids in saliva (representing a nonintrusive sampling of free rather than total hormone, for example, Turkes, Turkes, Joyce, & Riad-Fahmy, 1980) will have a phenomenal effect on hormone–aggression studies. Repeated, nonstressing sampling now appears within our grasp.

C. Use of Endocrine Gland Extirpation and Hormone Administration to Modify Human Aggression

1. Castration Studies

Several workers have concluded that castration (especially when combined with other therapeutic measures) is an effective means of curbing violence in sex offenders (reviewed by Brain, 1981c and Meyer-Bahlberg, 1981b). One should initially note that the reported studies are by no means as conclusive as is generally claimed. For example, Bremer (1959) followed up 224 Norwegian cases in which castration was employed as therapy for sex crimes. Surgery was said to drastically reduce sex drive in such cases, lowering the potential for further crime [note that Heim & Hursch, 1979, have cast doubt on this simple view that libido is reduced by castration—some studies, for example, Cornu (1973), maintain that castration has no deleterious effect on sex drive in a proportion of the sample]. Half these cases were considered by Bremer (1959) to be potentially dangerous, whereas the remainder were regarded merely as anti-social or troublesome (exhibitionists, etc.). Castration was most effective when excessive libido seemed to account for the criminal or disturbed behavior. Bremer (1959) reported, however, that surgery was ineffective in the control of hostility in schizophrenics (i.e., it had no specific pacifying effect).

Hawke (1950) attempted to curb sexual and other forms of aggression by castration in inmates of a Kansas institution. Many of the 330 individuals castrated in this study were "brutal homosexuals" who had proved unmanageable. Postoperative stabilization occurred, and they could be paroled or become helpful patients within the institution. Hawke (1950) also described a series of observations in which relatively large doses of T were given over several weeks to castrates. It often became necessary to terminate this treatment, because patients became "destructive." When T administration was stopped, the individuals became tractable once again within a few days and no longer "created disturbances."

Recidivism in sex criminals treated by castration seems to be impressively low. Danish statistics indicate that this rate is about one-tenth of that in unoperated subjects (Sturup, 1961). Similar data have been obtained for the Norwegian (Bremer, 1959) and Kansas (Hawke, 1950) samples. One should note, however, that measures of changed aggression are unsystematic and rather anecdotal, and use of this operation in therapy is difficult to support because it is:

1. Generally based on inconclusive studies
2. Irreversible
3. Difficult to establish informed free choice in such cases (see Section VII)
4. Likely to modify behaviors other than the intended hostility
5. Apparently efficacious (if at all) only in sex criminals (see, however, comments of Heim & Hursch, 1979).

Indeed, as can be seen, many of the studies are relatively old and in many cases the problems of the "patient's" changed expectations about self control and the fact that they age before release are not adequately dealt with. One must admit, however, that on purely empirical grounds, the operation is one of the most effective ways of ensuring that recidivism does not occur. The treatment is once-and-for-all and not dependent on repeated and continuous therapy.

2. Estrogens as Antihostility Agents

Clinical studies have shown that estrogens may be used to control aggressive tendencies in man. For example, Golla and Hodge (1949) claimed that estrogens could be used as "a form of clinical castration." This therapy was more efficient than surgery because it blocked the effects of both adrenal and gonadal androgens. Stilbestrol (a synthetic estrogen) lowered aggressive tendencies of adolescents and young adults (Foote, 1944; Sands, 1954; Whitaker, 1959). For example, Dunn (1941) reported that stilbestrol could be used to control hyperirritable aggression and "excessive libido" in a 27-year-old male under a maximum sentence for sexual offenses. Daily treatment with stilbestrol for 4 weeks improved the patient's mental and physical sexual responses, and he apparently remained relatively symptom-free for more than 3 months after cessation of therapy. Subsequently, remission occurred and therapy was resumed.

Stilbestrol has many unfortunate side-effects, including production of gynaecomastia (Chatz, 1972; Dunn, 1940), fluid retention, with ensuing headaches and phlebothrombosis. This treatment may also aggravate epilepsy and abolish reproductive drive. Consequently, Chatz (1972) and Field and Williams (1970) concluded that stilbestrol was unsuitable in the treatment of hyperaggressiveness. They used subcutaneous or intramuscular injections of long-acting estrogens (estradiol BPC and estradiol valerate) in order to avoid daily oral therapy. This approach permitted the release of otherwise highly dangerous individuals and did not depend on their continued cooperation in taking medication. Both reports indicated that aggressive and sexual drives were essentially eliminated while the patients were subject to this therapy.

In summary, estrogens seem useful in treating aggression but their side-effects create problems.

3. *Antiandrogens and the Control of Aggression*

Antiandrogenic therapy for human hostility has attracted considerable attention (reviewed in Brain, 1981c). A-Norprogesterone (Lerner, Bianchi, & Borman, 1960), chlormadione acetate (Rocky & Neri, 1968), cyproterone acetate (Neumann, von Berswordt-Wallrabe, Elger, & Steinbeck, 1968), and medroxyprogesterone (Servais, 1968) have all been said to antagonize androgenic secretion. These compounds are also reported to produce castration-like symptoms in intact animals. Cyproterone acetate (CA) appears to block endogenous T efficacy by competing with it for receptor sites (Neumann, Steinbeck, & Hahn, 1970). Conversely, medroxyprogesterone acetate (MPA) seems to lower endogenous T secretion (Money, 1970).

Excessive libido and sex-related aggression can be clinically controlled by CA application (Hoffet, 1968; Laschet & Laschet, 1967; Laschet, Laschet, Fetzner, Glaesel, Mall, & Naab, 1967). For example, seven individuals convicted of indecent assault and a sexual murderer showed successful responses to cyproterone therapy (Laschet *et al.*, 1967). Abel, Blanchard, and Becker (1976) provided limited support for CA and MPA therapy in rapists. These compounds depress sexual drive and interest, resulting in the rapist having behavioral control. Abel and co-workers (1976) noted, however, that these compounds may produce impotency and depression. They suggest that they should be used only in a crisis situation—"when the patient reports loss of control is imminent." These authors opined that these drugs indiscriminately reduced deviant and nondeviant arousal.

Eaton (1976) reviewed the results of CA therapy in "some persons jailed for violent sex-related offences in Germany." He pessimistically concluded that, as animal studies indicate that cyproterone *does not* reduce male sexual behavior, the initially encouraging clinical results may be "not due to the drug, but a placebo effect."

We have already noted that MPA is highly effective in lowering T levels. There is also evidence that it may be used to control excessive, impulsive sexual behavior and aggression in man. Sexually hyperactive and aggressive adolescent boys have been made more tractable by MPA therapy (Lloyd, 1964). This compound is said to suppress aggression without abolishing sexual motivation (Blumer & Migeon, 1975; Money, 1970), Itil (1981a,b) claimed that the partial improvements in aggressiveness induced in a variety of male subjects by antiandrogens are less predictable than effects on sexual behavior. Blumer and Migeon (1975) reported that MPA lowered "family-interview assessed aggression." Blumer (1971) also found the compound useful in treatment of temporal lobe epileptics with episodic bouts of aggressive behavior. Money (1972) recorded that MPA reduces criminal sexual behavior in male offenders. This suggests that these compounds may indirectly suppress aggression by reducing sexual motivation. This contradicts the initial statement by these same workers. Meyer-Bahlberg (1981b) notes that although MPA suppresses aggression at doses insufficient to depress androgen-dependent sexual behavior, "the various reports available to date make it seem unlikely that androgen depletion in adulthood leads to a marked diminuation in psychopathological aggression."

Money *et al.* (1976) reviewed their experiences with a combined program of MPA treatment and counselling on 46, XY and 47, XYY sex offenders. The XY subjects in this study were largely pedophils and exhibitionists (rapists were not referred to these workers). The XYY sample were individuals "many of them institutionalized with known histories of antisocial behavior," but the authors noted that a proportion of the XYY men were also actually or potentially sex offenders. Money *et al.* (1976) found that XY subjects were not overtly aggressive. MPA (100–400 mg/week) substantially lowered circulating T levels in both XY and XYY subjects as well as modifying behavior. The authors noted that "by and large, however, these partial improvements (in aggressive behavior) were less predictable than improvements in sexual behavior." They also believed that the improvements in aggression may be an indirect effect of hormonal treatment by relieving "a person of total personal moral responsibility for socially stigmatized behavior."

Despite the paucity of a direct aggression-suppressing action by antiandrogens in rodent species and generally pessimistic comments concerning clinical treatments (reviewed by Brain, 1978), some workers, for example, Itil and Reisberg (1978), recommend these preparations "when the violent–aggressive behavior is associated with pathological sexual hyperactivity."

VII. ETHICAL PROBLEMS ASSOCIATED WITH BIOLOGICAL APPROACHES TO THE CONTROL OF HUMAN AGGRESSION

Some of these difficulties have already been noted in text and reviews are provided by Adams (1981) and Ebling (1981). Adams, for example, notes that criticism of biological research on aggression is evident across a wide *political* spectrum and tends to be concerned with mistreatment of human subjects and cruelty to animals. He also suggests that criticism can be used as a form of political propaganda.

Robinson (1971) correctly identified the basic problem as, if treatments are to be applied, *who* will manipulate and *what* will be modified? Many grandiose claims are made concerning *who* should assume the responsibilities for applying or not applying therapy. Mark (1978a) claimed that biological violence is a public health problem, and the major thrust of any program dealing with violence must be toward its prevention—"a goal that will make a better and safer world for us all." Proud sentiments, but we have noted earlier that one may take issue with the view that every activity that can be labeled aggression is a disease and that the medical profession is the appropriate agent to correct such activities. Halleck (1978) put the onus for determining appropriateness on society, claiming that "the ethical question of how far society is entitled to go in changing an offender's psychology and physiology in the name of rehabilitation will, in my opinion, eventually become more important than the current simplistic debates as to whether we should punish or treat violent offenders." This is true, but it again seems to imply a homogeneous and static view of society. Conversely, Lion and Penna (1976) suggested that as "therapy involves some degree of modification of the patient's behavior, we are confronted with complex ethical and technical obstacles whenever we become agents of an institution rather than being directly hired by the patient." One might argue that the fact that an individual advocates treatment for him- or herself makes the situation no less difficult in ethical terms. Society generally does not approve of suicide, for example. Many workers have considered that the obtaining of informed consent is sufficient protection for individual rights. Kopelman (1978) noted that such consent has a moral function and gives the individual the right to choose to participate. There are, however, considerable problems, for example, in XYY screening where the infants cannot give consent (Kopelman, 1978); mental institutions where the patients' logic may be impaired; and in prison situations where Whitehead (1981) claimed that it is impossible to obtain free informed consent.

Razavi (1975) set out one of the more impressive protective schemes for prison inmates. The gathered data (on genetic factors) were not used for legal and custodial disposition; volunteers could join or withdraw at will; data were collected blind and not divulged to the medical staff, custodians, probation boards, or attorneys unless the inmate requested this. Despite these attempts at fairness, one could argue that the participant has certain expectancies concerning his or her cooperation–noncooperation.

There is a recurrent fear that the treatments may be used to stifle legitimate protest or even to bolster the effectiveness of inadequate institutions. Some individuals also feel strongly about the potential military uses of therapies of this type (discussed in Adams, 1981).

Muller–Oerlinghausen (1978) advocated a stronger partnership between the patient and the investigator to counteract the ongoing paternalism or legal formalism. One may note that an additional problem of clinical trials relates to the ethics of using control groups. If the intention to help the individual is used to justify the treatment, how can control groups be ethical?

In contrast to the corporate responsibility view, van den Haag (1975) suggested that in the current climate of public opinion, "bodies have become private, intimate things, not to be invaded without consent for any public purpose." This is reflected by Whitlock's (1977) claim (see Section I,D) that psychosurgery may be appropriate only when there is evidence of *physical* damage to the brain. It is most difficult to resolve the problem of balancing the rights of individuals and society—especially when these conflict dramatically.

What then of the problem of *what* is modified by biological treatments for aggression? Adams (1981) emphasized that as aggression is a value-laden term, extrapolations from animals to human behavior "may take the form of infering that violence in human culture cannot be solved because it is 'caused' by inborn biological errors." Conversely, the claim may be that as animal aggression can be modified by drugs, psychosurgery, and hormones, these approaches are appropriate to man. Further, Steadman (1976) pessimistically notes that in "no place in the research literature is there any indication of proven psychiatric accuracy in making clinical judgements of dangerousness." Despite this, prison populations are often viewed as a major source of subjects for treatment. Halleck (1978) suggested that large numbers of offenders might be rehabilitated (in the simplest sense) "by drastic interventions, some of which might involve physical and psychological mutilation."

VIII. CONCLUDING REMARKS

It must be commented that there is a considerable range of good and bad material in the area investigating the biology of human aggression. Some medical workers appear to have overly simplistic views of this complex concept and apply uniformly negative attributes to behaviors receiving this label (this is *not* a view held by biologists). Such individuals also appear selective in finding support from animal studies for their therapies. One may also comment that although associations have been found between aggression and genetic endowment, neuroanatomical treatments, drugs and hormones, there are considerable problems associated with most current treatments. The problems are partially technical and partially ethical. It is urged that more attention be paid to multifactorial approaches to aggression research, in which biological factors are merely an aspect. One may also claim that it seems unlikely (even if these problems are solved) that biological therapies will be appropriate in more than a small minority of cases. This is not to deny the importance of biology but to reiterate that treatments derived from such approaches should not be regarded as the only or indeed necessarily the most appropriate means of curbing aggression. A tendency to overemphasize such approaches (a) distorts the truth; (b) raises false expectations in many quarters; and (c) creates fears that are not easy to resolve.

References

Abel, G. G., Blanchard, B. B., & Becker, J. V. Psychological treatment for rapists. In S. Brodsky & M. Walker, (Eds.), *Sexual assault*, pp. 99–115. Lexington, Massachusetts: Lexington, 1976.

Adams, D. B. Brain mechanisms for offense, defense and submission. *The Behavioral and Brain Sciences*, 1979, **2**, 201–241.

Adams, D. B. The use and misuse of aggression research. In P. F. Brain & D. Benton (Eds.), *Multidisciplinary approaches to aggression research*, pp. 531–544. Amsterdam: Elsevier/North Holland, 1981.

Bandler, R. J., & Tork, I. Behavioural–anatomical techniques as a means of studying the neural control of aggression. In P. F. Brain & D. Benton (Eds.), *The biology of aggression*, pp. 367–382. Alphen aan den Rijn: Noordhoff/Sijthoff, 1981.

Bardwick, J. M. Psychological correlates of the menstrual cycle and oral contraceptive medication. In E. J. Sachard (Ed.), *Hormones, behavior and psychopathology*, pp. 95–103. New York: Raven Press, 1976.

Baron, R. A. *Human aggression: Perspectives in social psychology*, New York: Plenum, 1977.

Benson, R. M., & Migeon, C. J. Physiological and pathological puberty and human behavior. In B. E. Eleftheriou & R. L. Sprott (Eds.), *Hormonal correlates of behavior*, pp. 155–184. New York: Plenum, 1975.

Benton, D. The extrapolation from animals to man: The example of testosterone and aggression. In P. F. Brain & D. Benton (Eds.), *Multidisciplinary approaches to aggression research*, pp. 401–418. Amsterdam: Elsevier/North-Holland, 1981.

Benton, D., Kumari, N., & Brain, P. F. Mild hypoglycaemia and questionnaire measures of aggression. *Biological Psychology*, 1982, **14**, 129–135.

Berkowitz, L., & Frodi, A. Stimulus characteristics that can enhance or decrease aggression: Associations with prior positive or negative reinforcements for aggression. *Aggressive Behavior*, 1977, **3**, 1–15.

Blanchard, R. J., & Blanchard, D. C. Aggressive behavior in the rat. *Behavioral Biology*, 1977, **21**, 197–224.

Blumer, D. Das sexualverhalten der schlafen lappenepileptiker von und nach chirurischer behandlung. *Journal of Neurovisceral Relations*, 1971, **Suppl. x**, 469–476.

Blumer, D. Epilepsy and violence In D. J. Madden & J. R. Lion (Eds.), *Rage, hate, assault and other forms of aggression,* pp. 207–221. New York: Spectrum, 1976.

Blumer, D., & Migeon, C. Hormones and hormonal agents in the treatment of aggression. *Journal of Nervous and Mental Disease,* 1975, **160,** 127–137.

Brain, P. F. *Hormones and aggression* (Vol. 1). Montreal: Eden, 1977.

Brain, P. F. *Hormones and aggression* (Vol. 2). Montreal: Eden, 1978.

Brain, P. F. Dividing up aggression—Considerations in studying the physiological substrates of these phenomena. *The Brain and Behavioral Sciences,* 1979, **2,** 216–217. (a)

Brain, P. F. *Hormones, drugs and aggression* (Vol. 3). Montreal: Eden, 1979. (b).

Brain, P. F. Effects of the hormones of the pituitary–gonadal axis on behaviour. In K. Brown & S. J. Cooper (Eds.), *Chemical influences on behaviour,* pp. 255–328. New York: Academic Press, 1979. (c)

Brain, P. F. Effects of the hormones of the pituitary–adrenocortical axis on behaviour. In K. Brown & S. J. Cooper (Eds.), *Chemical influences on behaviour.* London: Academic Press, 1979. pp. 329–371. (d)

Brain, P. F. Steroidal influences on aggressiveness. In J. Obiols, C. Ballus, E. Gonzalez-Monclus, and J. Pujol (Eds.), *Biological psychiatry today,* pp. 1204–1208. Amsterdam: Elsevier/North-Holland, 1979. (e).

Brain, P. F. Adaptive aspects of hormonal correlates of attack and defence: A study in ethobiology. In P. S. McConnell *et al.* (Eds.), *Recent progress in brain research* (Vol. 53), pp. 391–413. Amsterdam: Elsevier/North-Holland, 1980.

Brain, P. F. Differentiating types of attack and defense in rodents. In P. F. Brain & D. Benton (Eds.), *Multidisciplinary approaches to aggression research,* pp.. 53–78. Amsterdam: Elsevier/North-Holland, 1981. (a)

Brain, P. F. Classical ethology and human aggression. In P. F. Brain & D. Benton (Eds.), *The biology of aggression,* Pp. 603–623, Alphen aan den Rijn: Noordhoof/Sijthoff, 1981. (b)

Brain, P. F. Diverse actions of hormones on "aggression" in animals and man. In L. Valzelli & I. Morgese (Eds.), *Aggression and violence: A psycho/biological and clinical approach,* pp. 99–149. St. Vincent, Italy: Edizioni Saint Vincent, 1981. (c)

Brain, P. F. Hormones and aggression in infra-human vertebrates. In P. F. Brain & D. Benton (Eds.), *The biology of aggression,* pp. 181–213. Alphen aan den Rijn: Noordhoff/Sijthoff, 1981. (d)

Brain, P. F. Alcohol and aggression: Some notes on the presumed relationship between the physiological and behavioural correlates of man's oldest drug. *British Journal of Alcohol and Alcoholism,* 1982, **17,** 39–45.

Brain, P. F. Human aggression and non-interpersonal aspects of the physical environment. In H. L. Freeman & G. Ashworth (Eds.), *Mental health and the environment,* pp. 97–120. London: Churchill–Livingstone, 1984.

Brain, P. F. Pituitary–gonadal influences on social aggression. In B. B. Svare (Ed.), *Hormones and aggressive behavior,* pp. 3–25. New York: Plenum, 1983.

Brain, P. F., & Benton, D. (Eds.). *The Biology of aggression.* Alphen aan den Rijn: Noordhoff/Sijthoff, 1981. (a)

Brain, P. F., & Benton, D. (Eds.). *Multidisciplinary approaches to aggression research,* Amsterdam: Elsevier/North-Holland, 1981. (b)

Brain, P. F., & Benton, D. Conditions of housing, hormones and aggressive behavior. In B. B. Svare (Ed.), *Hormones and aggressive behavior,* pp. 349–372. New York: Plenum, 1983.

Brain, P. F., & Bowden, N. J. Sex steroid control of intermale fighting in albino laboratory mice. In W. B. Essman & L. Valzelli (Eds.), *Current developments in psychopharmacology* (Vol. 5), pp. 403–465. New York: Spectrum, 1979.

Brain, P. F., Kamis, A., Haug, M., Mandel, P., & Simler, S. Studies on diverse models of aggression in drug research. *Acta Physiological et Pharmacologia Bulgarica*, 1982, **8**, 97–105. (a)

Brain, P. F., Parmigiani, S., & Childs, G. Further studies on "aggression" employing laboratory mice in different situations, In G. V. Caprara & P. Renzi (Eds.), *Experimental research on aggression*. Rome: Bulzoni Editore, 1982. (In press.) (b).

Breggin, P. R. Psychosurgery for the control of violence: A critical review. In W. S. Fields & W. H. Sweet (Eds.), *Neural bases of violence and aggression*, pp. 350–378. St. Louis: Warren H. Green, 1975.

Bremer, J. *Asexualization*. New York: Macmillan, 1959.

Carroll, D., & O'Callaghan, M. A. J. Psychosurgery and the control of aggression. In P. F. Brain & D. Benton (Eds.), *The biology of aggression*. pp. 457–472. Alphen aan den Rijn: Noordhoff/Sijthoff, 1981.

Chatz, T. L. Recognizing and treating dangerous sex offenders. *International Journal of Offenders and Therapy*, 1972, **2**, 109–115.

Christiansen, K. O. The genesis of aggressive criminality: Implications of a study of crime in a Danish twin study in: A danish twin study. In W. W. Hartup & J. de Wit (Eds.), *Origins of aggression*, pp. 99–120. The Hague: Mouton, 1978.

Collins, J. J. (Ed.), *Drinking and crime: Perspectives on the relationship between alcohol consumption and criminal behavior*. London: Tavistock, 1981.

Cools, A. Aspects and prospects of the concept of neuro-chemical and cerebral organization of aggression: Introduction of new research strategies in "brain and behaviour" studies. In P. F. Brain & D. Benton (Eds.), *The biology of aggression*, pp. 405–426. Alphen aan den Rijn: Noordhoff/Sijthoff, 1981.

Cornu, F. *Catamnestic studies on castrated sex delinquents from a forensic-psychiatric viewpoint*. Basel: Karger, 1973.

Dalton, K. *The premenstrual syndrome*. London: William Heinemann, 1964.

Daruna, J. H. Patterns of brain monoamine activity and aggressive behavior. *Neuroscience and Biobehavioral Reviews*, 1978, **2**, 101–113.

Delgado, J. M. R. Brain stimulation and neurochemical studies on the control of aggression. In P. F. Brain, & D. Benton (Eds.), *The biology of aggression*, pp. 427–456. Alphen aan den Rijn: Noordhoff/Sijthoff, 1981. (a)

Delgado, J. M. R. Neuronal constellations in aggressive behavior. In L. Valzelli & I. Morgese (Eds.), *Aggression and violence: A psycho/biological and clinical approach*, pp. 82–98. St. Vincent: Edizioni Saint Vincent, 1981. (b)

Doering, C. H., Brodie, H. K. H., Kraemer, H., Becker, H., & Hamburg, D. A. Plasma testosterone levels and psychologic measures in man over a two-month period. In R. C. Friedman, R. M. Richart, & R. L. Vande Wiele (Eds.), *Sex differences in behavior*, pp. 413–431. New York: Wiley, 1974.

Dunn, C. W. Stilbestrol-induced gynecomastia in the male. *American Journal of Medicine*, 1940, **115**, 2263–2264.

Dunn, C. W. Stilbestrol-induced testicular degeneration in hypersexual males. *Journal of Clinical Endocrinology and Metabolism*, 1941, **1**, 643, 648.

Earls, F. The social reconstruction of adolescence: Toward an explanation for increasing rates of violence in youth. *Perspectives in Biology and Medicine*, 1978, **22**, 65–82.

Eaton, G. G. Animal models and the study of human aggressive behavior. *Journal of American Medical Women's Association*, 1976, **31**, 345–348.

Ebling, F. J. G. Ethical considerations in the control of human aggression. In P. F. Brain & D. Benton (Eds.), *The biology of aggression*, pp. 473–486. Alphen aan den Rijn: Noordhoff/Sijthoff, 1981.

Ehrenkranz, J., Bliss, E., & Sheard, M. H. Plasma testosterone: Correlation with aggressive behavior and social dominance in man. *Psychosomatic Medicine*, 1974, *36*, 469–475.

Eibl-Eibesfeldt, I. Evolution of destructive aggression. *Aggressive Behavior*, 1977, *3*, 127–144.

Eleftheriou, B. E., & Scott, J. P. (Eds.). *The physiology of aggression and defeat*. New York: Plenum, 1971.

Engelmann, F., Dongier, M., & Reid, J. E. Cerebral event related slow potentials in antisocial personalities. In L. Beliveau, G. Canepa, & D. Szabo (Eds.). *Human aggression and dangerousness*. Montreal: 1978. Pp. 127–143.

Ervin, F. R. The treatment of rage—implications for the future. In J. S. Smith, & L. G. Kiloh (Eds.), *Psychosurgery and society*, pp. 75–78. Oxford: Pergamon, 1977.

Evans, C. M. Alcohol, violence and aggression. *British Journal of Alcohol and Alcoholism*, 1980, *15*, 104–117.

Feshbach, S., & Fraczek, A. (Eds.). *Aggression and behavior change*. New York: Praeger, 1979.

Field, L. H., & Williams, M. The hormonal treatment of sexual offenders. *Medicine, Science and the Law*, 1970, *10*, 27–34.

Flor-Henry, P. Psychosis, neurosis and epilepsy. *British Journal of Psychiatry*, 1974, *124*, 144–150.

Foote, R. M. Diethylstilbestrol in the management of psychopathological states in males. *Journal of Nervous and Mental Diseases*, 1944, *99*, 928–935.

Gandelman, R. Androgen and fighting behavior. In P. F. Brain, & D. Benton (Eds.), *The biology of aggression*, pp. 215–230. Alphen aan den Rijn: Noordhoff/Sijthoff, 1981.

Golla, F. L., & Hodge, R. S. Hormone treatment of the sexual offender. *The Lancet*, 1949, *1*, 1006–1007.

Groth, A. N., & Birnbaum, H. J. *Men who rape*. New York: Plenum, 1979.

Groth, A. N., & Loredo, C. M. Rape: The Sexual expression of aggression. In P. F. Brain, & D. Benton (Eds.), *Multidisciplinary approaches to aggression research*, pp. 465–475. Amsterdam: Elsevier/North-Holland, 1981.

Halleck, S. L. Violence: Treatment versus correction. In I. L. Kutash, S. B. Kutash, L. B. Schlesinger, *et al.* (Eds.), *Violence: Perspectives on murder and aggression*, pp. 377–393. San Francisco: Jossey-Bass, 1978.

Hamburg, D. A., & Trudeau, M. B. (Eds.), *Biobehavioral aspects of aggression*. New York, Liss, 1981.

Hamburg, D. A., & van Lawick-Goodall, J. Factors facilitating development of aggressive behavior in chimpanzees and humans. In W. W. Hartup, & J. de Wit (Eds.), *Origins of aggression*, pp. 57–84. The Hague: Mouton, 1978.

Hartup, W. W., & de Wit, J. (Eds.). *Origins of aggression*. The Hague: Mouton, 1978.

Hawke, C. C. Castration and sex crimes. *American Journal of Mental Deficiency*, 1950, *55*, 220–226.

Heath, R. G. The neural basis for violent behavior: Physiology and anatomy. In L. Valzelli & I. Morgese (Eds.), *Aggression and violence: A psycho/biological and clinical approach*, pp. 176–194. St. Vincent: Edizioni Saint Vincent, 1981.

Heim, N., & Hursch, C. J. Castration for sex offenders: Treatment or punishment? A review and critique of recent European literature. *Archives of Sexual Behavior*, 1979, *8*, 281–304.

Hinde, R. A. *Biological bases of human social behaviour*. New York: McGraw-Hill, 1974.

Hinton, J. W. Biological approaches to criminality. In P. F. Brain, & D. Benton (Eds.), *Multidisciplinary approaches to aggression research*, pp. 447–462. Amsterdam: Elsevier/North-Holland, 1981. (a)

Hinton, J. W. Adrenal cortical and medullary hormones and their psychophysiological correlates in violent and psychopathic offenders. In P. F. Brain, & D. Benton (Eds.), *The biology of aggression*, pp. 291–300. Alphen aan den Rijn: Noodhoff/Sijthoff, 1981. (b).

Hoffet, H. On the application of the testosterone blocker cyproterone acetate (SH 714) in sex deviants and psychiatric patients in institutions. *Praxis*, 1968, **7**, 221–230.

Hunter, H. Males: Some clinical and psychiatric aspects deriving from a survey of 1,811 males in hospitals for the mentally-handicapped. *British Journal of Psychiatry*, 1977, **131**, 468–477.

Itil, T. M. Drug therapy in the management of aggression. In L. Valzelli, & I. Morgese (Eds.), *Aggression and violence: A psycho/biological and clinical approach*, pp. 211–224. St. Vincent: Edizioni Saint Vincent, 1981,. (a)

Itil, T. M. Clinical psychopharmacology of aggression. In P. F. Brain, & D. Benton (Eds.), *Multidisciplinary approaches to aggression research*, pp. 489–502. Amsterdam: Elsevier/North-Holland, 1981. (b)

Itil, T. M., & Reisberg, B. Drug-treatment of violent-aggressive behavior. In *Proceedings of the Second World Congress of Biological Psychiatry*, Barcelona, 1978.

Jacobs, P. A., Brunton, M., & Melville, M. M. Aggressive behaviour, mental subnormality and the XYY male. *Nature (London)*, 1965, **208**, 1351–1352.

Jarvik, L. F., Klodin, V., & Matsuyana, S. S. Human aggression and the extra Y chromosome: Fact or fantasy? *American Psychologist*, 1973, **28**, 674–682.

Karczmar, A. G., Richardson, D. L., & Kindel, G. Neuropharmacological and related aspects of animal aggression. *Progress in Neuropsychopharmacology*, 1978, **2**, 611–631.

Karli, P. Conceptual and methodological problems associated with the study of brain mechanisms underlying aggressive behaviour. In P. F. Brain, & D. Benton (Eds.), *The biology of aggression*, pp. 323–362. Alphen aan den Rijn: Noordhoff/Sijthoff, 1981.

Kelly, D. D. Cautions in interpreting neurobehavioral data in terms of a biological impulse to aggress. In L. Beliveau, G. Canepa, & D. Szabo (Eds.), *Human aggression and dangerousness*, pp. 181–203. Montreal: 1978.

Kendenburg, D., Kendenburg, N., & Kling, A. An ethological study in a patient group. Paper presented at the American Psychological Association Annual Meeting. Honolulu, 1973.

Kiloh, L. G. The treatment of anger and aggression and the modification of sexual deviation. In J. S. Smith, & L. G. Kiloh (Eds.), *Psychosurgery and society*, pp. 37–49. Oxford: Pergamon Press, 1977.

Kling, A. Frontal and temporal lobe lesions and aggressive behavior. In W. L. Smith, & A. Kling (Eds.), *Issues in brain/behavior control*, pp. 11–22. New York: Spectrum, 1976.

Kopelman, L. Ethical controversies in medical research: The case of XYY screening. *Perspectives in Biology and Medicine*, 1978, **21**, 196–204.

Krebs, H. On the biology of juvenile delinquency: Comments on the essay by Felton Earls, "The Social Reconstruction of adolescence: Toward an explanation for Increasing Rates of Violence in Youth," *Perspectives in Biology and Medicine*, 1980, **23**, 179–188.

Kreuz, L. E., & Rose, R. M. Assessment of aggressive behavior and plasma testosterone in a young criminal population. *Psychosomatic Medicine*, 1972, **34**, 1321–1332.

Kutash, I. L., Kutash, S. B., Schlesinger, L. B., et al. (Eds.). *Violence: Perspectives on murder and aggression*. San Francisco: Jossey-Bass, 1978.

Laschet, U., & Laschet, L. Antiandrogentherapie der pathologisch gesteigerten und abartigen sexualitat des mannes. *Klinische Wochenschrift*, 1967, **45**, 324–325.

Laschet, U., Laschet, L., Fetzner, H. R., Glaesel, H. U., Mall, G., & Naab, M. Results in the treatment of hyper- or abnormal sexuality of men with antiandrogens. *Acta Endocrinologica*, 1967, **119**, 54.

Lerner, L. J., Bianchi, A., & Borman, A. A-Norprogesterone, an androgen antagonist. *Proceedings of Society for Experimental Biology and Medicine*, 1960, **103**, 172–175.

Lewis, D. O., & Shanok, S. S. Medical histories of delinquent and non-delinquent children. *American Journal of Psychiatry*, 1977, **134**, 1020–1025.

Lion, J. R., & Penna, M. W. Some scientific, clinical and ethical issues in the treatment of aggressive behavior. In D. J. Madden, & J. R. Lion (Eds.), *Rage, hate, assault and other forms of aggression*, pp. 249–262. New York: Spectrum, 1976.

Lloyd, C. W. Treatment and prevention of certain sexual behavioral problems. In C. W. Lloyd (Ed.), *Human reproduction and sexual behavior*. Philadelphia: Lea & Febiger, 1964.

Lloyd, C. W., & Weisz, J. Hormones and aggression. In W. S. Fields, & W. H. Sweet (Eds.), *Neural bases of violence and aggression*, pp. 92–113. St. Louis: Warren H. Green, 1975.

Madden, D. J., & Lion, J. Treating the violent offender. In I. L. Kutash, S. B. Kutash, L. B. Schlesinger, & Associates (Eds.), *Violence: Perspectives on murder and aggression*, pp. 404–412. San Francisco: Jossey-Bass, 1978.

Madden, D. J., & Lion, J. R. Clinical management of aggression. In P. F. Brain, & D. Benton (Eds.), *Multidisciplinary approaches to aggression research*, pp. 477–488. Amsterdam: Elsevier/North-Holland, 1981.

Malick, J. B. The pharmacology of isolation-induced aggressive behavior in mice. In W. B. Essman, & L. Valzelli (Eds.), *Current developments in psychopharmacology* (Vol. 5), pp. 1–27. New York: Spectrum, 1979.

Mandel, P., Haug, M., Puglisi, S., Kempf, E., & Mack, G. Involvement of the gabaergic system in aggressive behaviour. In P. F. Brain, & D. Benton (Eds.), *The biology of aggression*, pp. 169–174. Alphen aan den Rijn: Noordhoff/Sijthoff, 1981.

Mark, V. H. The study and treatment, on an open ward, of abnormally aggressive patients with focal brain disease. In L. Beliveau, G. Canepa, & D. Szabo (Eds.), *Human aggression and dangerousness*, pp. 169–178. Montreal, 1978. (a)

Mark, V. H. Sociobiological theories of abnormal aggression. In I. L. Kutash, S. B. Kutash, L. B. Schlesinger, & Associates (Eds.), *Violence: Perspectives on murder and aggression*, pp. 101–132. San Francisco: Jossey-Bass, 1978. (b)

Mark, V. H., & Sweet, W. H. The role of limbic brain dysfunction in aggression. In S. H. Frazier (Ed.), *Research publications: Association for research in nervous and mental disease 52 aggression*, pp. 186–200. Baltimore: Williams and Wilkins, 1974.

Mark, V. H., Sweet, W., & Ervin, F. Deep temporal lobe stimulation and destructive lesions in episodically violent temporal lobe epileptics. In W. S. Fields, & W. H. Sweet (Eds.), *Neural bases of violence and aggression*, pp. 379–400. St. Louis: Warren H. Green, 1975.

Martinius, J. A circumscribed lesion in the right temporal lobe and non-paroxysmal violent behavior. In *Proceedings of the Second World Congress of Biological Psychiatry*, Barcelona, 1978.

Mattsson, A., Schalling, D., Olweus, D., & Loow, H. Plasma testosterone, aggressive behavior and personality dimensions in young male delinquents. *Journal of American Academy of Child Psychiatry*, 1980, **19**, 476–490.

Maxson, S. C. The genetics of aggression in vertebrates. In P. F. Brain, & D. Benton (Eds.), *The biology of aggression*, pp. 69–104. Alphen aan den Rijn: Noordhoff-Sijthoff, 1981.

Meyer–Bahlburg, H. F. L. Aggression, androgens and the XYY syndrome. In R. C. Friedman, R. M. Richart, & R. L. Vande Wiele, (Eds.), *Sex differences in behavior*, pp. 433–453. New York: Wiley, 1974.

Meyer–Bahlburg, H. F. L. Sex chromosomes and aggression in humans. In P. F. Brain, & D. Benton (Eds.), *The biology of aggression*, pp. 109–124. Alphen aan den Rijn: Noordhoff/Sijthoff, 1981. (a)

Meyer–Bahlburg, H. F. L. Androgens and human aggression. In P. F. Brain, & D. Benton (Eds.), *The biology of aggression*, pp. 263–290. Alphen aan den Rijn: Noordhoff/Sijthoff, 1981. (b)

Meyer–Bahlburg, H. F. L., Nat, R., Boon, D. A. Sharma, M., & Edwards, J. A. Aggressiveness and testosterone in man. *Psychosomatic Medicine* 1974, **36**, 269–274.

Miczek, K. A., & Kzsiak, M. Drug effects on agonistic behavior. In T. Thompson & P. Dews (Eds.), *Advances in behavioral Pharmacology*, (Vol. 2), pp. 87–162. New York: Academic-Press, 1979.

Midgley, M. *Beast and man: The roots of human nature*. Brighton: Harvester, 1979.

Money, J. Use of an androgen-depleting hormone in the treatment of male sex offenders. *Journal of Sexual Research*, 1970, **6**, 165–172.

Money, J. The therapeutic use of androgen-depleting hormone. In H. L. P. Resnick, & M. F. Wolfgang (Eds.), *Sexual behavior: Social clinical and legal aspects*, pp. 351–360. Boston: Little Brown, 1972.

Money, J., and Schwartz, M. Fetal androgens in the early treated androgenital syndrome of 46 XX hermaphroditism: Influence on assertive and aggressive types of behavior. *Aggressive Behavior*, 1976, **2**, 19–30.

Money, J., Wiedeking, C., Walker, P. A., & Gain, D. Combined antiandrogenic and counseling program for treatment of 46, XY and 47, XYY sex offenders. In E. J. Sachar (Ed.), *Hormones, behavior and psychopathology*, pp. 105–120. New York: Raven Press, 1976.

Monroe, R. R. Drugs in the management of episodic behavioral disorders. In W. S. Fields, & W. H. Sweet (Eds.), *Neural bases of violence and aggression*, pp. 328–345. St. Louis: Warren H. Green, 1975.

Monti, P. M., Brown, W. A., & Corriveau, D. P. Testosterone and components of aggressive and sexual behavior in man. *American Journal of Psychiatry*, 1977, **134**, 692–694.

Moyer, K. E. Kinds of aggression and their physiological basis. *Communications in Behavioral Biology*, 1968, **2**, 65–87.

Moyer, K. E. The physiology of aggression and the implications for aggression control. In J. L. Singer (Ed.), *The control of aggression and violence*, pp. 61–92. New York: Academic Press, 1971. Pp. 61–92.

Moyer, K. E. The physiological inhibition of hostile behavior. In J. F. Knutson (Ed.), *The control of aggression*, pp. 9–38. Chicago: Aldine, 1973.

Moyer, K. E. A physiological model of aggression: Does it have different implications? In W. S. Fields, & W. H. Sweet (Eds.), *Neural bases of violence and aggression*, pp. 161–201. St. Louis: Warren H. Green, 1975.

Moyer, K. E. Biological substrates of aggression and implications for control. In P. F. Brain, & D. Benton (Eds.), *The biology of aggression*, pp. 47–67. Alphen aan den Rijn: Noordhoff/Sijthoff, 1981. (a)

Moyer, K. E. Neural and endocrine substrates of aggression. In L. Valzelli, & I. Morgese (Eds.), *Aggression and violence: A psycho/biological and clinical approach*, pp. 72–81. St. Vincent: Edizioni Saint Vincent, 1981. (b)

Muller-Oerlinghausen, B. Ethical problems in clinical psychopharmacology. *International Journal of Pharmacology*, 1978, **16**, 443–450.

Neumann, F., Von Berswordt-Wallrabe, R., Elger, W., & Steinbeck, H. Activities of anti-androgens. Experiments in prepuberal and puberal animals and in foetuses. In J. Tamm (Ed.), *Testosterone*, pp. 134–143. Stuttgart: Thieme Verlag, 1968.

Neumann, F., Steinbeck, H., & Hahn, J. D. Hormones and brain differentiation. In L. Martini, M. Motta, & F. Fraschini (Eds.), *The hypothalamus*, pp. 539–603. New York: Academic Press, 1970.

Neziroglu, F. Behavioral and organic aspects of aggression. In *Proceedings of the Second World Congress of Biological Psychiatry*, Barcelona, 1978.

O'Brien, M. J., Levell, M. J., & Hullin, R. P. Inhibition of aldosterone production in adrenal cell suspensions by serum from patients with manic–depressive psychosis. *Journal of Endocrinology*, 1979, **80**, 41–50.

Olivier, B. Selective anti-aggressive properties of DU 27725: Ethological analyses of inter-male and territorial aggression in the male rat. *Pharmacology Biochemistry and Behavior*, 1981, **14**, Suppl. 7, 61–77.

Olweus, D. Stability of aggressive reaction patterns in males: A review. *Psychological Bulletin*, 1979, **86**, 852–875.

Olweus, D., Mattsson, A. Schalling, D., & Loow, H. Testosterone, aggression, physical, and personality dimensions in normal adolescent males. *Psychosomatic Medicine*, 1980, **42**, 253–269.

Persky, H., Smith, K. D., & Basu, G. K. Relation of psychological measures of aggression and hostility to testosterone production in man. *Psychosomatic Medicine*, 1971, **33**, 265–277.

Persky, H., Zuckerman, M., & Curtis, G. C. Endocrine function in emotionally disturbed and normal men. *Journal of Nervous and Mental Diseases*, 1968, **146**, 488–497.

Rada, R. T., Laws, D. R., & Kellner, R. Plasma testosterone levels in the rapist. *Psychosomatic Medicine*, 1976, **38**, 257–268.

Razavi, L. Cytogenetic and somatic variation in the neurobiology of violence: Epidemiological, clinical and morphological considerations. In W. S. Fields, & W. H. Sweet (Eds.), *Neural bases of violence and aggression*, pp. 205–272. St. Louis: Warren H. Green, 1975.

Renfrew, J. W. Analysis of aggression produced by electrical brain stimulation. In P. F. Brain, & D. Benton (Eds.), *Multidisciplinary approaches to aggression research*, pp. 295–307. Amsterdam: Elsevier/North-Holland, 1981.

Robinson, B. W. Aggression: Summary and overview. In B. E. Eleftheriou, & J. P. Scott (Eds.), *The physiology of aggression and defeat*, pp. 291–305. New York: Plenum, 1971.

Rocky, S., & Neri, R. O. Comparative biological properties of SCH 12600 (6-chloro-4,6-pregnadien-16-methylene-17-α-o1-3,20-dione-17-acetate) and chlormadinone acetate. *Federation Proceedings*, 1968, **27**, 624.

Rodgers, R. J. Neurochemical correlates of aggressive behaviour: Some relations to emotion and pain sensitivity. In K. Brown, & S. J. Cooper (Eds.), *Chemical influences on behaviour*, pp. 373–419. London: Academic Press, 1979.

Russell, G. W. Aggression in sport. In P. F. Brain, & D. Benton (Eds.), *Multidisciplinary approaches to aggression research*, pp. 431–446. Amsterdam: Elsevier/North Holland, 1981.

Sands, D. E. Further studies on endocrine treatment in adolescence and early adult life. *Journal of Mental Science*, 1954, **100**, 211–219.

Sanjo, K. Posterior hypothalamic lesions in the treatment of violent behavior. In W. S. Fields, & W. H. Sweet, (Eds.), *Neural bases of violence and aggression*, pp. 401–428. St. Louis: Warren H. Green, 1975.

Servais, J. Etude clinique de quelques cas de troubles psychosexuels chez l'homme, traiters par un inhibiteur de la libido: Le methyloestrenolone. *Acta Neurologica et Psychiatrica Belgica*, 1968, **68**, 407–429.

Sharma, M., Meyer-Bahlburg, H. L. F., Boon, D. A., Slaunwhite, W. R., Jr., & Edwards, J. A. Testosterone production by XYY subjects. *Steroids*, 1975, **26**, 175–179.

Simeon, J. Biology and therapy of violent behaviour in children. In *Proceedings of the Second World Congress of Biological Psychiatry*, Barcelona, 1978.

Singer, J. L. (Ed.), *The control of aggression and violence*. New York: Academic Press, 1971.

Smith, D. F. *Lithium and animal behavior* (Vol. 1), Montreal: Eden, 1977.

Sosowsky, L. Explaining the increased arrest rate among mental patients: A cautionary note. *American Journal of Psychiatry*, 1980, **137**, 1602–1605.

Spellacy, F. Neuropsychological differences between violent and nonviolent adolescents. *Journal of Clinical Psychology*, 1977, **33**, 966–969.

Spellacy, F. Neuropsychological discrimination between violent and non-violent men. *Journal of Clinical Psychology*, 1978, **34**, 49–52.

Steadman, M. J. Predicting dangerousness. In D. J. Madden, & J. R. Lion (Eds.), *Rape, hate, assault and other forms of aggression*. New York: Spectrum, 1976, pp. 53–70.

Steiner, M., & Carroll, B. J. The psychobiology of premenstrual dysphoria: Review of theories and treatments. *Psychoneuroendocrinology*, 1977, **2**, 321–325.

Sterup, G. K. Correctional treatment and the criminal sexual offender. *Canadian Journal of Criminology and Correction*, 1961, **3**, 250–265.

Taylor, D. C. Aggression and epilepsy. *Journal of Psychosomatic Research*, 1969, **13**, 229–236.

Theilgaard, A. Aggression in man with XYY and XXY Karyotypes. In P. F. Brain, & D. Benton (Eds.), *The biology of aggression*, pp. 125–130. Alphen aan den Rijn: Noordhoff/Sijthoff, 1981.

Thiessen, D. D. *The evolution and chemistry of aggression*. Springfield, Illinois: C. C. Thomas, 1976.

Thinklenberg, J. R., & Woodrow, K. M. Drug use among youthful assaultive and sexual offenders. In S. H. Frazier (Ed.), *Research publications: Association for research in nervous and mental disease 52 aggression*, pp. 209–224. Baltimore: Williams and Wilkins, 1974.

Turkes, A. O., Turkes, A. Joyce, B. G., & Riad-Fahmy, D. A sensitive enzyme immunoassay with a fluorimetric end-point for the determination of testosterone in female plasma and saliva. *Steroids*, 1980, **35**, 89–101.

Ursin, H. Affective and instrumental aspects of fear and aggression. In M. Koukkou Lehmann (Ed.), *Functional states of the brain and their determinants*. Amsterdam: Elsevier/North-Holland, 1980.

Valenstein, E. S. *Brain control: A critical examination of brain stimulation and psychosurgery*. New York: Wiley, 1973.

Valenstein, E. S. Brain stimulation and the origin of violent behavior. In W. L. Smith, & A. Kling (Eds.), *Issues in brain/behavior control*, pp. 33–48. Englewood Cliffs, N.J.: Prentice-Hall, 1976.

Valzelli, L. Human and animal studies on the neurophysiology of aggression. *Progress in Neuro-psychopharmacology*, 1978, **2**, 591–610.

Valzelli, L. *An approach to neuroanatomical and neuro-chemical psychophysiology*. Torino: C. G. Edizioni Medico Scientifiche, 1980.

Valzelli, L. *Psychobiology of aggression and violence*. New York: Raven, 1981.

Valzelli, L., & Morgese, I. (Eds.). *Aggression and violence: A psycho/biological and clinical approach*. St. Vincent: Edizioni Saint Vincent, 1981.

Van Den Haag, E. *Punishing criminals: Concerning a very old and painful question*. New York: Basic Books, 1975.

Van Der Dennen, J. M. G. Problems in the concepts and definitions of aggression, violence and some related terms. *Internal Publication of the Polemologisch Instituut*, Groningen, Netherlands, 1980.

Weisfeld, G. E. An ethological view of human adolescence. *The Journal of Nervous and Mental Disease*, 1979, **167**, 38–55.

Welch, A. S., & Welch, B. L. Isolation, reactivity and aggression: Evidence for an involvement of brain catecholamines and serotinin. In B. E. Eleftheriou, & J. P. Scott (Eds.), *The physiology of aggression and defeat*, pp. 91–142. New York: Plenum, 1971.

Whitaker, L. H. Oestrogen and psychosexual disorders. *Medical Journal of Australia*, 1959, **2**, 547–549.

Whitehead, T. Sex hormone treatment of prisoners. In P. F. Brain, & D. Benton (Eds.), *Multidisciplinary approaches to aggression research*, pp. 503–551. Amsterdam: Elsevier/North-Holland, 1981.

Whitlock, F. A. The ethics of psychosurgery. In J. S. Smith, & L. G. Kiloh (Eds.), *Psychosurgery and society*, pp. 129–135. Oxford: Pergamon, 1977.

Witkin, H. A., Mednick, S. A., Schulsinger, F., Bakkestrom, E., Christiansen, K. O., Goodenough, D. R., Hirschhorn, K., Ludsteen, C., Owen, D. R., Philip, J., Rubin, D. B., & Stocking, M. Criminality in XYY and XXY men. *Science*, 1976, **196**, 547–555.

Woodman, D., & Hinton, J. W. Catecholamine balance during stress anticipation: An abnormality in maximum security hospital patients. *Journal of Psychosomatic Research*, 1978, **22**, 477–483.

Yaryura-Tobias, J. A. Behavioral-gluco-dysrhythmic triad. *American Journal of Psychiatry*, 1973, **130**, 825.

Yaryura-Tobias, J. A., & Neziroglu, F. Violent behavior, brain dysrhythmia and glucose dysfunction: A new syndrome. *Journal of Orthomolecular Psychiatry*, 1975, **4**, 182–188.

Yeudall, L. T. Neuro-psychological assessment of forensic disorders. *Canada's Mental Health*, 1977, **25**, 7–15.

Yeudall, L. T. Neuropsychological correlates of criminal psychopathy. Part I: Differential diagnosis. In L. Beliveau, G. Canepa, & D. Szabo (Eds.), *Human aggression and dangerousness*, pp. 205–256. Montreal: 1978.

Yeudall, L. T., & Wardell, D. M. Neuro-psychological correlates of criminal psychopathy. Part II: Discrimination and prediction of dangerous and recidivistic offenders. In L. Beliveau, G. Canepa, & D. Szabo (Eds.), *Human aggression and dangerousness*, pp. 257–282. Montreal, 1978.

Development of Stable Aggressive Reaction Patterns in Males

DAN OLWEUS

University of Bergen, Bergen, Norway

I. INTRODUCTION

The relative level of aggressive behavior a child or an adolescent displays in interpersonal contexts is fairly stable over time. This implies that individuals who are more aggressive than most of their peers at a particular point in time tend to be so at a later period (even if the absolute level of aggressive behavior for the group may have changed)

Advances in the
Study of Aggression, Volume 1

and vice versa. Furthermore, it has been found (e.g., Farrington, 1978; Robins, 1966, 1978) that marked aggressiveness toward peers and authorities, manifested as early as in the 8- to 12-year age range, is predictive of antisocial behavior years later. No doubt a habitually aggressive individual represents a problem both for society in general and for those individuals in the immediate environment who become the target of his or her aggression. In view of these facts, it is important to find out what factors are responsible for the *development* of an aggressive reaction pattern.

This is one of the main questions to which the present article is addressed. First, however, the issue of the stability or continuity of aggressive behavior will be dealt with in some detail. Some results and ideas about the possible role of testosterone in the development of aggressive reaction patterns will also be presented.

As aggressive and antisocial behavior is clearly more frequent in boys than in girls (Eme, 1979; Maccoby & Jacklin, 1974) and is generally a more serious problem in terms of the consequences for the environment, most of what follows will be restricted to males. Furthermore, the words *stability, continuity,* and *longitudinal consistency* are used as synonymous terms in the present context. They refer to the extent to which individuals in a group retain their relative positions on identical or similar dimensions for assessments at different periods of time (cf. Olweus, 1974, p. 536). As a rule, a correlation coefficient is used to give a numerical expression of the degree of stability (unless otherwise stated, all correlation coefficients in the present chapter are product–moment coefficients).

II. STABILITY OF AGGRESSIVE
REACTION PATTERNS

My own interest in the stability of aggressive behavior patterns was aroused in the context of a large-scale project on bully–whipping-boy problems in school (Olweus, 1973a, 1978). For instance, in one study I found that approximately 80% of boys whom teachers had nominated as marked bullies in Grade 6 were again picked out as bullies (marked or less marked) by a different set of teachers 1 year later. This finding suggested a considerable degree of continuity over time in aggressive behavior.

A. Review of Studies of Stability in Aggression

To see if this conclusion could be substantiated in other investigations, I made a review of all longitudinal studies of aggressive reaction patterns I was able to find (Olweus, 1977b, 1979). In addition, I initiated two short-term longitudinal studies of my own, to be described later. It should be noted that the focus of the review was on aggressive behavior patterns, as observed or inferred by individuals other than the subjects themselves. Thus studies using self-report data were not included. Only publications written in English were considered.

It was possible to locate 14 main publications containing 16 independent longitudinal studies (one English sample, two Swedish, and 13 American samples). A total of 24 stability coefficients were available (see Table I). The age of the subjects at the time of first assessment varied from 2 to 18 years, and they were followed for intervals varying from half a year to 21 years. The methods of data collection included direct observation, peer nominations, peer ratings, teacher ratings, and clinical ratings. The average number of subjects on which stability coefficients were based amounted to 116—quite a respectable number by usual psychological research standards. Most theoretical analyses in the review were carried out on attenuation-corrected stability coefficients, that is, correlation coefficients corrected for errors of measurement.

An overview can be gained from Fig. 1, which presents the stability coefficients as a joint function of the subjects' age at the time of the first measurement (T_1) and the interval between the two times of measurement $(T_2 - T_1)$. When the stability correlations were plotted as a function of the interval between the two times of measurement (Fig. 2), a relatively regular picture was obtained (see Olweus, 1977b, 1979, for details). As might be expected, the size of the stability coefficient tended to decrease as the interval covered increased. For an interval of 1 year the estimated disattenuated stability coefficient was as high as .76; for an interval of 5 years, .69.

For several reasons, I found it interesting to compare the results from the aggression studies with data from the intelligence domain. Thirteen studies on the stability of intelligence test measurements (of Binet type) compiled by Thorndike (1933) were used as a standard of reference. In this case, the regression line was based on 36 stability coefficients covering intervals up to 5 years. The subjects were mainly school-age children, and the average sample size was 111. The results showed that, although the stability in intelligence was higher than that for aggressive

Table I. Longitudinal Studies of Aggression[a,b]

Study	Method of data collection or integration	N	Reliability at T_1	Reliability at T_2	Age at T_1	Interval in years $(T_2 - T_1)$	Age ratio (T_1/T_2)	Raw correlation (uncorrected)	Correlation corrected for attenuation
		Subjects below age 6 at T_1							
Patterson, Littman, & Bricker (1967)	Direct observation	36[c]	.80	.80	3.5	.50	.88	.72	.90
Kohn & Rosman (1972)	Teacher ratings	70	.77	.73	4.0	.50	.89	.56	.74
Jersild & Markey (1935)	Direct observation	24[d]	.80	.80	3.0	.75	.80	.70	.88
Emmerich (1966)	Teacher ratings	53[e]	.85[f]	.85	3.5	.83	.81	.65	.76
Martin (1964)	Direct observation	53[e]	.80[f]	.80	3.5	.83	.81	.52	.65
Block, Block, & Harrington (1974)	Teacher ratings	41	.86	.74	3.5	1.00	.78	.70	.88
Kohn & Rosman (1972)	Teacher ratings	250	.77	.77	4.0	1.00	.80	.53	.69
Kohn & Rosman (1972)	Teacher ratings	250	.77	.83	4.0	1.50	.73	.48	.60
Kohn & Rosman (1973)	Teacher ratings	271	.70	.70	5.0	1.50	.77	.51	.73
Kagan & Moss (1962)	Clinical ratings	36	.70	.90[f]	5.0	18.00	.22	.22	.26
Kagan & Moss (1962)	Clinical ratings	36	.60	.90[f]	2.0	21.00	.09	.29	.36

Subjects above age 6 at T_1

Wiggins & Winder (1961)	Peer nominations	163	.87	.87	9.0	1.00	.90	.56	.65
Wiggins & Winder (1961)	Peer nominations	176	.81	.81	10.0	1.00	.91	.54	.67
Olweus (1977a)	Peer ratings	85	.81	.81	13.0	1.00	.93	.80	.98
Block (1971)	Clinical ratings	84	.66	.74	12.0	3.00	.80	.54	.69
Olweus (1977a)	Peer ratings	201	.85	.87	13.0	3.00	.81	.68	.79
Farrington (1978)	Teacher ratings	410	.80[f]	.80	9.0	4.00	.69	.51	.64
Eron, Huesmann, Lefkowitz, & Walder (1972)	Peer nominations	71	.90	.82	8.0	5.00	.62	.48	.56
Eron, Huesmann, Lefkowitz, & Walder (1972)	Peer nominations	71	.82	.85	13.0	5.00	.72	.65	.78
Eron, Huesmann, Lefkowitz, & Walder (1972)	Peer nominations	211	.90	.85	8.0	10.00	.44	.38	.44
Kagan & Moss (1962)	Clinical ratings	36	.85	.90[f]	13.0	10.00	.57	.56	.67
Kagan & Moss (1962)	Clinical ratings	36	.85	.90[f]	9.0	14.00	.39	.40	.48
Tuddenham (1959)	Clinical ratings	32	.75	.74	18.0	14.00	.56	.68	.91
Block (1971)	Clinical ratings	84	.74	.78	15.0	18.00	.46	.44	.53

[a] From Olweus (1979). Copyright 1979 by the American Psychological Association. Reprinted by permission.
[b] Samples on which stability correlations were based generally included males only, unless indicated otherwise. T_1 = time of first measurement; T_2 = time of second measurement.
[c] Subjects were 18 males and 18 females.
[d] Subjects were male and female.
[e] Subjects were 29 males and 24 females.
[f] See Olweus, (1977b) for details.

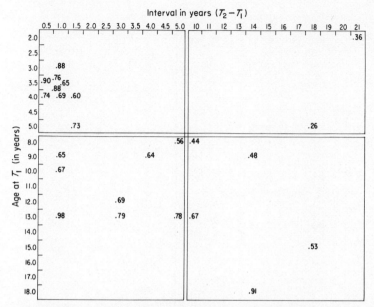

Figure 1. Summary of disattenuated stability correlations for different intervals in years $(T_2 - T_1)$ and different ages at time of first measurement (T_1). From Olweus (1979). Copyright 1979 by the American Psychological Association. Reprinted by permission.

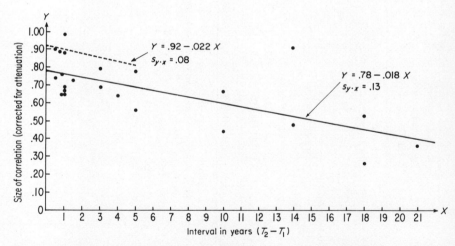

Figure 2. Regression line showing relationship between attenuation-corrected stability coefficients and time interval $(T_2 - T_1)$ in years (solid line). The regression line is based on 24 stability coefficients (plotted). For comparison, the regression line for attenuation-corrected stability coefficients in the area of intelligence is shown (broken line). This regression line is based on 36 stability coefficients (not plotted), from Thorndike, 1933. From Olweus (1979). Copyright 1979 by the American Psychological Association. Reprinted by permission.

variables, the difference in stability was not great. It could be generally concluded that *there is a substantial degree of stability in aggressive reaction patterns* (as well as in intelligence test behavior), often over many years.

1. Description of Selected Studies

For purposes of illustration, three of the longitudinal studies constituting the basis for the preceding conclusion will be briefly described (more detailed descriptions of these and the remaining studies shown in Table I are given in Olweus, 1977b).

a. Jersild and Markey (1935). In an early study (Jersild & Markey, 1935), 24 nursery-school children aged 2–4 years (average age = 3 years) were observed at two points in time, separated by approximately 9 months. The behavior of each child was recorded during 10 distributed 15-minute periods of free play. Marked individual differences in aggressive behavior were found, and the behavioral stability was striking. When calculated for all 24 children, the stability correlation over the 9-month period was .70 (ρ) for the variable of primary interest, "Frequency of being aggressor." When the correlations were determined separately for different groups (N varying from 7 to 15), the coefficients were even higher (range .71–.88). After correction for imperfect reliability, the stability correlation of .70 amounted to .88. This means that from the first to the second period of observation, very small changes had occurred among the children in their tendency to attack other children: Those children who were frequently aggressive toward their peers at the beginning of the study tended to behave in the same way 9 months later, and vice versa. It should be noted that this high degree of stability in aggressive behavior was obtained despite the fact that relatively marked changes in the composition of the peer groups had taken place from the first to the second time of observation.

b. Olweus (1977a). Two short-term longitudinal studies concerning a 1-year and a 3-year interval, respectively, were conducted by Olweus (1977a) on two samples of Swedish adolescent boys. In both studies the same two 7-point peer-rating scales were used; they concerned unprovoked physical aggression against peers ("He starts fights with other boys at school," abbreviated as "starts fights") and verbal aggression against a mildly criticizing teacher ("When a teacher criticizes him, he tends to answer back and protest," abbreviated as "verbal protest"). Each boy who served as a rater assessed all the boys in his class by placing cards with the names of his classmates below the points of the scale that referred to different frequencies of occurrence (from "very seldom" to "very often"). The rating procedure was individually administered.

In Study 1, the number of raters in each class was three on both occasions for Grades 6 and 7. In the second study, the number of raters in different classes varied somewhat, the average number being four for Grade 6 and five for Grade 9. In general, the raters were chosen on the basis of random selection from each class. The average of the ratings on a particular variable was used as the subject's value for that variable.

The subjects of the first study consisted of 85 boys from seven classes who were rated at the end of Grade 6, when their median age was 13 years, and also 1 year later. In this study only small changes in the composition of the peer groups took place between Grade 6 and Grade 7. All classes, however, had new teachers at Grade 7. Study 2 was composed of 201 boys from 18 classes who were rated at the end of Grade 6 and also 3 years later at the end of Grade 9, when their median age was 16 years. The subjects constituted roughly 75% of the whole population of school boys in the community in these grades. They represented a good deal of variation with respect to socioeconomic factors (relatively representative of greater Stockholm). Two classes to be mentioned underwent marked changes in the composition of the peer group. Furthermore, all classes had new teachers for Grade 9, and 11 of the classes had moved to other school buildings. A certain amount of environmental change thus occurred for this sample from Grade 6 to Grade 9.

The stability correlations in Study 1 were .81 for "starts fights" and .79 for "verbal protest." After correlation for attenuation these coefficients amounted to 1.01 (rounded to 1.00) and .96, respectively. In Study 2, covering a 3-year interval, the uncorrected stability correlations were .65 and .70, respectively. The disattenuated coefficients were .77 and .81, respectively.

As mentioned, two classes in the second study are of particular interest from a stability–change point of view. In one of these, the original Grade-6 class, consisting of 10 boys, was split into two at the beginning of Grade 8 (5 boys were transferred to another class for unknown reasons). At the second period of rating, the original class had been augmented by eight new boys (with no previous connections with one another), which thus represented a very marked change in the composition of the class. This change notwithstanding, the stability correlations for the original five boys were very high and were, in fact, even higher than the corresponding correlations for the total sample. Also, the transfer of the five boys to a new class consisting of nine boys did not seem to reduce the stability of behavior of the latter: The across-time correlations for the core of nine boys in this class were for both variables higher than the coefficients for the whole sample (for details, see Olweus, 1977a).

It should also be mentioned that change of school did not seem to appreciably affect the degree of stability over time. There were small and inconsistent differences between the across-time correlations for the 11 classes who moved to other school buildings and the 7 classes who did not move.

c. Block (1971). The final study to be described was carried out by Block (1971) and presented in *Lives Through Time.* The subjects of this study were 84 adolescent males (and 87 females), participants in the well-known Oakland Growth and Berkeley Guidance longitudinal studies. By means of the Q-sort method, the subjects were assessed for three different periods of time, the junior high school years (JHS), the senior high school years (SHS), and when they were in their middle thirties (Adult). For each subject, three independent sets of data, one for each period, were developed, and this material was used to characterize each subject on a number of variables. The characterizations of the subjects were made by clinical psychologists who worked independently and who were assigned to "cases" in systematically permuted combinations, in order to avoid judge biases. At least two of the variables included are directly concerned with aggressive reactions and behavior: "Overreactive to minor frustrations; irritable" (No. 34) and "Tends to be rebellious and nonconforming" (No. 62).

The stability correlations for the first of these variables, "Overreactive to minor frustrations; irritable" were .45 for the JHS–SHS period (an interval of 3 years) and .29 for the SHS–Adult period (an interval of approximately 18 years). After correction for attenuation, these coefficients were .78 and .40, respectively. For the variable "Tends to be rebellious and nonconforming," the stability correlations for the JHS–SHS and the SHS–Adult periods were .58 and .29, after attenuation correction .72 and .37, respectively. When a composite was formed to these two variables, the disattenuated stability correlations were .69 for the JHS–SHS period and .53 for the SHS–Adult period.

In evaluating these results, it should be noted that a good deal of environmental change had occurred in the lives of the subjects during the 20 or so years from the high school years to the time of the adult follow-up. Among other things, 95% of the subjects had married, and 19% had been divorced. The majority of them had become parents. Roughly half of the subjects had also served in the armed forces during World War II.

2. More Specific, Descriptive Conclusions

The substantial degree of regularity manifested in Fig. 2 is particularly impressive considering the great variation in sample composition, definition of variables, research setting, method of data collection and integration, and the researcher's theoretical orientation in these studies. There was also a very great range in the ages and intervals studied. After having emphasized the regularity of the data as a general finding, it is appropriate to examine the results more closely for a number of more specific conclusions.

It is obvious that marked individual differences in habitual aggression level manifest themselves early in life (certainly by age 3) and may show a high or very high degree of stability for periods of at least $1\frac{1}{2}$ years at this developmental level (in nursery school settings). Data from one study (Kagan & Moss, 1962) suggested that ratings of aggression in relation to the period from 0 to 3 years may have some predictive value of aggression variables assessed as long as 20 years later. However, to what extent aggressive reaction patterns observable during the preschool years can predict related patterns some 10 years later must for the time being remain an open question, as data for such an assessment are not available.

Furthermore, in contrast with the common belief that the method of direct observation gives evidence of much more "behavioral specificity" and less stability than ratings of different kinds, no such tendencies were found in the present material. The average stability correlation for the three studies using direct observation (Jersild & Markey, 1935, Martin, W. E., 1964; Patterson, Littman, & Bricker, 1967) was .81, which can be compared with the average value of .79 for the three comparable studies by Block, Block, and Harrington (1974), Emmerich (1966), and Kohn and Rosman (1972; first study in Table I) employing teacher ratings. The average stability correlations for the two sets of studies, using uncorrected coefficients, were .65 and .64, respectively. Judging from these studies, there seems to be no difference in the degree of stability over relatively limited periods of time (up to a year) for aggression data collected by means of direct observation and teacher ratings.

Passing on to the school years, it is obvious that aggressive reaction patterns observable at ages 8 or 9 can be substantially correlated with similar patterns observed 10–14 years later (some 25% of the variance accounted for). It should also be noted that such patterns can be used with some success to predict certain forms of antisocial behavior, for example, violent delinquency (Farrington, 1978), that occurs 10–12 years later.

Aggressive behavior at ages 12 and 13 may show a high degree of stability for periods of 1–5 years (from 50% to more than 90% of the variance accounted for). Also, for periods as long as 10 years the stability is high (some 45% of the variance accounted for). Furthermore, aggressive reaction patterns at these ages have considerable predictive capacity for later antisocial aggression, as evidenced by the studies of Eron, Huesmann, Lefkowitz, and Walder (1972) and Farrington (1978).

Finally, aggressive behavior (chiefly verbal) and reactivity in the mid-30s are substantially correlated with similar patterns observed some 15–18 years earlier, when the subjects were teenagers.

In evaluating these results, the general adequacy and validity of the data should also be considered. One should recall that in several investigations a considerable degree of correspondence has been found between the aggression variables studied and teacher ratings of the same or related behaviors. This was true for teacher ratings and nominations versus peer ratings (Olweus, 1978; Walder, Abelson, Eron, Banta, & Laulicht, 1961; Wiggins & Winder, 1961) as well as for teacher ratings versus direct observation (Jersild & Markey, 1935). If the latter variables were corrected for attenuation, the correlation between them would very likely exceed .75, indicating a quite substantial relationship. In some investigations, the aggression variables studied also manifested relationships of considerable magnitude with self-report data on similar patterns (Olweus, 1973b, 1977b, 1978) and related, but more antisocial, forms of behavior (Eron *et al.*, 1972; Farrington, 1978). In addition, clear associations were obtained between two of the peer nomination instruments used in the stability studies and overt aggressive behavior in a contrived, naturalistic setting (Winder & Wiggins, 1964) and in a controlled, experimental situation, respectively (Williams, Meyerson, Eron, & Selmer, 1967). Finally, the possible existence of rater biases and stereotypes was carefully examined in some studies, in particular those by Block (1971) and Olweus (1977a). In the latter study it was concluded on the basis of several different analyses that "the rating data to an overwhelming degree reflect characteristics of the boys under study, rather than the biases and cognitive schemas of the raters irrespective of ratee characteristics" (p. 1310).

All in all, these results, derived by different methods and under a wide variety of conditions, constitute strong evidence of the validity and general adequacy of the aggression data on which the stability correlations were based. They also attest to a substantial degree of cross-situational consistency in the sense that there is a considerable correspondence between aggression data obtained from independent sources or assessments at about the same point in time. (The issue of cross-situational consistency in aggression studies will not be pursued further in this article, for further discussion see Olweus, 1980b.)

3. Interpretation of the Stability Data

The conclusion that there is a substantial degree of stability in aggressive behavior cannot, however, without further analyses be taken as evidence of the corresponding stability of some reaction tendencies or motive systems within individuals. In particular, it might be argued that the observed consistency primarily reflects consistently different conditions for different individuals in the settings studied. Thus, in the first place, the stated conclusion can be said to apply under typical conditions, that is, under a degree of environmental variation (or stability) and pressure for change (or nonchange) typically found in the settings of the subjects for the periods studied (cf. Olweus, 1977a). Accordingly, it is important to examine the conditions characterizing the settings and periods under study, maybe particularly for the highly aggressive individuals, as their relative lack of change is a prerequisite to high stability coefficients.

The issue of environmental stability and change in these studies will not be analyzed here (see Olweus, 1977b, 1979, for a discussion). I will limit myself to the conclusion derived from one set of analyses, drawing particularly on the extensive findings regarding a group of highly aggressive schoolboys, bullies, selected on the basis of the fact that they often attacked and harassed other children, whipping boys (Olweus, 1978). Specifically, the question was considered whether there were particular aversive situations or conditions in the immediate, proximal (i.e., school) environment of the habitually aggressive subjects that might explain their behavior.

Combining several lines of evidence concerning the possible existence of frustrations, failures, and rejections in the school as well as other psychological, physical, and socioeconomic conditions of the bullies, it was concluded that it is very difficult to explain the behavior of these highly aggressive boys as a consequence of their being exposed to unusually aversive situations or conditions in the school environment (Olweus, 1978, p. 136). All in all, there was little evidence to support a view that stable differences in aggression level resulted from consistently different environmental conditions for different individuals in the situation in which the aggressive behavior was studied. (However, there is considerable evidence showing that the conditions in other situations, for example, within the family, have been and may still at the time of the study be quite different for more and less aggressive boys.)

4. General Conclusions

On the basis of the results and analyses presented (Olweus, 1979) two general conclusions can be drawn.

1. The degree of stability or continuity in aggressive behavior is much greater than has been maintained (e.g., Kohlberg, LaCrosse, & Ricks, 1972, p. 1222; Mischel, 1968, 1969). The across-time stability was not, in fact, much lower than that found in the intelligence domain. However, to avoid misunderstanding, I want to make it clear that when pointing out similarities between results from the intelligence domain and those from the aggression area, I restrict my comparison to the degree of stability over time. I am in no way implying assumptions about similar developmental and operating mechanisms or, for instance, that the degree of genetic influence is the same in the two areas (see Olweus, 1978, Chap. 8).

2. The results and analyses strongly suggest that important determinants of the observed continuity in aggressive behavior over time are to be found in relatively stable, individual-differentiating reaction tendencies or motive systems, however conceptualized, within individuals (personality variables). These reaction tendencies or motive systems very likely compose a cognitive component, which in highly aggressive individuals may involve a biased perception of the environment. Such perceptions probably affect the likelihood of aggressive reactions from the individual and, as a consequence, from his or her social environment.

These conclusions should not be taken to imply that situational factors are considered unimportant for the evocation of aggressive behavior (see, e.g., Olweus, 1973b). Nor do they imply that aggressive behavior is independent of rewarding and maintaining conditions in the immediate, proximal environment. However, it is contended here that the explanatory and predictive value of such factors has been exaggerated in the last decade. As concluded, relatively stable, internal reaction tendencies are important determinants of behavior in the aggressive motive area, and they should be given greater weight than has been done. In line with this argument, it also seems quite reasonable to assume that the inferred, internal reaction tendencies or motive systems within an individual are essential codeterminants of what the individual will perceive as reinforcing. In fact, the analyses presented suggest that highly aggressive individuals to a considerable degree actively select and create the kind of situations in which they are often observed (cf. Bowers, 1973; Wachtel, 1973).

B. Stability of Aggressive Behavior in Females

It is commonly maintained that there is practically no stability over time for aggressive behavior in females. This generalization is mainly based on the Kagan and Moss (1962) study of 35 girls and 36 boys, who were followed from early childhood to adulthood (average age of 24 years). The differential stability in males and females has been interpreted as a function of traditional sex-role standards to the effect that aggressive behavior in a boy is accepted and even positively valued whereas such behavior is discouraged in girls.

A preliminary analysis of the findings in the (English) research literature revealed quite a different picture (see Olweus, 1984). Without going into detail, it can be mentioned that six studies on the stability of aggressive behavior in comparable male and female samples (up to age 19 years) were found. A total of 21 stability coefficients were available for each sex. The average age of the subjects was approximately 7 years, and the subjects were followed for intervals varying from half a year to 10 years. The average interval was 2.8 years.

Though statistically significant and fairly consistent, the difference in stability for males and females was not marked. The average r for males was .497, whereas the corresponding value for females was .439 (coefficients not corrected for attenuation), giving an average difference of .058 correlation points. It can thus be concluded that, in contrast to what is commonly believed, there is a fairly high degree of stability in aggressive reaction patterns also in females, at least for intervals of 10 years up to age 19. It should be noted that this conclusion is based on six different studies with relatively large samples (the average sample size was approximately 200). The somewhat lower stability in females as compared with males may partly reflect the fact that, for whatever reason, there are far fewer highly aggressive girls than boys (see, e.g., Maccoby & Jacklin, 1974). This will result in lower variability in the female distributions, thereby reducing the size of the correlation coefficient. The difference-in-variability interpretation is supported by the standard deviation data presented in Kohn (1977, Table 6.1).

C. Stability of Conduct Problem Behavior

As aggressive behavior can be regarded as part of a more general antisocial reaction pattern, it may be of interest to consider briefly a few studies on the stability of (probably) more serious forms of acting-out behavior or conduct problems.

The results reported in the literature are in good agreement with the general conclusion derived from studies of aggressive behavior. In the Isle of Wight study (Rutter, Tizard, & Whitmore, 1970), for example, approximately 60% of the children with conduct disorders at age 10 were classified as having conduct problems 4 years later. Similarly, Robins

(1966, 1978) found that the prognosis was quite poor for children referred to a child guidance clinic for antisocial behavior such as fighting,
theft, alcohol abuse, and truancy. When followed up 30 years later, at an
average of 43 years, a considerable portion of them still exhibited serious
antisocial tendencies and 28% were diagnosed as sociopaths. These
findings differed radically from the outcome for children referred to the
clinic for nonantisocial symptoms and for a control group.

These studies, in particular the ones conducted by Robins, suggest
that antisocial behavior in childhood may be an almost necessary but not
sufficient condition for later antisocial problems of some severity. Thus,
nearly all of Robins' adult antisocial subjects had a history of antisocial
behavior in childhood (1978). In the Isle of Wight study, it is noteworthy
that no children who had neurotic problems when younger developed
into antisocial adolescents (Graham & Rutter, 1973).

In conclusion, aggressive and related acting-out behavior shows a
substantial degree of stability often over long periods of time. The degree of stability seems to vary inversely both with the length of the
interval covered and the subject's age at the time of first assessment.

III. DEVELOPMENT OF AGGRESSIVE REACTION
PATTERNS IN BOYS

In view of the preceding findings and conclusions it is of great importance to try to find out what the causative factors are in the development
of a highly aggressive reaction pattern. Using a path-analytic approach
(see e.g., Duncan, 1975; Heise, 1975; Wright, 1934), I attempted to identify some of these factors in an empirical research study. An outline of
this study and its main findings will be presented in what follows (for
details, see Olweus, 1980a). Subsequently, the role of some other potentially important factors will be briefly discussed.

A. Are Highly Aggressive Boys Anxious and Insecure
under the Surface?

Before describing this empirical study, it may be of interest to try to
answer this question. Such an answer will provide information on one
important aspect of what characterizes highly aggressive boys (other
aspects are reported in Olweus, 1978). This question is highlighted by
means of research contrasting several different samples of teacher-nominated bullies with groups of normal control boys and whipping boys
(see Olweus, 1978, for details). Although there is not a one-to-one rela-

tionship between teacher-nominated bullies and, for example, boys rated as very aggressive by their peers, it has been found that bullies by and large have very high values on rating dimensions of physical and verbal aggression and also that they constitute a substantial portion of the boys rated as highly aggressive.

It is not uncommon among psychologists and psychiatrists to assume that aggressive and tough behavior represents a kind of defensive reaction against underlying insecurity and anxiety. One implication of this view is that if only the surface behavior were bypassed by means of suitable techniques, a quite different, often directly reversed picture of the individual's personality characteristics would emerge.

Presumably, there is some support for such an assumption, both from clinical experience and empirical studies. At least some aggressive individuals are likely to show this discrepancy between surface and depth. However, can these somewhat tenuous findings be generalized to all or most aggressive individuals? Are the bullies, in reality, insecure and anxious behind a facade of violent and self-confident behavior?

The answer is clearly *no* for the bullies considered as a group. The bullies' self-reports on a number of inventories as well as their mothers' descriptions agreed in portraying the bullies as less anxious and less insecure than (sometimes at the same level as) randomly selected control boys (see Olweus, 1978). In addition, and maybe more important, use of projective techniques in two independent studies (Olweus, 1978, p. 116, and unpublished), the Defence Mechanism Test (Kragh, 1960) and the Holzman Inkblot Test, respectively, did not indicate a higher level of anxiety or neurotic conflicts in the bullies; there was even a trend in the opposite direction. Finally, endocrinologic measurements of Grade-9 boys in a novel and somewhat threatening situation revealed that the bullies excreted significantly lower amounts of the stress hormone, adrenaline (in the urine). Adrenaline is generally considered to be a good indicator of emotional arousal, stress, and anxiety. Thus, the results from the more indirect, projective and endocrinologic, measures were in essential agreement with the findings based on more direct and possibly somewhat more superficial methods of assessment.

In this context, it is also interesting to refer briefly to a Finnish study (Ekman, 1977) that used some of the measurement techniques developed in my project as well as other methods. In this study, composing approximately 400 students in Grades 8 and 9, the subjects were asked about their feelings and reactions when they witnessed a peer being attacked or harassed by others. The responses from the bullies clearly differed from those of the whipping boys and the control boys. Nearly 50% of the bullies checked one of the response alternatives "is exciting" or "he/she deserves it," whereas these responses were very infrequent in the other groups. Similarly, the response distributions were highly different for the question "Do you usually have a bad conscience after having participated in harassing a peer?" More than 60% of the bullies answered "almost never" or "fairly seldom," whereas much lower percentages of subjects in the other groups endorsed these alternatives. Generally, the picture of the bullies that emerged from analysis of these and related questions was very consistent with my own findings (Olweus, 1978). The bullies were characterized by a lack of empathy and negligible feelings of guilt in response to harassment of whipping boys by themselves or by others.

In summary, the following conclusion, which runs counter to common belief, may be drawn. There is no evidence to suggest that the highly aggressive boys, the bullies, are anxious, sensitive, and insecure under the surface. The available data, obtained with a number of reliable and valid methods, clearly point in the opposite direction (to avoid overinterpretation, however, it should be cautioned that this conclusion does not preclude that a small proportion of the bullies may also be characterized by some degree of anxiety and insecurity).

With this conclusion as a background, I shall now describe the empirical research on the development of aggressive reaction patterns (as measured by peer ratings of interpersonal aggressive behavior).

B. Empirical Study

1. Some Information on Procedure

The subjects in this study were two roughly random samples of school boys from greater Stockholm. One group, Sample 1, consisted of 76 boys from Grade 6 (with a median age of 13 years); the other, Sample 2, of 51 boys from Grade 9 (with a median age of 16 years). In addition, all the mothers and approximately two-thirds of the fathers participated.

Peer ratings were used to obtain information about the boys' habitual level of interpersonal aggressive behavior. (It should be noted that the boys showed great variation in terms of aggressive behavior, from quite nonaggressive to highly aggressive boys.) Three dimensions were combined into a composite measure of aggression: "starts fights" (unprovoked physical aggression against peers); "verbal protest" (verbal aggression against teachers); and "verbal hurt" (verbal aggression against peers). This composite variable is called "boys' aggression" (X_5). Its reliability was .900 in Sample 1 and .923 in Sample 2.

To provide detailed information about the boys' rearing conditions during childhood and the parents' disciplinary practices and personality qualities, extensive, partly retrospective interviews were carried out with the mothers and fathers, independently. Analysis of the measurement characteristics of the interview data indicated that generally the information obtained was both reliable, accurate, and relatively free from biases of different kinds.

On the basis of previous research and theoretical considerations, four variables were regarded as potentially central in a causal model for the development of an aggressive reaction pattern in a boy. (These variables will be briefly described.) In addition, the possible influence of the family's socioeconomic condition as measured by several indexes combining parental income, education, housing conditions, and social class (three categories) was examined. These indexes had low and nonsignificant correlations with the main dependent variable, "boy's aggression." The correlations with the theoretically selected variables were also quite small, thus precluding a meaningful use of socioeconomic variables in the model.

The following four variables were included in the path model, in addition to the final dependent variable, "boy's aggression":

1. *Mother's negativism* (X_1), the principal caretaker's basic emotional attitude to the boy during the first 4–5 years of his life. None of the fathers was the principal caretaker. A negative basic attitude could be manifested in hostility and rejection as well as in coldness and indifference.
2. *Boy's temperament* (X_2), a composite of the boy's general level of activity and the intensity of his temperament (calm–hot tempered) in early years. This variable was included in view of the likely possibility that the boy might in various ways "contribute to his own socialization" (Bell, 1968; Bell & Harper, 1977).
3. *Mother's permissiveness for aggression* (X_3), the principal caretaker's degree of permissiveness or laxness with regard to aggressive behavior toward mother, peers, and siblings.
4. *Mother's and father's use of power-assertive methods* (X_4), in particular, physical punishment and strong affective reactions such as threats and violent outbursts. Low values on this variable indicate an absence of such methods as well as the presence of more love-oriented techniques such as reasoning, withdrawal of love, or deprivation of privileges.

To examine whether some other potentially important, though less clearly relevant, variables significantly increased the amount of variance explained in the ultimate dependent variable, a hierarchical strategy was adopted (Cohen & Cohen, 1975). For each such variable, the amount of variance explained by the four path-model variables plus the new variable was compared with the variance accounted for the path-model variables alone. The variables included in these analyses were "father's negativism" (during the boy's first 4–5 years), "identification with father," "seriousness of separations during childhood," "amount of time in day-care institution(s)," and "parental divorce."

2. Main Results

Results for the Grade 6 sample are presented in Fig. 3. The figure portrays a reduced, trimmed model in which two causal paths have been eliminated. With regard to direct causal effects, the path coefficients for the four arrows leading to X_5 are of particular interest. However, path analysis also permits the determination of indirect causal effects. There is an indirect effect of one variable, say X_2, on another, say X_5, when the first variable has a causal effect on an intervening variable, for instance, X_3, which in turn exerts a causal influence on X_5. In other words, part or all of the effect of one variable on another is mediated by an intervening variable. The magnitude of the indirect effect is obtained through multiplication of the path coefficients involved—in the present case the coefficient for X_2 to X_3 with the one from X_3 to X_5. The figure

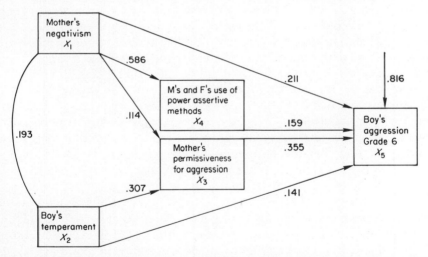

Figure 3. Path diagram for trimmed causal model. (Sample 1 in Grade 6, $N = 76$, $R = .579$, $R^2 = .335$; M's = mother's, F's = father's.) A path coefficient—a standardized regression coefficient, β—above or below a unidirectional straight arrow indicates the direct causal effect of one variable on another while all other causal variables are held constant. From Olweus (1980a). Copyright 1980 by the American Psychological Association. Reprinted by permission.

next to the vertical arrow pointing to X_5 (.816) is $(1 - R^2)^{1/2}$, indicating the causal effects on X_5 of all variables not included in the model (residuals). To facilitate reading of the diagram, the corresponding figures for X_3 and X_4 were omitted.

As is evident from Fig. 3, two causal paths, from X_2 to X_4 and from X_3 to X_4, have been deleted (set to 0) in the reduced model. In both cases, the effect of the causally prior variable was less than 1% of the variance in the dependent variable. The absence of a relationship between mother's permissiveness for aggression and mother's and father's use of power-assertive methods was anticipated on theoretical grounds. For all other paths, the coefficients were large enough to account for 1% or more of the variance of the respective dependent variables. Accordingly, it was decided not to modify the model further.

The following comments relate to the results for the Grade-6 sample, although the findings on the Grade-9 sample were on the whole very similar. The path coefficient of .211 for the link between "mother's negativism" and "boy's aggression" in Fig. 3 shows that the basic emotional attitude of the principal caretaker contributes directly to the boy's development of an aggressive reaction pattern. If the mother is negative, rejecting, and indifferent to the boy when he is young (and later), this is likely to result in the adolescent boy becoming relatively more aggressive and hostile toward his environment. Also, there is a substantial indirect effect (.568 × .159 = .093) of "mother's negativism" via the variable "mother's and father's use of power-assertive methods." A negative basic attitude thus entails more frequent use of power-assertive disciplinary techniques such as corporal punishment and strong threats, which, in turn, contribute to a higher aggression level in the boy.

Variable X_2, the boy's temperament when he was young, also has a direct causal effect (.141) on the boy's later aggression level. That is, a boy with an active and hot-headed temperament, as manifested in early years, is more likely to develop aggressive modes of reaction than a calm and quiet boy. For the temperament variable there is also a marked indirect effect via the "mother's permissiveness for aggression" (.307 × .355 = .109).

As is evident from Fig. 3, the mother's degree of permissiveness for aggressive behavior from the young boy—directed at herself, peers, and siblings—is a variable of great causal importance (.355). A highly accepting, tolerant, or lax attitude without clear limits for the boy's aggressive behavior contributes substantially to the development of an aggressive reaction pattern in the boy.

The fourth variable, "mother's and father's use of power-assertive methods," has a direct causal effect (.159) on the boy's aggression level in adolescence. Thus, the parents' use of physical punishment and strong threats contributes to a higher level of aggression in the boy, independent of effects from other causal variables.

When the previous causal model was applied on the Grade-9 sample, the path coefficients shown in Fig. 4 were obtained. In general, the results were strikingly similar to those derived from the Grade-6 sample. The correlation between the seven pairs of path coefficients (Figs. 3 and 4) was .92. However, the path coefficients were somewhat lower for Grade 9, as was the amount of variance explained. For the ultimate dependent variable, "boy's aggression," the proportion of variance explained by the four variables in the model was .335 in Grade 6, $F(4, 71) = 8.92$, $p < .001$, and .212 in Grade 9, $F(4, 46) = 3.09$, $p < .02$.

3. Effects of Other Potentially Relevant Variables

The correlations of the other variables of potential relevance (see p. 121) with "boy's aggression" were by and large in the expected direction, though several of them were quite small. None of these variables, when added to the four basic variables included in the path model, significantly increased the amount of variance explained in "boy's aggression." A number of demographic variables such as size of the family, the boy's ordinal position, number of brothers, and age of mother and father and their age difference were also examined but found to be of negligible importance.

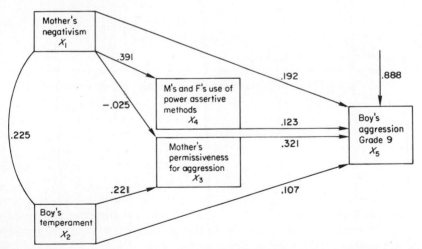

Figure 4. Path diagram for trimmed causal model. (Sample 2 in Grade 9, $N = 51$, $R = .460$, $R^2 = .212$; M's = mother's, F's = father's.) From Olweus (1980a). Copyright 1980 by the American Psychological Association. Reprinted by permission.

4. Relative Importance of Variables

An approximate measure of the total causal influence of a variable on the boy's level of aggression can be obtained by summing direct and indirect effects (e.g., Alwin & Hauser, 1975). This has been done in Table II. Examination of the "total effect" columns shows that the rank order of the four variables in terms of causal importance for boy's aggression is the same in both samples: "mother's permissiveness for aggression," "mother's negativism," "boy's temperament," and "mother's and father's use of power-assertive methods." In Grade 6, the difference between the first two variables is negligible.

The proportion of variance explained in the ultimate dependent variable (X_5) is good or very good according to usual standards in psychological research ($R = .579$ and $R^2 = .335$ in Grade 6 and $R = .460$ and $R^2 = .212$ in Grade 9). It should be recalled that the data on the causal variables and the aggression variable, respectively, were obtained through completely different informants and methods.

As is well known, empirical relationships between different variables are attentuated by errors of measurement. As inter-rater reliability estimates were available for all variables in the model, it was also possible to calculate path coefficients on the basis of disattenuated correlations. Generally, the path coefficients leading to "boy's aggression" became somewhat larger (with the exception of the path from X_2 to X_5), as might be expected. The amount of variance explained in the aggression variable rose to .433 ($R = .658$) in Grade 6 and to .278 ($R = .527$) in Grade 9.

Table II. Direct, Indirect, and Total Causal Effects of Different Causal Variables on Boys Aggression[a]

	Sample 1 ($N = 76$)			Sample 2 ($N = 51$)		
Variable	Direct effect	Indirect effect	Total effect	Direct effect	Indirect effect	Total effect
X_1 Mother's negativism	.211	.134	.345	.192	.040	.232
X_2 Boy's temperament	.141	.109	.250	.107	.071	.178
X_3 Mother's permissiveness for aggression	.355		.355	.321		.321
X_4 Mother's and father's use of power-assertive methods	.159		.159	.123		.123

[a]From Olweus (1980a). Copyright 1980 by the American Psychological Association. Reprinted by permission.

It should be noted that these analyses correct for only one source of unreliability (in the rating procedure).

In summary, it can be concluded that the results of the path analyses conducted on the two samples were in good agreement. The reduced causal model that was developed on the basis of the analyses on the Grade-6 sample and that could satisfactorily reproduce the empirical correlations in this sample functioned in much the same way for the Grade-9 sample. This concordance of findings on two independent samples is remarkable in view of the fact that the subject groups were of limited size and, accordingly, the estimated parameters relatively susceptible to chance variations.

5. Discussion

a. Methodological Issues. Use of path analysis presupposes that the relations among the variables in the model are linear and additive. Plots of the bivariate distributions showed that the relations involved were essentially linear. In addition, a number of analysis of variance tests failed to reveal any significant two-way interactions. Accordingly, the data fulfilled the statistical assumptions underlying path analysis.

Causal relations can never be definitely proven but only inferred, with greater or lesser certainty, on the basis of theoretical considerations and an analysis of the conditions surrounding the assumed causal connections. In such an undertaking, the following three basic issues need to be examined: Is the causal ordering among the variables reasonable? Are there variables not included in the model that can account for the results obtained? Are there particular biases associated with the methods used in collecting the data that, partially or wholly, can explain the findings?

In the present context only the second issue will be considered, the other two are discussed in detail in Olweus (1980a).

There is always the possibility that important causal variables have been neglected in the construction of the model. If an omitted causal variable correlates positively with one or more of the causal variables in the model and *comes early in the causal sequence,* two broad kinds of consequences can be discerned (the consequences of more complex patterns of relations are not discussed here): The new variable has no direct effect of its own but exerts an influence on "boy's aggression" exclusively through indirect effect(s). In such a case, the path coefficients from all variables coming later in the causal scheme will remain the same (as will R^2). Another situation with potentially serious consequences is one in which an omitted causal variable has a direct effect on "boy's aggression." This implies that part(s) or all of what has been previously

interpreted as direct causal effects from later variables now becomes a
spurious (noncausal) component(s). Depending on the magnitude of the
spurious component(s), this may result in marked changes in the path
coefficients and in the interpretive conclusions.

If omitted *variables come late in the causal sequence,* the consequences of
such omissions are generally not problematic. Inclusion of such a variable implies that part(s) or all of what has been previously interpreted as
direct effects from causally prior variables will now become indirect
effects via the new causal variable. However, the total causal impact of
all variables in the previous model will be the same. In relation to the
present model, several recent causal variables can be imagined, for instance, a variable measuring presence or absence of bad companions.
Although the inclusion of such a recent causal variable is likely to result
in more complete determination of "boy's aggression," it would not
lead to radical changes in the basic causal structure.

Many potentially relevant causal variables (including minimal brain
dysfunction, MBD) in addition to those incorporated in the model have
been examined. None of them, if included, would have appreciably
affected the model.

b. Substantive Results. It is natural to compare this article with *Patterns of Child Rearing* by Sears, Maccoby, and Levin (1957). In their final
analyses (pp. 482–488), Sears and colleagues emphasized the importance of the following three factors for the development of an aggressive
reaction pattern in younger children: mother's warmth (reversed), use
of physical punishment, and permissiveness for aggression. Obviously,
the findings in this article are in very good general agreement with these
results.

Without making detailed comparisons, it can be asserted that the
results of two other major American studies in this area—those of
Lefkowitz, Eron, Walder, and Huesmann (1977) and of McCord, Mc-
Cord, and Howard (1961)—as well as the integrative reviews of Becker
(1964) and Martin (1975) clearly agree in pointing up the relevance of
three of the variables found to be important in the present research:
mother's negativism or rejection, permissiveness for aggression, and
parental use of power-assertive disciplinary methods. None of these
studies, however, included a measure of the nature of the temperament
in the young boy, nor did they use an explicit causal model to impose
structure on the data.

The results of the research reported here showed that four main intrafamilial factors can explain a considerable amount of variance in the
habitual level of aggression displayed by Swedish adolescent boys. The
effects of these factors were largely additive, which implies that the
more of the negative childhood conditions a young boy is exposed to

and the more active and hot-headed his temperament, the more likely he is to develop into an aggressive adolescent. The pattern of intercorrelations indicated a trend toward pairwise association of the four factors: "mother's negativism" and "mother's and father's use of power-assertive methods" tended to occur together as did "boy's temperament" and "mother's permissiveness for aggression."

The fact that highly similar results were derived in two independent samples increases the credence that can be attached to the constructed causal model and the empirical findings. "Mother's negativism" and "mother's permissiveness for aggression" had the greatest causal effects (Table II). The implication of this finding is that a young boy who gets too little love and interest from his mother and too much freedom and lack of clear limits with regard to aggressive behavior is particularly likely to develop into an aggressive adolescent.

The great influence of the mother has been stressed; what of the role of the father? The effect of the father's basic emotional attitude on the boy's aggression level was weaker than that of the mother, and it appeared only in Sample 1. Similarly, the correlations of the individual components of the composite variable, "mother's and father's use of power-assertive methods," with "boy's aggression" showed stronger and more consistent effects for the mother component. These findings are not surprising in view of the fact that Swedish fathers as a rule took negligible part in the care of their young children in the late 1950s and the early 1960s when the boys of the study were in their childhood. Findings regarding father's effects may be expected to change as fathers take a more active role in the care and rearing of their children.

Also, the absence of strong effects of the father on the boy's aggression level does not preclude the possibility that he may exert an influence via the mother (cf. Lewis & Weinraub, 1976). In the present research, a measure of the emotional relationship between the mother and father at the time of the study correlated substantially with "mother's negativism" (.56 in Sample 1 and .31 in Sample 2). These results are consistent with the view that a conflictful mother–father relationship may increase the mother's negative feelings for the boy, which, in turn, may affect the boy's aggression level.

The analyses indicated that the parent's use of power-assertive disciplinary techniques such as physical punishment contributed to the boy's level of aggression in adolescence. This result gives some support to the view that "physical violence generates violence." However, as shown in the analyses of total effects, this influence was secondary in importance to the negative effect of the basic emotional attitude of the mother. Accordingly, what may be called the *silent violence* toward a boy exerted by means of a negative, indifferent attitude and lack of positive regard seems to be more detrimental to the boy's personality development than the use of physical punishment. At the same time, it should be emphasized that a negative basic attitude and use of power-assertive disciplinary methods often occurred together.

The temperament dimension had a direct effect, though not particularly strong, on the boy's later level of aggression. Perhaps more important from a theoretical point of view, however, was the fact that the analyses demonstrated an *indirect* effect of the boy's temperament on aggression via the mother's permissiveness for aggression: A boy with an impetuous and active temperament may to some extent exhaust his mother, resulting in her becoming more permissive of the boy's aggression, which, in turn, may be conductive to a higher level of aggression in the boy. Generally, these analyses point to the importance of isolating such child–parent–child effects (Bell, 1968). Application of path analysis to this key problem seems to be a promising strategy.

It is reasonable to assume that the temperament dimension is to some extent determined by genetic factors (Thomas & Chess, 1977). This assumption is supported by the fact that a correlation of .34 was obtained between "boy's temperament" and a slightly shortened form of Eysenck's extraversion–introversion scale (Eysenck & Eysenck, 1975), which was administered to the subjects of Sample 1 in Grade 9. As has been shown by Eaves and Eysenck (1975), for example, extraversion–introversion has a considerable genetic component.

It is noteworthy that the socioeconomic conditions of the family were generally unrelated to the boy's level of aggression and to the causal variables of the model. In addition, an analysis of the relation between the boy's aggression level and the family's social status for the whole population of Sample 2 (approximately 290 boys) yielded an approximately zero correlation. This shows that aggressive boys as well as poor and good rearing conditions can exist in all kinds of families, independent of their position in the social hierarchy. As the samples studied are roughly representative of large segments of the Swedish society with respect to socioeconomic conditions, the results obtained cast considerable doubt on the validity of the "social heritage" theory (e.g., Jonsson, 1967), at least for countries such as Sweden.

C. Some Other Potential Determinants

1. Genetic Factors

The causal analysis reported suggests that genetic factors may play some, but not a marked, role in determining a boy's level of aggressive behavior in adolescence, via his temperamental makeup. However, is there any more direct evidence, for example, from twin or adoption studies, to suggest that individual differences in aggression, or generally, in antisocial behavior are to some extent determined by genetic factors?

With regard to aggressive behavior, it must be emphasized that, for the present, very little is known about the possible impact of genetic factors. Whereas in animal studies the effects of selective breeding on aggressive behavior have been demonstrated in a large number of species (e.g., Becker, 1962; Scott, 1958), surprisingly little research has been directed to studying possible genetic influences in the area of human aggression (see Cattell, Blewett, & Beloff, 1955; Heise, 1973; Jinks & Fulker, 1970; Shields, 1977).

As regards antisocial behavior or criminality, the evidence available (see, e.g., Mednick, Moffit, Gabrielli, & Hutchings, 1985; Rutter, 1983; Shields, 1977) suggests that genetic factors play a minor role in juvenile delinquency but have more marked, though still fairly modest effects on antisocial personality disorders (psychopathy) persisting into adult life. In this context it should be underlined that only a small proportion of the boys in a random sample from a school population can be expected to develop serious antisocial disorders as adults.

In sum, although the paucity of research findings prevents any definite conclusions, it can be tentatively assumed that individual differences in aggression level among boys are only to a fairly small extent determined by genetic factors. It is reasonable to assume that the possible effects of such factors are to some degree mediated via the boy's temperamental makeup.

2. Peers

When a boy starts to interact regularly with other children, the behaviors of his companions are likely to affect the probability that the boy will develop or maintain an aggressive reaction pattern. First, it appears that aggressive behavior is rewarded in many interpersonal contexts, with concrete benefits such as the attainment of desirable objects as well as in the form of approval from peers and prestige (Bandura, 1973; Patterson et al., 1967). Such behavioral consequences can be assumed to increase the likelihood of aggressive behavior in similar situations in the future. In addition, peers also function as models whose behavior may, in varying degrees, be imitated (e.g., Bandura, 1973). Day-care center and nursery school groups are likely to provide a good deal of rewarding conditions as well as aggressive models for a boy with a tendency to be aggressive toward his environment.

In adolescence, the peer group tends to be an important source of influence of a boy's behavior. If aggressive behavior is positively valued in the group to which the boy belongs or wishes to belong, this may reduce the boy's possible inhibitions against aggression and increase his readiness to behave aggressively in a number of situations. The previously mentioned mechanisms of rewards and modeling are likely to be operative also at these age levels.

Little research has been directed to a systematic comparison of the effects of the peer group versus familial factors on the development of aggressive reaction patterns. Even if these influences are often seen as countervailing forces, particularly in adolescence, it appears reasonable to assume that they in many instances work in the same direction and, furthermore, that previous and current parent–child relations and the rearing conditions in the family will to some extent determine the boy's choice of companions and the kind of influences he is exposed to. For example, if the boy has experienced negative familial conditions in his childhood and later on (as described in the causal model), this is likely to make him more susceptible to the influence of peers with aggressive and antisocial tendencies, and vice versa. In this view, at least part of the negative impact from bad companions may be seen as indirect effects (cf. Section III,B,2) of prior unsatisfactory family conditions.

To a limited extent, this possibility will be explored in later analyses within the empirical research project described earlier.

3. Television

This is not the place to review the considerable amount of research on the possible effects of television on aggressive behavior (see Murray, 1980, for a bibliography; and Eron and Huesmann, Section II, this volume). There have often been reported positive, but fairly weak relationships between exposure to television violence and frequency of aggressive behavior (of the order of $r = .20-.25$). Most of these studies have been conducted on samples of children or adolescents from the United States where viewers are exposed to a good deal of violence on television.

The interpretation of this association has been a matter of considerable controversy. However, considering all the evidence available, it seems reasonable to conclude that repeated exposure to television violence is likely to entail at least some increase in aggressive (and antisocial) behavior in certain predisposed individuals. At the same time, it has been found (Fenigstein, 1979) that the expression of aggression leads to a preference for violent films to watch. Accordingly, it may be assumed that the association is made up of bidirectional effects, from television violence to aggressive behavior as well as vice versa (Eron & Huesmann, 1985).

All in all, television violence is not likely to be a major factor in the development of highly aggressive reaction patterns, at least not in countries (such as the Scandinavian countries) where fairly little violence is allowed on television (see Olweus, 1978, p. 162).

D. The Possible Role of Testosterone

Finally, the possible effect of the male sex hormone, testosterone, will be considered. This will be done in somewhat greater detail than has been the case with the factors discussed in Section III,C.

On the basis of animal research (e.g., Brain, this volume; Rose, 1975), it has been hypothesized that the habitual level of testosterone present in an adolescent or human male at a particular time affects his readiness to engage in aggressive as well as in more generally antisocial behavior. The empirical evidence collected so far has been somewhat conflicting (see e.g., Olweus, Mattsson, Schalling, & Löw, 1980).

In order to test this and related hypotheses, a detailed study (Olweus et al., 1980) was made of 58 normal adolescent Swedish boys, aged 16 (they all belonged to Sample 1, described in Section III,B,1, followed-up in Grade 9). The boys provided two sets of blood samples for plasma testosterone assays (separated by a month, $r = .63$) as well as data on a number of personality inventories and peer-rating scales assessing aggression, lack of frustration tolerance, impulsiveness, extraversion–introversion, and anxiety. Physical variables such as pubertal stage, height, weight, and physical strength were also measured.

Some of the empirical findings were as follows. The relationship of average testosterone level with peer-rated aggression in Grade 9 (previously denoted as "boy's aggression") was not very strong ($r = .21$). A closer association was found with the self-report scales of verbal and physical aggression, mainly reflecting responsiveness to provocation and threat ($r = .44$). Thus, the boy's testosterone levels were more strongly related to a readiness to respond to threat and insults, a sort of defensive aggression, than to aggressive behavior of a more negative and destructive kind. This finding is clearly meaningful from an evolutionary point of view.

Also the short self-report scale measuring lack of frustration tolerance showed a clear correlation ($r = .28$) with testosterone (and fairly independently of the verbal and physical aggression scale). Adolescent boys with higher levels of testosterone thus tended to be habitually more impatient and irritable than boys with lower testosterone levels.

In interpreting the observed testosterone–(destructive) aggression relationship, one must consider the possibility that testosterone is also an "effect" variable, that is, a variable that is influenced (reduced) by environmental factors such as aversive and stressful events (see Olweus *et al.*, 1980). In this study, however, there was little indication that a high level of habitual anxiety or repeated aversive stimulation associated with low peer status in school lead to a decrease in testosterone.

Furthermore, it should be noted that there was substantial stability in aggressive behavior (measured by peer ratings) from Grades 6 (age 13) to 9 (uncorrected $r = .62$). This result as well as the findings on the stability of aggression just reported show that the relative level of aggression of a 16-year-old boy is in considerable measure determined already before puberty. In light of these facts, it is reasonable to expect that differences in circulating testosterone will not lead to very marked changes in the boy's relative levels of aggressive behavior.

The reported modest correlation of .21 (uncorrected for attenuation) between testosterone and peer-rated aggression is in line with this expectation but, at the same time, it should be underlined that the contribution of testosterone in predicting "boy's aggression" (Grade 9) was largely independent of the contributions of the other factors in the causal model. It may therefore be of some interest to briefly discuss a possible pathway mediating the testosterone–aggression relation, namely, lack of frustration tolerance.

In doing so, I want to emphasize that the reasoning is based on the assumption that testosterone is primarily a causal variable in this context. Also, and maybe needless to say, even if the empirical data reported here are consistent with the arguments presented, the findings should be replicated on other samples before the suggested line of explanation can be considered reasonably tenable.

As previously mentioned, testosterone was positively correlated with the "lack of frustration tolerance" scale. Furthermore, the latter variable was clearly related to "boy's aggression" at Grade 9 ($r = .41$). The associations of testosterone with "lack of frustration tolerance" and "boy's aggression," respectively, are likely to be primarily nonspurious, as the correlations of testosterone with these variables measured at earlier time periods were quite low, $-.08$ for "lack of frustration tolerance" (Grade 7) and .11 for "boy's aggression" (Grade 6). Thus, the boys' testosterone levels were not "determined" by their positions on these variables at earlier periods of time.

Considering this pattern of relations, it is natural to assume that a high level of testosterone in puberty makes a boy more impatient and irritable, which, in turn, increases his readiness to behave aggressively toward his environment. Thus, in this view, at least part of the relation of testosterone with "boy's aggression" is an indirect effect effect via the mediating variable, "lack of frustration tolerance." The latter part of this supposed chain of influences is, of course, in good agreement with what has been maintained for a long time in different variants of the frustration–aggression theory.

A similar line of reasoning can be followed in the case of antisocial behavior. Included in the battery of self-report instruments was a factorially homogeneous, nine-item scale of antisocial behavior, referring to how often the boy had engaged in such things as petty thefts, minor frauds, and vandalism. This scale showed evidence of good validity in that it correlated substantially with "boy's aggression" and with school grades (negatively).

The relation of the antisocial scale with testosterone was fairly weak, $r = .17$. However, this scale showed a marked association ($r = .57$) with "lack of frustration tolerance" and the latter scale correlated .28 with testosterone, as reported earlier. Thus, parallelling the previous line of reasoning, it can be assumed that an increase in testosterone level lowers an adolescent boy's tolerance of frustration, leading to a heightened probability of engaging in generally antisocial behavior. (More detailed analyses using a casual–analytic framework are reported in Olweus, 1985).

This argument appears intuitively reasonable and is consistent with the fact that boys who behave in an antisocial way seem to do so in part out of a desire for excitement, change, and thrills (to avoid boredom). It should be noted that these relationships cannot be explained by reference to differences in age or pubertal stage (as measured by pubic hair development) as the latter variables correlated approximately zero with "lack of frustration tolerance" and the scale of antisocial behavior.

Considering the magnitude of the reported associations with testosterone, it is obvious that testosterone is only one out of many factors— and a fairly weak one—that may affect an adolescent boy's readiness to behave in aggressive-destructive and antisocial ways. At the same time, it should be made clear that the reported correlations, based on fallible variables, underestimate the true relations. Whereas "boy's aggression" and the scale of antisocial behavior were sufficiently reliable, both the testosterone measure (Spearman–Brown-corrected reliability of .77) and the "lack of frustration tolerance" scale ($\alpha = .59$) had somewhat lower reliabilities than desirable. If more reliable measures were used in assessing these variables (or correction for attenuation was applied), the relationships with testosterone would be higher, though maybe not dramatically so. In addition, as previously noted, the contribution of testosterone seems to be fairly independent of the effects of other causal variables. Accordingly, it can be concluded on the basis of this analysis that the role of testosterone in the development of aggressive and anti-social behavior patterns certainly merits further study.

IV. CONCLUDING COMMENTS

A major focus of the research presented in this article has been on relatively early factors contributing to the development of stable aggressive reaction patterns in boys. Even if these basic factors can explain a considerable amount of variance in adolescent boys' aggression level, there is still a substantial portion of variance not accounted for (Figs. 1 and 2). This shows that additional, perhaps in particular later, factors also play an important role in the determination of aggressive behavior in an adolescent boy. Accordingly, it is essential to a more complete understanding that later factors related to the peer group, to structural properties of the relevant environment (such as the school), and to the individual's neuroendocrinological reaction patterns be considered in future research. It is to be expected, however, that at least some of these factors are associated with and to some extent causally determined by factors that come earlier in the developmental sequence.

The determinants discussed in this article refer primarily to fairly broad categories of behaviors and emotional attitudes such as mother's negativism and use of power-assertive methods in childrearing. How these factors operate more specifically has not been explored in detail so far. One may ask, for instance, what the precise mechanisms are that underlie the negative effects of use of power-assertive methods. Is the explanation that repeated physical punishment involves considerable pain and humiliation that disturb the emotional bonds of the boy to his parents and make him generally hostile and aggressive toward his environment? Or is the boy primarily modeling his behavior on the punishing, aggressive parent? Or maybe both kinds of processes are implied? A further specification of the mechanisms involved in the development of aggressive reaction patterns as well as more fine-grained theoretical analyses of the mediating processes are certainly among the important tasks that need to be considered in future research on aggression.

References

Alwin, D. F., & Hauser, R. M. The decomposition of effects in path analysis. *American Sociological Review*, 1975, **40**, 37–47.
Bandura, A. *Aggression. A social learning analysis.* Englewood Cliffs, N.J.: Prentice-Hall 1973.
Becker, W. C. Developmental psychology. *Annual Review of Psychology*, 1962, **13**, 1–34.
Becker, W. C. Consequences of different kinds of parental discipine. In M. L. Hoffman &

L. W. Hoffman (Eds.), *Review of child development research* (Vol. 1). New York: Russell Sage, 1964.

Bell, R. Q. A reinterpretation of the direction of effects in studies of socialization. *Psychological Review*, 1968, **75**, 81–95.

Bell, R. Q., & Harper, L. V. *Child effects on adults*. Hillsdale, N.J.: Erlbaum, 1977.

Block, J. *Lives through time*. Berkely, Calif.: Bancroft, 1971.

Block, J., Block, J. H., & Harrington, D. M. Some misgivings about the Matching Familiar Figures Test as a measure of reflection–impulsivity. *Developmental Psychology*, 1974, **10**, 611–632.

Bowers, K. S. Situationism in psychology: An analysis and a critique. *Psychological Review*, 1973, **80**, 307–336.

Catell, R. B., Blewett, D. B., & Beloff, J. R. The inheritance of personality. A multiple variance analysis determination of approximate nature–nurture ratios for primary personality factors in Q-data. *American Journal of Human Genetics*, 1955, **7**, 122–146.

Cohen, J., & Cohen, P. *Applied multiple regression/correlation analysis for the behavioral sciences*. Hillsdale, N. J.: Erlbaum, 1975.

Duncan, O. D. *Introduction to structural equation models*. New York: Academic Press, 1975.

Eaves, L., & Eysenck, H. J. The nature of extraversion: A genetical analysis. *Journal of Personality and Social Psychology*, 1975, **32**, 102–112.

Ekman, K. *Skolmobbning*. Pro gradu arbete. Abo Akademi, Finland, 1977.

Eme, R. F. Sex differences in childhood psychopathology: A review: *Psychological Bulletin*, 1979, **86**, 574–595.

Emmerich, W. Continuity and stability in early social development: II. Teacher ratings. *Child Development*, 1966, **37**, 17–27.

Eron, L. D., & Huesmann, L. R. The role of television in the development of prosocial and antisocial behavior. In D. Olweus, J. Block, and M. Radke-Yarrow (Eds.), *Development of antisocial and prosocial behavior: Research theories and issues*. New York: Academic Press, 1985, in press.

Eron, L. D., Huesmann, L. R., Lefkowitz, M. M., & Walder, L. O. Does television cause aggression? *American Psychologist*, 1972, **27**, 253–263.

Eysenck, H. J., & Eysenck, S. *Manual of the Eysenck Personality Questionnaire*. London: Hodder & Stoughton, 1975.

Farrington, D. P. The family backgrounds of aggressive youths. In L. A. Hersov, M. Berger, & D. Schaffer (Eds.), *Aggression and anti-social behavior in childhood and adolescence*. Oxford: Pergamon, 1978.

Fenigstein, M. P. Does aggression cause a preference for viewing media violence? *Journal of Personality and Social Psychology*, 1979, **37**, 2307–2317.

Graham, P., & Rutter, M. Psychiatric disorder in the young adolescent: A follow-up study. *Proceedings of the Royal Society for Medicine*, 1973, **66**, 1226–1229.

Heise, D. R. The heritability of personality. In D. R. Heise (Ed.), *Personality: Biosocial bases*. New York: Rand McNally, 1973.

Heise, D. R. *Causal analysis*. New York: Wiley, 1975.

Jersild, A. T., & Markey, F. V. Conflicts between preschool children. *Child Development Monograph*, 1935, No. 21.

Jinks, J. L., & Fulker, D. W. Comparison of the biometrical genetical, MAVA, and classical approaches to the analysis of human behavior. *Psychological Bulletin*, 1970, **75**, 311–349.

Jonsson, G. Delinquent boys, their parents, and grandparents. *Acta Psychiatrica Scandinavia*, Suppl. 95, 1967.

Kagan, J., & Moss, H. A. *Birth to maturity: A study in psychological development*. New York: Wiley, 1962.

Kohlberg, L., LaCrosse, J., & Ricks, D. The predictability of adult mental health from childhood behavior. In B. Wolman (Ed.), *Manual of child psychopathology*. New York: McGraw-Hill, 1972.

Kohn, M. *Social competence, symptoms and underachievement in childhood: A longitudinal perspective*. Washington, D. C.: Winston, 1977.

Kohn, M., & Rosman, B. L. A social competence scale and symptom checklist for the preschool child: Factor dimensions, their cross-instrumental generality, and longitudinal persistence. *Developmental Psychology*, 1972, **6**, 430–444.

Kohn, M., & Rosman, B. L. Cross-situational and longitudinal stability of social-emotional functioning in young children. *Child Development*, 1973, **44**, 721–727.

Kragh, U. The Defence Mechanism Test: A new method for diagnosis and personnel selection. *Journal of Applied Psychology*, 1960, **44**, 303–309.

Lefkowitz, M. M., Eron, L. D., Walder, L. O., & Huesmann, L. R. *Growing up to be violent*. New York: Pergamon, 1977.

Lewis, M., & Weinraub, M. The father's role in the child's social network: In M. E. Lamb (Ed.), *The role of the father in child development*. New York: Wiley, 1976.

Maccoby, E. E., & Jacklin, C. N. *The psychology of sex differences*. Palo Alto: Stanford University Press, 1974.

McCord, W., McCord, J., & Howard, A. Familial correlates of aggression in nondelinquent male children. *Journal of Abnormal and Social Psychology*, 1961, **62**, 79–93.

Martin, B. Parent–child relations. In F. D. Horowitz, E. M. Hetherington, S. Scarr-Salapatek, & G. M. Siegel (Eds.), *Review of child development research* (Vol. 4). Chicago: Chicago University Press, 1975.

Martin, W. E. Singularity and stability of the profiles of social behavior. In C. B. Stendler (Ed.), *Readings in child behavior and development*. New York: Harcourt, Brace & World, 1964.

Medwick, S. A., Moffit, T., Gabrielli, W., & Hutchings, B. Genetic factors in criminal behavior: A review. In D. Olweus, J. Block, & M. Radke-Yarrow (Eds.), *Development of antisocial and prosocial behavior: Research, theories, and issues*. New York; Academic Press, 1985, in press.

Mischel, W. *Personality and assessment*. New York: Wiley, 1968.

Mischel, W. Continuity and change in personality. *American Psychologist*, 1969, **24**, 1012–1018.

Murray, J. P. *Television and youth. Twenty-five years of research and controversy*. Boys Town: The Boys Town Center for the Study of Youth Development, 1980.

Olweus, D. *Hackkycklingar och översittare: Forskning om skolmobbing*. Stockholm, Sweden: Almqvist & Wiksell, 1973. (a)

Olweus, D. Personality and aggression. In J. K. Cole & D. D. Jensen (Eds.), *Nebraska Symposium on Motivation, 1972* (Vol. 20). Lincoln: University of Nebraska Press, 1973. (b)

Olweus, D. Personality factors and aggression: With special reference to violence within the peer group. In J. de Wit, & W. W. Hartup (Eds.), *Determinants and origins of aggressive behavior*. The Hague: Mouton, 1974.

Olweus, D. Aggression and peer acceptance in adolescent boys: Two short-term longitudinal studies of ratings. *Child Development*, 1977, **48**, 1301–1313. (a)

Olweus, D. *Longitudinal studies of aggressive reaction patterns in males: A review*. (Report No. 2). Bergen, Norway: University of Bergen, Institute of Psychology, 1977. (b)

Olweus, D. *Aggression in the schools: Bullies and whipping boys*. Washington: Hemisphere, 1978.

Olweus, D. Stability of aggressive reaction patterns in males: A review. *Psychological Bulletin*, 1979, **86**, 852–875.

Olweus, D. Familial and temperamental determinants of aggressive behavior in adolescent boys—a causal analysis. *Developmental Psychology,* 1980, **16,** 644–660. (a)

Olweus, D. The consistency issue in personality psychology revisited—with special reference to aggression. *British Journal of Social and Clinical Psychology,* 1980, **19,** 377–390. (b)

Olweus, D. Stability in aggressive and withdrawn, inhibited behavior patterns. In R. M. Kaplan, V. J. Konecni, & R. W. Novaco (Eds.), *Aggression in children and youth.* The Hague: Nijhoff, 1984.

Olweus, D. Aggression and hormones. Behavior relationships with testosterone and adrenaline. In D. Olweus, J. Block, & M. Radke-Yarrow (Eds.), *Development of antisocial and prosocial behavior: Research, theories, and issues.* New York, Academic Press, 1985, in press.

Olweus, D., Mattsson, A., Schalling, D., & Löw, H. Testosterone, aggression, physical, and personality dimensions in normal adolescent males. *Psychosomatic Medicine,* 1980, **42,** 253–269.

Patterson, G. R., Littman, R. A., & Bricker, W. Assertive behavior in children: A step toward a theory of aggression. *Monographs of the Society for Research in Child Development,* 1967, **32** (5).

Robins, L. N. *Deviant children grown up.* Baltimore: Williams & Wilkins, 1966.

Robins, L. N. Sturdy childhood predictors of adult anti-social behavior: Replications from longitudinal studies. *Psychological Medicine,* 1978, **8,** 611–622.

Rose, R. M. Testosterone, aggression and homosexuality: A review of the literature and implications for future research. In E. J. Sachar (Ed.), *Topics in endocrinology.* New York: Grume and Stratton, 1975.

Rutter, M. Disturbances of conduct. In E. M. Hetherington (Ed.), *Carmichael's Manual of child psychology* (4th Ed.). New York: Wiley, 1983.

Rutter, M., Tizard, J., & Whitmore, K. *Education, health, and behavior.* London: Longman, 1970.

Scott, J. P. *Aggression.* Chicago: University of Chicago Press, 1958.

Sears, R. R., Maccoby, E. E., & Levin, H. *Patterns of child rearing.* Evanston, Ill.: Row, Peterson, 1957.

Shields, J. Polygenic influences. In M. Rutter & L. Hersov (Eds.), *Child Psychiatry: Modern approaches.* Oxford: Blackwell Scientific, 1977.

Thomas, A., & Chess, S. *Temperament and development.* New York: Brunner/Mazel, 1977.

Thorndike, R. L. The effect of interval between test and retest on the constancy of the IQ. *Journal of Educational Psychology,* 1933, **24,** 543–549.

Tuddenham, R. D. The constancy of personality ratings over two decades. *Genetic Psychology Monographs,* 1959, **60,** 3–29.

Wachtel, P. L. Psychodynamics, behavior therapy, and the implacable experimenter: An inquiry into the consistency of personality. *Journal of Abnormal Psychology,* 1973, **83,** 324–334.

Walder, L. O., Abelson, R. P., Eron, L. D., Banta, T. J., & Laulicht, J. H. Development of a peer-rating measure of aggression. *Psychological Reports,* 1961, **9,** 497–556.

Wiggins, J. S., & Winder, C. L. The Peer Nomination Inventory: An empirically derived sociometric measure of adjustment in preadolescent boys. *Psychological Reports,* 1961, **9,** 643–677.

Williams, J. F., Meyerson, L. J., Eron, L. D., & Selmer, I. J. Peer rated aggression and aggressive responses elicited in an experimental situation. *Child Development,* 1967, **38,** 181–190.

Winder, C. L., & Wiggins, J. S. Social reputation and social behavior: A further validation of the Peer Nomination Inventory. *Journal of Abnormal and Social Psychology,* 1964, **68,** 681–684.

Wright, S. The method of path coefficients. *Annals of Mathematical Statistics,* 1934, **5,** 161–215.

The Control of Aggressive Behavior by Changes in Attitudes, Values, and the Conditions of Learning

LEONARD D. ERON *and*
L. ROWELL HUESMANN

University of Illinois at Chicago, Chicago, Illinois

I. INTRODUCTION

It has been pointed out previously that aggression is a trait that is stable over long periods of time in a person's life (Eron, Huesmann, Dubow, Romanoff, & Yarmel, 1984; Huesman, Eron, Lefkowitz, & Walder, 1984a; Olweus, 1979). The more aggressive children are at age 8, the more likely they are to be aggressive at age 19 and at age 30. Childhood

Advances in the
Study of Aggression, Volume 1

aggression, as observed in the school situation, is predictive of serious antisocial behavior in late adolescence and adulthood. Individuals who are aggressive in one kind of situation are likely to be aggressive in other kinds of situations. Those who engage in physical aggression are also likely to be verbally aggressive and to engage in various forms of anti-social behavior. Whatever the causes of aggression, and they are many—including probably genetic, constitutional, physiological, and social/experiential factors—aggression is a way of obtaining gratification and solving interpersonal problems which is adopted very early in life. By the time a youngster is in middle childhood, consistent patterns of acting aggressively or not have already been firmly incorporated into his or her repertoire of responses and are difficult to extinguish.

Thus it is necessary, if we are ever to reduce the extent of aggressive behavior in society, to arrange conditions so that youngsters do not learn, or at least do not overlearn, aggressive problem solving strategies in the first place. It is also essential that society provide at least equal or better opportunities for the learning of prosocial behavior in these early years.

Our research over the past 30 years has identified numerous factors in the child's sociocultural environment, in the child's family interactions, and in the child's personality that promote the learning of aggression. Three of these factors seem more amenable to influence and change by society than do the others. The first of these is the extent to which the child is exposed to prominent examples of persons who obtain attractive goals and gain adulation from their peers through use of physical force and other coercive techniques. Although aggression within the family and among peers may teach this lesson to some children, television is the primary source of such models for many children. The second factor is the extent to which both the family and society at large foster the idea that aggressive behavior is normative and expected, at least for males, and therefore to be encouraged in boys. Society's differential gender role expectations are the basis for this emphasis in training. The third factor is the extent to which the child is monitored and nurtured by his family as he matures. The neglected, rejected child whose parents ignore his aggression is highly at risk for engaging in severe antisocial behavior. Thus, changes in the parent's child rearing practices have the potential for reducing the child's aggression. In this article, we will summarize the research findings that suggest that each of these factors—television pro-gramming, gender role expectations, and child rearing practices—is an important determinant of aggressive behavior, and we will suggest ways in which their effects can be mitigated.

II. TELEVISION VIOLENCE AND AGGRESSION

A. Findings

In 1972, The Surgeon General concluded that there was "a causal relation between viewing violence on television and aggressive behavior," which could no longer be denied (Comstock & Rubinstein, 1972). It was maintained (Chaffee, 1972) that in reaching this conclusion one of the influential studies was our own (Eron, Huesmann, Lefkowitz, & Walder, 1972). In this study, we followed a large group of 8-year-old subjects for 10 years and found that among a host of variables investigated, the best single predictor to how aggressive a young male would be in late adolescence was the violence of the television programs he watched when he was in middle childhood. It is true that the relation was not a powerful one, explaining a major portion of the variance. But the fact that it held up over a number of years was impressive since it corroborated the short-term laboratory studies which had demonstrated the same causal effect under controlled conditions (e.g., Bandura, Ross, & Ross, 1963; Berkowitz, 1962).

Ten years of extensive and intensive research following the issuance of the Surgeon General's report has provided further evidence of the relation between television violence viewing and aggression. This research has been summarized and evaluated in a chapter written for the new Surgeon General's report by Huesmann (1983). Among the new field studies was a project by Belson (1978), funded by the Columbia Broadcasting System (CBS), in which data were collected on 1650 adolescent boys in London. Belson concluded that "the evidence is very strongly supportive of the hypothesis that high exposure to television violence increases the degree to which boys engage in serious violence" (p. 15).

Another study done in the United States with a different age group was that of Singer and Singer (1980) who followed a group of nursery school children over the course of a year and carefully measured a number of variables at four different times. A variety of different multivariate analyses of these data all point to the same conclusion: television viewing, particularly violence viewing, is a cause of heightened aggressiveness in children of that age.

A third study was conducted by researchers at the National Broadcasting Company (NBC) (Milavsky, Kessler, Stipp, & Rubens, 1982) who used peer nominations of aggression as their dependent measure. They also reported significant correlations between aggression and violence viewing among elementary school children.

Finally, over the past 7 years, we have been conducting a number of new studies investigating TV violence and aggression in natural settings (Eron, Huesmann, Brice, Fischer, & Mermelstein, 1983; Huesmann, Eron, Klein, Brice, & Fischer, 1983; Huesmann, Lagerspetz, & Eron, 1984b). The purpose of this research has been to investigate further the boundary conditions of the causal relation that had been demonstrated in the 10-year longitudinal study noted previously. On the basis of those results, we had surmised that there must be a sensitive period in a child's development, probably around age 8 to 12, when youngsters are especially susceptible to the influence of violent television. This supposition was based on our finding that there was no relation between the violence of programs these subjects watched at age 19 and their aggressive behavior at that time, although there had been a significant contemporaneous relation for the same subjects at age 8. Further, the correlation over time was larger than the early contemporaneous one. This suggested that there might be a cumulative effect at least into late childhood or the early adolescent years.

To check on these suppositions we undertook a new 3-year longitudinal study in which we investigated the television habits and aggressive behaviors of a group of 672 youngsters in Oak Park, Illinois, a socially and economically heterogeneous suburb of Chicago, and 86 children from two inner city parochial schools in Chicago (Eron et al., 1983; Huesmann et al., 1983). Half of the subjects were in the first grade (age 6) and half in the third grade (age 8) at the beginning of the data collection. During the first year of the study, the youngsters were tested in their classrooms with a variety of paper and pencil procedures, and their parents were interviewed individually. The children were subsequently tested again in both the second and third years of the study with the same procedures. With this overlapping, longitudinal design, it was possible to separate age effects from cohort effects and trace the development of both television habits and aggressive behavior, as well as the relation between them, from age 6 to 10. This study has now been replicated in five other countries, Finland, Poland, Australia, the Netherlands, and Israel (Fraczek, 1983; Huesmann, Lagerspetz, & Eron, 1984b; Sheehan, 1984).

In general, we found that, indeed, the relation between television violence viewing and aggression is already emerging at age 6, but the relation is not as substantial and consistent across samples of that age as in samples of 9 to 11 year olds. Such a finding is consistent with the theory that the effect of violence is cumulative (Eron *et al.*, 1983). As noted above, the Singers found an effect as early as ages 3 and 4. In regard to the upper end of the age range of susceptibility, we had argued earlier (Eron *et al.*, 1972) that once an individual reached adolescence, behavioral predispositions and inhibitory controls would have become so well developed that it would be difficult for television to influence patterns of characteristic behavior such as aggression. However, Belson (1978) who, as noted above, collected data on teenage boys in London, showed the television violence/aggression relation certainly extended to that age range. Also, in a study of adolescents in the United States, Hartnagel, Teevan, and McIntyre (1975) found a significant, though low, correlation between violence viewing and aggressive behavior. Thus, it seems likely that the television violence and aggression relation extends over a wider age spectrum than we previously suspected.

However, because of a number of converging developmental trends, as demonstrated in our recent developmental study (Eron *et al.*, 1983), it is likely that children around age 8 in the United States are especially susceptible to the influence of violent television. From grades 1 to 5, children are becoming increasingly aggressive; also during that period the amount of television violence viewed increases from grade 1 to 3 and then starts to decline. However, the child's perception of television violence as realistic declines from grade 1 to 5. Thus, in the United States, the third grade may be the center of an especially sensitive period when the factors are just right for television violence to have an effect. Some of the strongest relations between television violence and both simultaneous and later aggression have been reported for children about this age (Chaffee, 1972; Lefkowitz, Eron, Walder, & Huesmann, 1977). Interestingly, however, the developmental trends for aggression, violence viewing, and realism are somewhat different in some of the other countries investigated (Huesmann *et al.*, 1984b). Thus, one effect of the specific socialization processes employed in a culture may be to alter the time of the sensitive period when television can have its greatest effects. However, the relation between violence viewing and aggression holds up consistently across countries despite these differences in socialization practices as well as differences in political/economic systems and extent of government control over television programming.

While the correlations by themselves help pinpoint the age of greatest effect, they do not indicate what the psychological processes are that cause the relation between aggression and violence viewing. However, path analyses of the data from our recent studies in the United States, Finland, Israel, and Poland have reinforced our earlier conclusion that the process is more one of TV violence engendering aggression than vice versa. Furthermore, though subject to differing interpretations, we find that similar path analyses of the recent NBC data (Milavsky *et al.*, 1982) suggest a similar conclusion. While the demonstrable causal effects over short periods are not strong, TV violence does appear to engender aggressive behavior. The cumulative effect over time can become large, since violence viewing stimulates aggression and aggressive children turn to violence to validate their own behavior. This bidirectional causal process model seems the most plausible, given our current data.

One criticism of our findings has been that the aggression criterion in many of these studies has been a measure based on peer ratings of behavior in the school setting. Thus, it has been contended by some skeptics (Cook, Kendzierski, & Thomas, 1984) that while these studies may indicate a small effect of televised violence on subsequent behavior of youngsters, the type of behavior observed has little to do with the kind of real-life violence that is of concern to most persons. According to Cook *et al.*, the peer nomination measure of aggression which we developed reflects no more than youthful "boisterousness and incivility." However, the data indicate otherwise. It is true that the original peer nomination measure taps into the kinds of aggressive behaviors which show up in the classroom and, although this measure samples physical fighting, stealing, and verbal abuse, it does not directly measure violent crime. There can be little doubt, however, that it predicts the incidence of such crimes in the future. The construct and empirical validities of this instrument as a measure of real-life aggression have been documented extensively over the years (Lefkowitz *et al.*, 1977). Recently obtained data are even more striking.

In 1981, we completed a follow-up of the 875 subjects who participated in our original Rip Van Winkle study in 1960. We succeeded in reinterviewing 409 of them, 165 of their spouses, and 82 of their children. The modal age of the subjects was 30 years. During the interview, the subjects were administered the Minnesota Multiphasic Personality Inventory (MMPI). The sum of scales *F, 4,* and *9* of this inventory has been demonstrated to be a valid indication of antisocial behavior (Huesmann, Lefkowitz, & Eron, 1978). The subjects were also asked a number of questions during this interview about how they punished their children. Spouses were asked about any physical aggression directed against them by the subjects. The latter questions were taken from the Strauss Home Violence Questionnaire (Strauss, Giles, & Stein-metz, 1979). In addition, we obtained data from the New York Division of Criminal Justice Services and the Division of Motor Vehicles as to the number and seriousness of crimes for which the subjects had been con-victed in New York State as well as the number of moving violations and convictions for driving while intoxicated. In all, we had some data on 632 of the original 875 subjects.

The correlations between the early peer nominations and these later measures of aggression are shown in Table I. It is apparent that over 22 years there is moderately good predictability from early aggression to later aggression, especially in the case of males. Especially impressive is the correlation between aggression at age 8 and later encounters with the law as indicated by driving and criminal offenses.

Since a disproportionate number of the original subjects who moved out of the state subsequent to the original testing were from high-ag-gressive groups (Lefkowitz *et al.*, 1977), and were thus unavailable for testing, the range of aggression scores has been truncated and the cor-relations are probably a minimal estimate of the relation between aggres-sion at age 8 and later antisocial behavior of the type that brings indi-viduals into contact with the law. The 1960 aggression score of males not interviewed was significantly higher than the aggression score of those males who were interviewed (Huesmann *et al.*, 1984a). Another reason

Table I. Correlations of Peer Nominated
Aggression at Age 8 with Aggression at Age 30

Age 30 aggression measures	Age 8 aggression	
	Males	Females
MMPI scales $F + 4 + 9$	.30***	.16*
Rating of subject by spouse	.27**	—
Punishment of child by subject	.24*	.24*
Criminal justice convictions	.24***	—
Seriousness of criminal offense	.21***	—
Moving traffic violations	.21***	—
Driving while intoxicated	.29***	—

$*p < .05.$
$**p < .01.$
$***p < .001.$

why the Pearson *r* may be an underestimation of the true relation between variables presented here is that the distributions of many of the
measures are skewed (e.g., peer nominated aggression has a pileup of
scores at the low end of the scale). A more representative demonstration
of the relations can be obtained by dividing the subjects into low, medi-
um, and high groups according to the original peer nomination measure
and calculating mean scores on each of the criterion variables separately
for each of the three groups.

These relations are seen much more graphically in Figs. 1–4. Figure 1
shows the relation between early peer nominated aggression and a self-
rating of aggression 22 years later; Fig. 2 refers to another self-disclosure
measure, how severely the subject punishes his or her own child 22
years later. Figure 3 on the left demonstrates the relation between peer
nominated aggression of boys at age 8 and how aggressive they were
toward their wives, as rated by their wives, when they are age 30. On
the right is the relation of the number of criminal convictions in the past
10 years to peer nominated aggression at age 8. And finally, in Fig. 4, we
have the relation to moving traffic violations and convictions for driving
while intoxicated. When tested by analysis of variance, the differences
among the means on each of the criterion variables are highly significant, again especially in the case of males. It is obvious that while the
peer nomination items, on their face, may refer to no more than "boisterousness or incivility," they do, indeed, predict the kinds of aggressive and violent behavior that are of interest to law enforcement
officials, social agencies, and concerned citizens.

Furthermore, the TV violence scores at age 8 do themselves predict
these serious antisocial behaviors 22 years later. Tables II and III present
the correlations between TV viewing and aggression over time for males

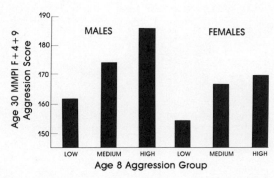

Figure 1. Relation of aggression at age 8 to aggression at age 30 as measured by MMPI.

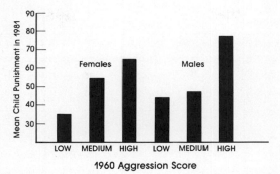

Figure 2. Relation of aggression at age 8 (1960) to severity of child punishment at age 30 (1981).

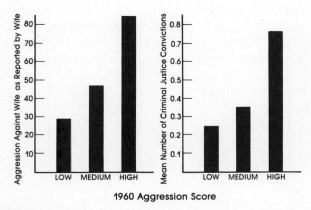

Figure 3. Relation of male aggression at age 8 (1960) to number of criminal convictions and aggression against wife by age 30 (1981).

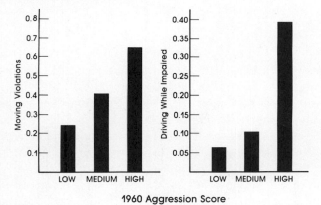

Figure 4. Relation of male aggression at age 8 (1960) to mean number of traffic violations in New York state by age 30 (1981).

Table II. Correlations between Subject's Aggression and TV Viewing over Time for Males

	Age 8 peer nominated aggression	Age 19 peer nominated aggression	Age 30			
			Aggressive habits	Seriousness of crimes	Punishment of child by subject	Aggression under alcohol
Age 8						
Parent's report of subject's TV violence viewing	.23*	.28**	.19*	.15*	.26	.19*
Parent's report of subject's TV viewing frequency	−.11†	—	—	.20***	.23†	—
Age 19						
Self-report of subject's TV violence viewing	—	—	—	—	—	—
Self-report of subject's TV viewing frequency	—	.13†	—	.12**	.39*	—
Age 30						
Self-report of subject's TV violence viewing	—	—	—	—	—	—
Self-report of subject's intensity of TV viewing	.12†	−.19*	—	.17*	—	—

†$p < .10.$
*$p < .05,$
**$p < .01,$
***$p < .001.$

and females. It can be seen that for male subjects, the violence of their favorite programs at age 8 related 22 years later to their self-ratings of how severely they punished their own children, how physically aggressive they themselves were, and how aggressively they acted while drinking. Even more impressive than the relation of TV violence at age 8 to these self-ratings of aggressive behavior at age 30 is the relation of both early TV violence and frequency of viewing to the seriousness of crimes committed, as reported by the New York Division of Criminal Justice. Equally, if not more, impressive is the canonical correlation of .41 when predicting from both TV violence viewing and frequency of

Table III. Correlations between Subject's Aggression and TV Viewing over Time for Females

	Age 8 peer nominated aggression	Age 19 peer nominated aggression	Age 30			
			Aggressive habit	Seriousness of crimes	Punishment of child by subject	Aggression under alcohol
Age 8						
Parent's report of subject's TV violence viewing	—	—	—	—	—	.13†
Parent's report of subject's TV viewing frequency	—	—	.15	.18*	.18	—
Age 19						
Self-report of subject's TV violence viewing	—	—	—	—	.18	—
Self-report of subject TV viewing frequency	—	—	—	.21*	.20	—
Age 30						
Self-report of subject's TV violence viewing	—	—	.14*	—	.16	—
Self-report of subject's intensity of TV viewing	.14*	—	.24***	.17*	—	—

†$p < .10$.
*$p < .05$.
***$p < .001$.

TV viewing at age 8 to self-reported aggression, seriousness of crimes committed, and extent of aggressive behavior while drinking at age 30. For females, there were many fewer significant relations, although frequency of TV viewing of females at age 8 correlated significantly with the seriousness of crimes measure at age 30. Further, what is remarkable for females is that TV violence and/or frequency measures taken at each phase of the study correlated positively with ratings at age 30 of how severely they punished their children. Although these sizable correlations are not significant (because N is small), the consistency with which the finding appears at each stage (ages 8, 19, and 30) bolsters our confi-

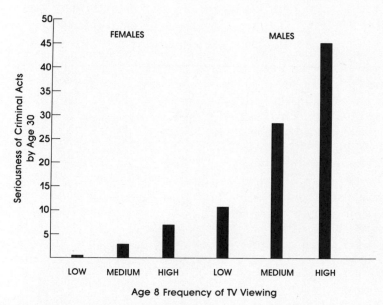

Figure 5. Relation of TV viewing frequency at age 8 to seriousness of crimes committed by age 30.

Table IV. Correlations Relating Subject's TV Viewing and Aggression to Subject's Child's TV Viewing and Aggression 22 Years Later

| | Subject's child age 6–12 | | | |
| | Aggression | | TV viewing | |
	Self-rating of aggression	Aggressive fantasy	Self-report of violence	Self-report of frequency
Subject at age 8				
Peer-nominated aggression	.29**	.34**	—	—
TV violence viewing	.41**	.27*	.26*	—
Subject at age 30				
MMPI scales $F+4+9$	.26*	.27*	—	—
Criminal justice convictions	—	.24*	.22†	—
TV violence viewing	—	—	—	—

$^†p < .10.$
$^*p < .05.$
$^{**}p < .01.$

dence in the reality of the relation for females between TV viewing and aggression as measured by severity of child punishment. Figure 5 graphically represents the relation between the early TV measure and seriousness of subjects' offenses at age 30 for both males and females.

These data leave little doubt that the kind of aggression of which early TV viewing habits are predictive is not just trivial behavior, that is, "boisterousness and incivility" as it has been characterized (Cook *et al.*, 1984). The continued viewing of TV violence by children can have a lasting effect on their character and personality, leading to serious criminal behavior and antisocial violence of all types.

However, even more striking than the previously mentioned results are the findings with regard to the subjects' own children. Table IV shows the relation obtained between the subjects' TV viewing and aggression and their childrens' TV viewing and aggression. There is a correlation of .26 between the subjects' violence viewing at age 8, and their childrens' violence viewing 22 years later. Even more impressive is the correlation of .41 between the subjects' violence viewing at age 8, and their childrens' self-rated aggression 22 years later. Television is indeed a powerful teacher. What the subject learns about life from the television screen seems to be transmitted to the next generation.

B. Proposed Remedies

It would seem that, given the preponderance of evidence, the television networks would assume some social responsibility and start to lower the level of violence and mayhem with which they are loading the airwaves. They refuse to do this and insist the link between television viewing and subsequent behavior has not been proved. This is a strange claim to come from executives working in commercial television whose chief purpose it is to persuade people to purchase specific products. They do this very often by showing high status, glamorous, and/or sexy individuals using those products. It is unlikely one will ever hear a TV sales representative tell a prospective purchaser of TV time that television does not influence behavior. In support of their anomalous position the television people now cite a single longitudinal study which purports to show no causal relation between television violence and subsequent aggressive behavior (Milavsky *et al.*, 1982). The authors of this study base their conclusion of no relation between TV violence and subsequent aggression on a single analysis in a whole series of analyses they performed in which they were searching for possible third variables to explain the relation between television violence viewing and aggression. Using an unconventional measure of social class, they claim to demonstrate that the relation disappears when social class is controlled. However, none of the other studies mentioned thus far, including our own, which have been carried out in two different sections of the United States, one urban and one semirural, and in five different countries, have found a diminution in effect when social class was controlled. It should be noted that this was the only one of many analyses which these researchers did controlling for possible third variables, which showed a significant diminution. Actually, as mentioned earlier, the Milavsky *et al.* results are very similar to our own, showing a cumulative causal process that produces only small changes over a few years.

With such persistent opposition to facing facts, it is unlikely that the networks will be persuaded to regulate themselves and change their programming so that there is a lessening of the level of aggression displayed on the TV screen. Aggression is a cheap and easy way to attract and maintain viewers' attention. Thus, barring government censorship, which no one seriously advocates, it is up to parents, educators, and other interested persons to devise procedures to counteract the harmful effects of television violence. Efforts at devising such procedures have been going on in at least two places. Jerome and Dorothy Singer (1980) of the Yale University Television Research Center have been preparing curricula to teach young children and their parents how to be intelligent television consumers. However, their early efforts at training parents to control and limit their children's TV viewing habits were not too successful. They say "television has become so entrenched in the daily life of children and families that direct efforts to influence parents to restrict viewing in any drastic way are doomed to meet strong resistance" (pp. 145–146). However, they were optimistic about the efficacy of providing parents with materials which they could use to encourage imagination and cognitive skills in their children. They provide tentative evidence that the use of these materials caused a lowering over time in the relation between TV violence and aggression in their preschool subjects.

A somewhat more successful intervention was one we conducted in Oak Park, Illinois, a socially and economically heterogeneous suburb of Chicago. This experiment (Huesmann *et al.*, 1983) was conducted within the framework of the 3-year longitudinal study described above. We took 170 youngsters, both boys and girls, who were already high violence viewers and divided them randomly into an experimental and control group. Over the course of 2 years, the experimental subjects were exposed to two treatments designed to reduce the likelihood of their imitating the aggressive behaviors they observed on TV. The control group received comparable neutral treatments. By the end of the second year, the experimental subjects were significantly less aggressive than the control subjects as rated by their peers. Furthermore, the relation between violence viewing and aggressiveness disappeared in the experimental group.

The procedures we developed for the experimental group were based on the assumption that aggression is facilitated by the youngster's attitudes about aggression as an acceptable way of solving problems. Thus, the youngster is more apt to copy the aggressive behaviors he sees on television if he perceives the television violence as realistic, if he identifies closely with the TV characters, and if he believes society approves of aggressive ways of solving problems. If a child perceives that the problem solving strategy used by the actor is unrealistic and ineffective in the real world or cannot identify with the actor or believes an aggressive response is unacceptable, then the child might be less likely to remember the sequence and act that way when he is in a similar situation or in one in which he feels such a response will be effective. On the other hand, even if the child remembers such a sequence, he will be less likely to respond that way if he believes that kind of action is unrealistic and unacceptable.

Thus, we believed that we could reduce the effect of violence on television by changing children's attitudes both about television and about aggression. We proposed to do this by teaching them first that television is an unrealistic portrayal of the real world; second, that aggressive behaviors are not as universal and acceptable in the real world as they appear on television, and third, that it is just not good to behave like the aggressive characters on TV. The actual procedures are described in some detail in the article by Huesmann *et al.* (1983). Both the experimental and control subjects were seen in small groups for three sessions in the first year and two sessions in a second year.

Four months after the second intervention, the final wave of data on all of the children in the study was collected. Remarkably, it was found that the mean peer nominated aggression score for the experimental group was now significantly lower than the score for the control group, although a year previously the two groups were approximately equal in score. The difference was highly significant, as evaluated by analysis of covariance with sex, grade, and pretreatment aggression score as covariates (Huesmann *et al.*, 1983).

Even more striking was the lack of relation between television violence and aggression in the experimental group and the continued positive relation in the control group, almost the same degree of relation as in the general population. The best predictor in the experimental group, however, was identification with TV characters. Another good predictor was judgment of TV realism. Those subjects who had higher self-rated identification with TV characters had higher peer nominated aggression scores. The more realistic the experimental subjects thought TV was, the more aggressive they were. In the control group there was no significant independent relation between realism or identification and aggression. For all boys in the Oak Park Study ($N = 375$), however, there was an interaction between identification and TV violence, so those who watched violent television and also identified with the aggressive characters were the most aggressive of all subjects.

Why were those subjects who identified with TV characters less susceptible to the treatment? The treatment attempted to change attitudes about television and about aggression as well. As a manipulation check, six attitudinal questions were asked before and after treatment; for example, "How much of what kids see on television shows would make a kid meaner?" The subjects responded to these questions on a 5-point scale. The score was the sum of the weighted responses. A change score was calculated for each child by subtracting the pretreatment score from the posttreatment score. The larger the score, the more the child changed toward the desired attitude. We found that the most important predictor of change was identification with TV characters. The more the subjects identified with TV characters, the less likely they were to change their attitudes toward television as a result of the intervention. It will be remembered that the more the youngsters identified with TV characters, the more aggressive they were. Extent of identification with TV characters is thus demonstrated to be an important mediating variable in the relation between television violence and aggression. The only other significant predictor was a self-report on the extent to which the subjects read fairy tales or had fairy tales read to them. The more extensive the reading of fairy tales, the more likely was the attitude toward television to change. This latter finding is in keeping with the Singers' (Singer & Singer, 1980) contention that training in fantasy can affect the relation between television violence and behavior.

This, of course, is just one study, which demands replication. But it certainly suggests that we are not helpless in the face of that insidious teacher in our living rooms. There are simple instructional procedures that can be used by parents and teachers to counteract the negative effects television has on our children. If efforts fail at getting the networks to change their programming so as to deemphasize unnecessary aggression and violence, and if parents find it impossible to limit and monitor their children's TV viewing, then at least psychologists, educators, and other trained professionals can devise and widely disseminate similar kinds of procedures with which to inoculate our children and thereby, perhaps, our children's children against the malevolent effects of the virulent epidemic of violence spreading across the airwaves.

III. GENDER ROLE EXPECTATIONS AND AGGRESSION

A. Findings

There is no doubt that, in general, males are more aggressive than females and specifically engage in more physically violent behavior. No matter how aggression is expressed or what specific measures of aggression are used, whether in laboratory situations or real life, males as a group always display more of it and get higher scores than females as a group. Nevertheless, we have found that there are some females who are just as aggressive as males both in real life and in the laboratory. These are usually girls who have been socialized like boys. For example, when they were growing up, they preferred boys' games to girls' games, and as adults they like to watch contact sports on television, and tend to endorse the behaviors which go along with high masculinity scores on interest inventories (Eron, 1980).

Such findings can be taken as evidence that over and above any innate, biological, or hormonal factors which may account for the differential rate and magnitude of aggressive behavior between males and females, there are learning and experiential factors that also contribute to the difference. Actually, it has been demonstrated that among neonates, there is little difference at birth between males and females on any variety of physiological and behavioral characteristics (Birns, 1976). The most outstanding characteristic of infant behavior is its instability and variability (Moss, 1967, 1974). However, differential handling of the same behavior in boys and girls starts immediately after birth. Boys receive more physical stimulation from their mothers while girls receive more verbal stimulation (Moss, 1967). Boy and girl infants are also perceived differently despite the lack of any real differentiation in their actual behavior or appearance. In an experiment by Seavey, Katz, and Zalk (1975), the very same infant, when identified as a girl, was described as round, soft, and fragile; and when labeled as a boy, was described as having a strong grasp and no hair. By the time children have passed a year of life, definite behavioral differences between boys and girls can be observed, due in part at least to differential handling by parents. Goldberg and Lewis (1969), observing 13-month-old young-sters, noted that boys were more physically active and independent and cried less than girls. They related this difference to differential handling of these boys and girls by their mothers when they had previously been observed by the researchers when the infants were 6 months of age.

By the time youngsters are in preschool, wide differences in level of aggressive behavior (Ankeny & Goodman, 1976; McGurk, & Lewis, 1972; McGurk, 1973), as well as differential adult response to such be-havior (Serbin, Connor, & Citron, 1978), are apparent. Among nursery school children, when girls are aggressive, they are usually softly repri-manded while boys are often scolded loudly, restrained physically, and given specific directions about what to do (Serbin, O'Leary, Vente, & Tonick, 1973). The teachers, however, in the latter study, were not aware that they were responding differentially to boys and girls.

In the primary grades, the difference in aggression between boys and girls is even more prominent and this difference is not limited to phys-ical aggression (Eron, Walder, & Lefkowitz, 1971; Maccoby, & Jacklin, 1974) but encompasses all manner of expression of aggression, verbal, physical, indirect, and acquisitive. By the time children have reached middle school age, they have formed definite attitudes about passive behavior as appropriate for girls but not for boys (Connor, Serbin, & Ender, 1978). Girls of this age consider a passive approach as the best way to solve problems while boys devalue such an approach.

Some hint of the effect of the differential socialization to which boys and girls are subjected as they grow older can be detected in the TV findings mentioned above. In the 10-year follow-up study, the relation between television violence and aggression was true only for boys; for girls there was no relation between television violence and aggression either contemporaneously at age 8 or longitudinally over a 10-year lag. One of the reasons given to explain this difference is that boys are encouraged and reinforced in the direct and overt expression of aggres-sion while most girls learn that physical aggression is an undesirable behavior for girls and so acquire other behaviors more suitable to expec-tations for girls (Eron, 1980). As indicated in the previously cited stud-ies, this learning transpires very early in their lives so that subsequently very few occasions arise in which they emit aggressive behaviors. There-fore, they are seldom either rewarded or punished for aggression. As a consequence, they may not be responsive to aggressive cues in the environment (Edwards, 1967) including aggressive displays on televi-sion. Studies by Bandura *et al.* (1961, 1963) have shown consistently that boys perform significantly more imitative aggression than girls. He also found that when girls are positively reinforced for imitating aggressive behavior, they significantly increase such behavior and respond in a manner more similar to boys who are reinforced for the same behaviors. The results of Hokanson and Edelman (1966) would support this contention that lowered aggression levels in females occur because aggression is nonreinforcing for females. They found that females did not demonstrate the quickened reduction of physiological arousal after the opportunity to counteraggress against a confederate of the experimenter who had aggressed against them. However, such quickened reduction of heart rate and blood pressure to basal levels was routinely seen in male subjects after engaging in aggressive behavior directed against the experimenter's confederate. For boys, aggression seems to reduce drive and thus has reinforcing properties for them. This is not so for girls. In summary, most girls may be trained to be nonaggressive to such an extent that aggressive models have little effect on them.

Results of the Rip Van Winkle longitudinal study suggest another reason for the lack of relation between television violence and aggression in girls. Girls, it seems, see television as less realistic than boys (Lefkowitz *et al.*, 1977). Thus, boys are more likely than girls to model the behavior they observe on television, especially if they believe this is normative behavior for their gender. Data collected in the Oak Park and cross-national studies (Huesmann *et al.*, 1984b) confirm these findings. In general, girls believe television is significantly less realistic than boys do. However, the more aggressive girls are, both at ages 8 through 10 and at 19, the more realistic they think television programs are. Furthermore, girls who see themselves as having masculine interests and attitudes at age 19, that is, girls who obtain high scores on the *masculinity* scale of the MMPI, tend to perceive television as more realistic and also tend to be more aggressive. Thus, the more girls see television as realistic, the more they are like boys in other respects and the more aggressive they are.

Two related findings are the significant positive relation for girls between aggression and masculine interest patterns as measured by the *masculinity–femininity* (*M–F*) scale of the MMPI (Lefkowitz *et al.*, 1977), as well as the significant positive relation between aggression scores for girls and the extent to which they watch contact sports on television (Lefkowitz, Eron, Walder, & Huesmann, 1973). Both of these scores which are related to aggression reflect attitudes and behaviors which are normative for boys. For boys, however, there was no relation between viewing contact sports on TV and aggression score, nor was there a relation for boys between masculinity on the *M–F* scale and aggression. It is very probable that the reason for lack of relation with aggression for boys lies in the minimal variability for boys on these variables. *Most* boys, whether low or high aggressive, watch contact sports and also endorse the attitudes and interests comprising the *masculinity* items on the *M–F* scale. Overall, these results indicate that the interests and activities of aggressive females tend to be deviant from their gender norms and similar to the behavior of the male gender group.

In 1981, when the Rip Van Winkle subjects were 30 years old and they were reinterviewed, we found a significant relation, as noted previously in Table I and Figs. 1–4, between peer rated aggression at age 8 and various measures of aggression at age 30. For females, however, the only significant relation of early aggression to later aggression was in the area of child punishment. Those girls who were high in aggression, as rated by their peers at age 8, reported at age 30 that they punished their children more severely than did those 30-year-old subjects who were low aggressive at age 8. Furthermore, as noted above, the more the female subjects watched television at each stage of the research (ages 8, 19, and 30), the more likely were they to be severe child punishers. This relation did not hold for males. Child punishment is probably the only arena in which a female can express aggression without fear of social censure or retaliation—unless she goes too far, inflicts serious harm, and is detected by the authorities. Then we call it child abuse. In this regard, it is interesting to note that child abuse by mothers is significantly more frequent than child abuse by fathers (Gelles, 1973). Of course, the fact that mothers spend more time with the children also contributes to these statistics.

It should be remembered that these subjects were girls growing up during the 1950s (modal year of birth, 1951). In 1965, Minuchin reported a study in which she found that boys and girls from traditional homes and schools differed more on aggression experienced both in fantasy and play than boys and girls from more modern homes and schools. There is some indication from our 3-year longitudinal Oak Park study, begun 17 years after the first phase of the 22-year Rip Van Winkle study, that socialization of little girls may have been undergoing some change in the intervening years and that boys and girls are indeed becoming more similar in a number of previously more severely sex-typed behaviors. While girls of primary school age are still significantly less aggressive than boys, they do not differ in the amount of time spent watching television or in how realistic they believe television to be (Eron *et al.*, 1983). Furthermore, there is now a positive relation for girls between television violence viewing and aggressive behavior in school, which previously had been found only for boys (Huesmann *et al.*, 1984b).

In our earlier study conducted over 20 years ago, we argued that an important reason for not finding a TV–violence–aggressive behavior relation for girls might have been that there were far fewer aggressive females on television for a girl to imitate than there were aggressive males for a boy to imitate. This would not seem to be the case. In the recent Oak Park study, we compared how much girls copied aggressive females on television with how much they copied male models. Although female models were copied to some extent by girls, the male models were copied more (Huesmann *et al.*, 1984b).

It may be that more important than the sex of the model are the behaviors the model is performing and that if masculine activities are intrinsically more appealing to subjects of either sex, then all subjects would be more likely to attend to male characters and imitate their activities. It has been demonstrated that the more powerful the model, the more likely are the model's behaviors to be attended to and copied, regardless of sex (Bandura *et al.*, 1963). Similarly, it is suggested now that the more appealing are the general activities of the model, the more likely will the observer be to attend to the model and therefore to copy the model's behaviors. Indeed, there is some evidence for this in our data on preference for sex-typed activities among these subjects. Our measure of preference for sex-typed activities in the Oak Park study comprised a booklet of four pages, each of which contained six pictures of children's activities. Two pictures of each set had been previously rated masculine, two feminine, and two neutral by 67 college students who had designated the activities as popular for boys and girls. The 24 pictures finally used in this procedure had been designated as boys' or girls' games with good reliability. The task for the children was to select the two activities they liked best on each page, and the children recieved a score for the number of masculine, feminine, and neutral pictures they chose. The reason for including a neutral category was that it is much easier for boys to admit to liking neutral activities than to admit to liking feminine ones. Similarly for girls, we anticipated that it would be difficult to admit to liking boys' activities. Here, however, we were surprised. One of our most interesting findings is that both boys and girls prefer more traditionally masculine activities as they get older (Eron *et al.*, 1983). The mean increase in score is highly significant in both sexes. Therefore, since boys' traditional activities have increasingly more appeal for both boys and girls as they grow older, it is not surprising that male figures stand out as models for both sexes.

Furthermore, the relation between preference for masculine activities and aggression is significant for both boys and girls. Regardless of sex, subjects who score high on preference for masculine activities are likely to be more aggressive. And the relation is stronger over the time lag than contemporaneously. The cumulative effect of the socialization ex-

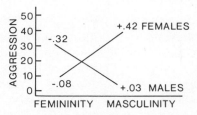

Figure 6. Correlations between aggression and masculinity or femininity in male and female college students.

perience is obvious. We see the culmination of this socialization experience in Figs. 6 and 7. These figures describe the results of an experiment
by one of our students, Esther Kaplan-Shain (1979), who related scores
of men and women college students on scales of masculinity and femininity (Bem, 1974) to performance on an aggression machine. This was
an adaptation of the Buss-type (Buss, 1961) apparatus, whereby the
subject signals a confederate by delivering loud sounds to the confederate's earphones rather than by electric shock—the louder the sound
delivered, the more aggressive is the response (Williams, Meyerson,
Eron, & Semler, 1967). In Fig. 6, we see that while masculinity in males
has little relation to aggressive responding, femininity in males is significantly negatively related to aggression. Similarly, while femininity in
females is not predictive of lack of aggression, masculinity in females is
positively correlated with the intensity of aggression response. Thus, it
would seem that men—regardless of the masculine attitudes they
have—are inhibited from responding aggressively if they also have traditionally feminine attitudes and values, while women who subscribe to
masculine attitudes and values are facilitated in aggressive responding
regardless of their feminine attitudes.

Figure 7 shows the mean aggression scores according to whether the
subjects are high or low masculine or high or low feminine. There is little
difference between aggressive responses of high- and low-masculine

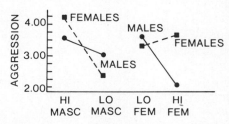

Figure 7. Mean aggression scores of high and low masculine and feminine college
students.

men, but there is a significant difference in the aggressive response of high- and low-feminine men ($p < .02$). Similarly, there is little difference in the responses of high- and low-feminine women but a large and significant difference between high- and low-masculine women ($p < .01$). The most aggressive responders of all are the high-masculine women. Women can learn to be as aggressive as men, despite their low levels of testosterone. There is further indication of this relation between aggression and masculinity/femininity as opposed to maleness/femaleness in our 22-year longitudinal study. Those female subjects who at age 30 scored in a masculine direction on scale 5 of the MMPI tended to get high scores ($r = .15$, $p < .05$) on the Strauss Spouse Abuse measure; while those male subjects who at age 30 scored in the feminine direction tended to get low scores ($r = -.19$, $p < .01$).

Finally, IQ and aggression were significantly related for both boys and girls age 8 in the 22-year Rip Van Winkle study ($r = -.27$ and $-.32$, respectively). Differences were found between males and females, however, in correlations from early IQ and aggression to later intellectual

Table V. Correlations of Peer Nominated Aggression and IQ at Age 8 with Aggression and Competence at Age 30

Age 30 measures	Age 8 aggression		Age 8 IQ	
	Males	Females	Males	Females
Aggression measures				
MMPI scales $F+4+9$	.30***	.16*	−.19**	—
Rating of subject by spouse	.27**	—	—	—
Punishment of child by subject	.24*	.24*	—	−.21*
Criminal justice convictions	.24***	—	−.15**	—
Seriousness of criminal offence	.21***	—	−.14*	—
Moving traffic violations	.21***	—	—	—
Driving while intoxicated	.29***	—	—	—
Competence measures				
WRAT spelling	−.30***	−.35***	.54***	.44***
WRAT reading	−.20*	−.37***	.56***	.47***
WRAT arithmetic	−.19*	−.35***	.55***	.42***
Education	−.25***	−.25***	.33***	.29***
Occupational status[a]	−.17*	−.28***	.36***	—
Social incompetence	.15*	.28***	−.24**	−.27***
Ego strength	−.15*	−.21**	.30***	.24***

[a]Occupational status was recorded so that higher numbers indicate higher status.
*$p < .05$.
**$p < .01$.
***$p < .001$.

and social competency and aggression, as indicated in Table V. For both males and females, it can be seen that later social and intellectual competency correlates more strongly with early aggression than later aggression correlates with earlier intellectual competence. The relative contribution of earlier aggression and IQ to later aggression and competency can be evaluated more precisely by multiple regression analysis. These analyses revealed some interesting gender differences. After partialing out the effects of early IQ, early aggression was predictive of educational attainment and adult Wide Range Achievement Test (WRAT) levels for both males and females. However, for females, aggression and not IQ predicted occupational status, with less aggressive females achieving higher status; while for males, IQ and not aggression predicted occupational status. The same differential predictions obtained for ego development and social incompetence; it would seem that for females, aggression is as incapacitating as low IQ, so that females who characteristically engage in aggressive behaviors are impaired in many areas. For males, perhaps because aggression is more socially acceptable than it is for females, the effect on competency, either social or intellectual, is only minimal, and intelligence is the primary determinant of later intellectual competency.

B. Proposed Remedies

These findings of a direct positive relation between aggression and traditional masculine attitudes and the fact that most criminal acts in the United States, at least most violent criminal acts, are committed by young males in late adolescence (Mulvihill, & Tumin, 1969), suggest an obvious remedy, albeit one which would probably be difficult to impose. The results of our studies to date, as well as those of other researchers, point to differential socialization as crucial in determining the different levels of aggression usually found in the two sexes. But there are some males and some females who have not learned the culturally prescribed lessons and they respond with levels of aggression characteristic of the other gender. The significant variables are the values and expectations a society holds for the expression of aggressive behavior in one sex rather than another and the rewards it provides or withdraws when that behavior is displayed. We have already discussed the ways in which society discourages aggressive behavior in girls from very early in their lives and rewards them for engaging in other kinds of activity. We must reexamine what it means to be a man or masculine in our society, since the preponderance of violence in our society is perpetrated by males or by females who are acting like males. It is our contention that if we want to reduce the level of aggression in society, we should also discourage boys from aggression very early in life and reward them for other behaviors. In other words, we should socialize boys more in the manner that we have been socializing girls. Rather than insisting that little girls should be treated like little boys and trained to be aggressive and assertive, it should be the other way around. Boys should be socialized the way girls have been traditionally socialized; boys should be encouraged to develop socially positive qualities like tenderness, sensitivity to feelings, nurturance, cooperativeness, and empathy. Such prosocial behaviors and attitudes are incompatible with aggressive behaviors. Empathy, for example, has been demonstrated to be negatively correlated with aggression (Feshbach & Feshbach, 1969). Furthermore, it has been shown that while such attributes as empathy may be more characteristic of girls (Feshbach, 1982) it is possible to train these attributes in children of both genders (Feshbach, 1979; Feshbach, Feshbach, Fauvre, & Ballard-Campbell, 1983). The level of individual aggression in society will be reduced only when male adolescents and young adults, as a result of socialization, subscribe to the same standards of behavior as have been traditionally encouraged for women.

IV. CHILD-REARING PRACTICES AND AGGRESSION

A. Findings

As has been suggested before, aggression is an overdetermined behavior. Whether an individual will act to do harm to another at any given moment is the final resultant of any number of factors, including genetic, biological, experiential, and situational antecedents. Thus far, we have discussed two antecedents, the observation of violence on television and the expectations for gender appropriate behavior which a society imposes. Both of these are experiential. We will now turn our attention to a third set of experiential variables, parental child-rearing practices. It can be assumed that most parents would like to bring up their children so they will be law abiding adults, respecting the personal and property rights of others. Unfortunately, some parents engage in behaviors with their children which have just the opposite effect. Gerald Patterson and his associates, in an impressive series of studies in which families with delinquent youngsters have been observed, assessed, and monitored in great detail, have documented the frequency with which parents engage in behaviors which both indirectly and directly encourage the antisocial delinquent behaviors of their sons (Patterson, Chamberlain, & Reid, 1982). They have found that parents of antisocial children are deficient in one or more of the following parenting skills: (1) monitoring the whereabouts of the child, (2) disciplining the child for his antisocial behavior, (3) negotiating and solving problems within the family, and (4) modeling of effective prosocial "survival skills."

Joan McCord (1979), in a long-term follow-up of more than 500 boys who had been selected to participate in a delinquency prevention program, related the incidence of criminal behavior by the time the subjects reached adulthood to lax and inconsistent discipline on the part of their parents and to the lack of warm, affective, and cohesive atmosphere in their homes.

West and Farrington (1973) did a long-term longitudinal study of 411 boys chosen at random from a working class section of London. They found that by the time the subjects had reached age 25, one-third had criminal records. Five factors seemed to be characteristic of this group— large family size, low family income, low intelligence, parental criminality, and faulty child-rearing practices. Among the latter were lax discipline and careless supervision, a failure "to explore or to formulate fixed rules about such things as punctuality, manners, bedtime, television viewing or tidying up."

In our own research, we found similar parental practices related especially to how aggressive the youngsters were in school concurrently but also over time to how aggressive they were at ages 19 and 30. Among the most potent predictors of concurrent aggression at age 8 were rejection by one or both parents, extensive use of physical punishment, lack of nurturance, and parental disharmony (Eron et al., 1971). Also important were internalization of parental standards and identification with parents. Punishment for aggression served as a deterrent to such behavior only for those boys who were closely identified with their fathers (Eron et al., 1971). For all others, punishment had the opposite of the desired effect—that is, increased punishment for aggression of boys who were poorly or only minimally identified with their fathers led to increased aggression.

By the time the subjects were 19 years of age, the efficacy of some of these antecedent conditions in leading to aggressive behavior had diminished (Lefkowitz et al., 1977). Punishment for aggression at age 8 was still seen to be important in predicting aggression at age 19. However, the relation was not monotonic. It seems that over the long-run, moderate punishment by parents produced less aggressive young adults than either no punishment or harsh punishment. One implication of this finding is that punishment, when used in moderation, seems to be effective in lowering the level of aggressive behavior. However, when harsh punishment is used, especially with children who only weakly identify with their parents, aggression is increased—probably as a result of modeling. At the same time, permisiveness, as indicated by no punishment at all or very little punishment, is equally harmful (Lefkowitz *et al.*, 1977). Thus, these findings are related to those of Patterson (1982) and of West and Farrington (1973) in regard to laxness of discipline.

Another child-rearing variable which had a strong contemporaneous relation to aggression and still showed some effectiveness over 10 years was parental nurturance (Lefkowitz *et al.*, 1977). Our measure of nurturance was heavily loaded with items having to do with how much the parent knows about the child's activities, needs, and feelings and how much time the parent spends with the child (Eron *et al.*, 1971). In this regard, our nurturance variable is similar both to McCord's warmth variable and Patterson's ideas about monitoring of the child's behavior. Lack of nurturance was related to aggression both at age 8 and at age 19.

A long-term effect of rejection by parents on aggressive behavior was not maintained over the 10-year period, even though it was the best single predictor to aggression contemporaneously. However, rejection did relate to the extent of psychopathology at age 19 (Eron, Lefkowitz, Walder, & Huesmann, 1974).

Identification with parents, as indicated by how much the youngsters copied their parents' behaviors as well as by how much they internalized parental standards, also related to aggression over the 10-year period (Lefkowitz *et al.*, 1977). The prosocial behaviors implied by these latter measures no doubt serve to replace and inhibit use of aggressive strategies in solving interpersonal problems.

This is seen much more clearly in the 22-year follow-up done when the subjects were 30 years old. It would be almost too much to expect the early parent–child rearing variables to retain a direct relation to aggressive behavior of the subjects over 22 years. This is not to say that the effect of parental practices would not influence subsequent behavior of the child; however, this would largely be through its interaction with the myriad of other variables impinging on an individual over the course of development into adulthood. Indeed, the direct effect of most of the specific parenting variables on aggressive behavior did diminish over the years. However, at least one parental practice retained a direct effect on child's aggressive behavior up until 30 years of age. Punishment of the subject for aggression, which related concurrently at age 8 to the subject's aggression in school ($r = .25$, $p < .001$) and related to the subjects' self-rating of aggression at age 19 ($r = .13$, $p < .05$), still related to subjects' self-rating of aggression at age 30 ($r = .14$, $p < .01$). Further-more, how severely the subjects were punished by their parents relates significantly to how severely the subjects punish their own children ($r = .25$, $p < .01$), further testimony to the common observation that abusive parents often have themselves been abused. It is also interesting that at age 19, before the subjects had any children, they were asked a suppositional question: if they had children, how they would punish them (the same series of objective questions that had been asked of their parents were used with the subjects). Responses to this question yielded the same order of relation to parental punishment and to how the subjects now actually do punish their own children (Lefkowitz, Huesmann, & Eron, 1978).

It has been demonstrated that aggression and prosocial behavior are uniformly negatively correlated (Eron, & Huesmann, 1984; Feshbach & Feshbach, 1969). If a child learns prosocial ways of solving problems, he tends not to adopt aggressive strategies. Furthermore, prosocial behavior is as stable across time and situations as aggression (Rushton, 1981; Eron & Huesmann, 1984). In our study, prosocial behavior at age 30 was measured by a number of variables including educational attainment, ego development, and social success. The parent variables measured in the first phase that correlated with these prosocial criteria 22 years later were identification, low parental authoritarianism, and low parental disparagement of the child. These same parental variables related in the opposite direction to aggression and social failure (Eron & Huesmann, 1984).

Aggression, as has been pointed out, is a way of solving problems and gaining gratification which is learned early in life, well before the eighth year. Thus, any meaningful program of prevention and control would have to start very early. Because aggression is learned so early in life, it is learned primarily within the home. The primary targets, therefore, in a program of prevention and control would be the parents.

B. Proposed Remedies

How does one instruct parents that they must love and nurture their children if they want to avert the development of antisocial behavior? Although it is impossible to command parents to love their children and not to reject them, it is possible to instruct them on how to use appropriate disciplinary practices without resorting to physical force as well as to teach them other child-rearing skills which would discourage the development of aggressive behaviors and encourage prosocial behaviors in their children.

Using social learning principles (Bandura, 1977), Patterson (1982), and others have developed a treatment program which teaches parents to monitor what the child does both within and outside the home. Further, they teach parents to reinforce prosocial behavior whenever it occurs and to use nonphysical punishment consistently for all forms of antisocial behavior. Parents are also taught crisis management and negotiation skills. This program has been effective in helping parents reduce the antisocial behavior of their preadolescent children (Patterson, 1979; Patterson *et al.*, 1982). Thus, changes in child behavior can be produced by teaching parents more effective child-rearing skills, although it is a long and arduous process and is based on the supposition that you can get parents to come in and cooperate.

Is working with children directly a viable alternative? It has been demonstrated in our longitudinal study that if children learn prosocial behaviors early in their development, they are less likely to adopt aggressive problem solving strategies and over the years are not apt to engage in antisocial behavior (Eron & Huesmann, 1984). Children with well-practiced social skills who were concerned about not harming other children grew up to be adults with positive social attainments and few encounters with law enforcement officials. It is our contention that these alternative ways of behaving are learned very early in life and become deeply ingrained in the individual's character structure, making attempts at correction and rehabilitation unlikely to succeed. However, a number of researchers have tried to intervene directly with youngsters already identified as delinquents and predelinquents. Arnold Goldstein (1981), believing, as do we and others, that youngsters who use coercive strategies have social skills deficits, has designed a program of social skills training for such individuals. Like Patterson's work with families, social skills training with individual youngsters consists of procedures derived from social learning theory (Bandura, 1977), for example, modeling, behavioral rehearsal, and performance feedback or reinforcement. A sample of the type of skills taught to aggressive adolescents would include such simple things as how to start a conversation or say "thank you," give a compliment, or ask for help, to more difficult social interactions such as dealing with embarassment, or dealing with an accusation, responding to failure, or setting a goal.

One of the chief criticisms of this kind of social skills training has to do with the amount of transfer to real-life situations from the training sessions. To date, the evidence has not been convincing (Goldstein & Kanfer, 1979).

It would seem that the Patterson approach has more practical potential for reducing the level of violence and aggression in society. Patterson and his colleagues propose to intervene early in the lives of young children by identifying those who are at risk for developing coercive strategies. The early identification is accomplished through a "multiple gating" or stepwise screening procedure (Loeber, Dishion, & Patterson, 1984). The initial screening is a low-cost procedure which uses teacher ratings. The second screening is a more expensive procedure in which parents are contacted by telephone and asked to report on any conduct problems in those children already selected on the first screening. A third gate would include observation in the homes of those children who were selected at the second screening as well as assessment of disciplinary practices used by the parents. This stepwise procedure improves predictions because at each successive stage, the delinquency base rate is increased. Since delinquency in general is a low base rate event, it would not be cost effective to start out immediately with a high-cost procedure such as house-to-house canvassing. Once youngsters have been identified as delinquent or predelinquent, Patterson starts to work with their families to change their intrafamilial behaviors. It was noted above that parents can be trained to improve their observational and monitoring skills and their disciplinary practices, and this has been shown to have a significant effect in reducing the delinquent and coercive behavior of their children. As our data on the stability of aggressive behavior imply, it is important to intervene early in the lives of youngsters who are beginning to show signs of developing an aggressive, antisocial life style. By the time they reach adolescence, it may already be too late.

Acknowledgments

This research has been supported by Grants MH 1726 and MH 34410 to the first author and Grants MH28280 and MH 31866 to the second author from the National Institute of Mental Health. We gratefully acknowledge the contributions to this research program of Monroe M. Lefkowitz and Leopold O. Walder. Thanks are also due to Eric Dubow, Evelyne Seebaur, and Patty Yarmel for assistance in collection and analysis of the data.

References

Ankeny, M. A., & Goodman, G. Passive aggression versus active aggression in preschool children. *Child Study Journal*, 1976, **6**, 235–244.
Bandura, A. *Social Learning Theory*. New York: Prentice-Hall, 1977.
Bandura, A., Ross, D., & Ross, S. A. Transmission of aggression through imitation of aggressive models. *Journal of Abnormal and Social Psychology*, 1961, **63**, 575–582.
Bandura, G., Ross, D., & Ross, S. Imitation of film mediated aggressive models. *Journal of Abnormal Psychology*, 1963, **66**, 3–11.
Belson, W. A. *Television violence and the adolescent boy*. Westmead, England: Saxon House, 1978.

Bem, S. L. The measurement of psychological androgyny. *Journal of Consulting and Clinical Psychology,* 1974, **42**, 155–162.

Berkowitz, L. Aggression: A social psychological analysis. New York: McGraw-Hill, 1962.

Birns, B. The emergence and socialization of sex differences in the earliest years. *Merrill-Palmer Quarterly,* 1976, **22**, 229–254.

Buss, G. H. *The Psychology of Aggression.* New York: Wiley, 1961.

Chaffee, S. H. Television and adolescent aggressiveness. In G. A. Comstock, & E. A. Rubinstein (Eds.), *Television and Social Behavior,* (Vol. 3) Washington, DC: U.S. Government Printing Office, 1972.

Comstock, G. A., & Rubinstein, E. A. (Eds.), *Television and Social Behavior,* Washington, DC: U.S. Government Printing Office, 1972.

Connor, J., Serbin, L., Ender, R. Responses of boys and girls to aggressive, assertive and passive behaviors of male and female characters. *Journal of Genetic Psychology,* 1978, **133**, 56–69.

Cook, T. D., Kendzierski, D. A., & Thomas, S. V. The implicit assumptions of television research: An analysis of the NIMH report on television and behavior. *Public Opinion Quarterly,* 1984 (in press).

Edwards, N. L. *Aggressive expression under threat of retaliation.* Unpublished doctoral dissertation, University of Iowa, 1967.

Eron, L. D. Prescription for the reduction of aggression. *American Psychologist,* 1980, **35**, 244–252.

Eron, L. D., & Huesmann, L. R. The relation of prosocial behavior to the development of aggression and psychopathology. *Aggressive Behavior,* 1984 (in press).

Eron, L. D., Huesmann, L. R., Brice, P., Fischer, P., & Mermelstein, R. Age trends in the development of aggression, sex typing and related television habits. *Developmental Psychology,* 1983, **19**, 71–77.

Eron, L. D., Huesmann, L. R., Dubow, E., Romanoff, R., & Yarmel, P. Aggression and its correlates over 22 years. In D. H. Crowell, I. M. Evans, & C. R. O'Donnell (Eds.), *Childhood Aggression and Violence: Sources of influence, prevention and control.* New York: Plenum, 1985 (in press).

Eron, L. D., Huesmann, L. R., Lefkowitz, M. M., & Walder, L. D. Does television violence cause aggression? *American Psychologist,* 1972, **27**, 253–262.

Eron, L. D., Lefkowitz, M. M., Walder, L. O., & Huesmann, L. R. Relation of learning in childhood to psychopathology and aggression in young adulthood. In A. Davids, *Child Personality and Psychopathology,* New York: Wiley, 1974.

Eron, L. D., Walder, L. O., & Lefkowitz, M. M. *Learning of aggression in children.* Boston: Little Brown, 1971.

Feshbach, N. D. Empathy training: A field study in affective education. In S. Feshbach & A. Fraczek (Eds.), *Aggression and behavior change: biological and social processes.* New York: Praeger, 1979.

Feshbach, N. D. Sex differences in empathy and social behavior in children. In N. Eisenberg (Ed.), *The development of prosocial behavior.* New York: Academic Press, 1982.

Feshbach, N. D. & Feshbach, S. The relationship between empathy and aggression in two age groups. *Developmental Psychology,* 1969, **1**, 102–107.

Feshbach, N. D., Feshbach, S., Fauvre, M., & Ballard-Campbell, M. *Learning to care: Classroom activities for social and affective development.* Glenview, IL: Scott, Foresman, 1983.

Fraczek, A. Age and sex related trends in patterns of TV violence viewing and interpersonal aggression in children. *Polish Psychology Bulletin,* 1983, **1**.

Gelles, J. R. Child abuse as psychopathology. *American Journal of Orthopsychiatry,* 1973, **43**, 611–621.

Goldberg, S. & Lewis, M. Play behavior in the year old infant. *Child Development*, 1969, **40**, 21–31.

Goldstein, A. P. Social skill training. In A. P. Goldstein, E. G. Carr, W. S. Davidson II, & P. Wehr, *In Response to Aggression*. New York: Pergamon, 1981.

Goldstein, A. P., & Kanfer, F. H. *Maximizing Treatment Gains*. New York: Academic Press, 1979.

Hartnagel, T. F., Teevan, J. J., & McIntyre, J. J. Television violence and violent behavior. *Social Forces*, 1975, **54**, 341–351.

Hokanson, J. E., & Edelman, R. Effect of three social responses on vascular processes. *Journal of Personality and Social Psychology*, 1966, **3**, 442–447.

Huesmann, L. R. Television violence and aggressive behavior. In D. Pearl, L. Bouthilet, & J. Lazar (Eds.), *Television and behavior: Ten years of scientific progress and implications for the 80's, Volume II, Technical Reviews*. Washington, DC: U.S. Government Printing Office, 1983.

Huesmann, L. R., Eron, L. D., Klein, R., Brice, P., & Fischer, P. Mitigating the imitation of aggressive behaviors by changing children's attitudes about media violence. *Journal of Personality and Social Psychology*, 1983, **44**, 899–910.

Huesmann, L. R., Eron, L. D., Lefkowitz, M. M., & Walder, L. O. The stability of aggression over time and generations. *Developmental Psychology*, 1984 (in press). (a)

Huesmann, L. R., Lagerspetz, K., & Eron, L. D. Intervening variables in the television violence-aggression relation: Evidence from two countries. *Developmental Psychology*, 1984 (in press). (b)

Huesmann, L. R., Lefkowitz, M. M., & Eron, L. D. Sum of MMPI scales F, 4 and 9 as a measure of aggression. *Journal of Consulting and Clinical Psychology*, 1978, **46**, 1071–1078.

Kaplan-Shain, E. Masculinity, femininity and overt aggression in male and female college students. Unpublished paper, University of Illinois at Chicago, Department of Psychology, Chicago.

Lefkowitz, M. M., Eron, L. D., Walder, L. D., & Huesmann, L. R. Preference for televised contact sports as related to sex differences in aggression. *Developmental Psychology*, 1973, **9**, 417–420.

Lefkowitz, M. M., Eron, L. D., Walder, L. O., & Huesmann, L. R. *Growing Up to be Violent*. New York: Pergamon, 1977.

Lefkowitz, M. M., Huesmann, L. R., & Eron, L. D. Parental punishment: A longitudinal analysis of effects. *Archives of General Psychiatry*, 1978, **35**, 186–191.

Loeber, R., Dishion, T., & Patterson, G. R. Multiple-gating: A multi-stage assessment procedure for identifying youths at risk for delinquency. *Crime and Delinquency* 1984 (in press).

Maccoby, E. E., & Jacklin, G. H. *The psychology of sex differences*. Stanford, CA: Stanford University Press, 1974.

McCord, J. Some child rearing antecedents of criminal behavior in adult men. *Journal of Personality and Social Psychology*, 1979, **9**, 1477–1486.

McGurk, J. M. Aggression and sociometric status with preschool children. *Sociometry*, 1973, **36**, 542–549.

McGurk, H., & Lewis, M. Birth order: A phenomenon in search of an explanation. *Developmental Psychology*, 1972, **7**, 366.

Milavsky, J. R., Kessler, R., Stipp, H., & Rubens, W. S. Television and aggression: Results of a panel study. In D. Pearl, L. Bouthilet, & J. Lazar (Eds.), *Television and behavior: Ten years of scientific progress and implications for the eighties*. (Vol. 2: *Technical Reviews*) Washington, DC: U.S. Government Printing Office, 1982.

Minuchin, P. Sex-role concept and sex typing in childhood as a function of school and home environments. *Child Development*, 1965, **36**, 1033–1048.

Moss, H. A. Sex, age and state as determinants of mother-infants interaction. *Merrill-Palmer Quarterly*, 1967, **13**, 19–36.

Moss, H. A. Early sex differences and mother-infant interaction. In R. D. Friedman, R. M. Richart, & R. C. Vanderviek (Eds.), *Sex Differences in Behavior*. New York: Wiley, 1974.

Mulvihill, D. J., Tumin, M. M. *Staff Reports to the National Commission on the Causes and Prevention of Violence, 12, Crimes of Violence*, Washington, DC: U.S. Government Printing Office, 1969.

Olweus, D. The stability of aggressive reaction patterns in human males: A review. *Psychological Bulletin*, 1979, **85**, 852–875.

Patterson, G. R. A performance theory for coercive family interactions. In R. Cairns (Ed.), *Social interaction: Methods, analyses and illustrations*. Hillsdale, NJ: Erlbaum, 1979.

Patterson, G. R. *A social learning approach. Vol. 3: Coercive family process*. Eugene, OR: Castalia Publishing Company, 1982.

Patterson, G. R., Chamberlain, P., & Reid, J. B. A comparative evaluation of parent training procedures. *Behavior Therapy*, 1982, **13**, 638–650.

Rushton, J. P. The altruistic personality. In J. P. Rushton and R. M. Sorrentino (Eds.), *Altruism and social behavior: Social, personality, and developmental perspectives*. Hillsdale, N J : Erlbaum, 1981.

Seavey, C. A., Katz, P. A., & Zalk, S. R. Baby X: The effect of gender labels on adult responses to infants. *Sex Roles*, 1975, **1**, 103–109.

Serbin, L., Connor, I., & Citron, C. Environmental control of independent and dependent behaviors in preschool girls and boys: A model for early independence training. *Sex Roles*, 1978, **4**, 867–875.

Serbin, L., O'Leary, K., Vente, R., & Tonick, I. A comparison of teacher response to the preacademic and problem behavior of boys and girls. *Child Development*, 1973, **44**, 796–804.

Sheehan, P. Age trends and correlates of children's television viewing. *Australian Journal of Psychology*, 1984 (in press).

Singer, J. L., & Singer, D. G. *Television, imagination and aggression*. Hillsdale, NJ: Erlbaum, 1980.

Strauss, M. A., Giles, R. J., & Steinmetz, S. K. *Behind closed doors: Violence in the American family*. New York: Doubleday/Anchor, 1979.

West D. J., & Farrington, D. P. *Who becomes deliquient?* London: Heinemann, 1973.

Williams, J. F., Meyerson, L. J., Eron, L. D., & Semler, I. J. Peer-rated aggression and aggressive responses elicited in an experimental situation. *Child Development*, 1967, **38**, 181–190.

Siblings: Fellow Travelers in Coercive Family Processes[1]

Oregon Social Learning Center, Eugene, Oregon

I.	Introduction	174
II.	Violence in the Home	175
III.	Coercive Processes	175
	A. Chains as Dependent Variables	178
	B. Contexts	180
IV.	Some Hypotheses about Siblings	180
	A. Labeling	181
	B. Coercion Variables	185
V.	Procedures	187
	A. Samples	187
	B. Observations	187
	C. Dependent Variables	189
	D. Decision Rules	191
VI.	Analyses	192
	A. Who Is Deviant?	192
	B. Victim Selection by Siblings	195
	C. Mothers' Payoffs for Sibling Coercion	200
VII.	Interaction of the Problem Child with His or Her Siblings	203
	A. Context	203
	B. Final Outcomes for Coercive Episodes	205
	C. Duration of Episodes	207
VIII.	Discussion	210
	References	213

[1]The manuscript was prepared while the author was in residence at the Center for Advanced Study in the Behavioral Sciences, Berkeley, California.

Advances in the
Study of Aggression, Volume 1

Copyright © 1984 by Academic Press, Inc.
All rights of reproduction in any form reserved.
ISBN 0-12-037701-2

I. INTRODUCTION

Modern theories on child pathology treat siblings as a mild psychological irritant. At most, siblings constitute that part of the family that contributes to "sibling rivalry." The writings published in the last half century have provided a consistent matrifocal perspective in considering determinants for deviant child behavior. Whereas the current stance in developmental psychology is to study bilateral effects as they relate to child pathology, the content of these investigations largely ignores sibling (and paternal) contributions to this process. By and large, the published literature gives siblings short shrift in terms of their possible contribution to deviant family interaction.

The purpose of this chapter is to provide a modest redress for these oversights. Data will be presented that describe the coercive interactions of siblings and parents as well as those for siblings and identified problem children. The analyses will also focus on differences in sibling reactions between normal and distressed families together with the relationship of these differences to increased rates of coercive behaviors in distressed families.

There are three general assumptions characterizing the perspective from which sibling contributions are viewed. The first assumption is that families are the source of much more violence than has been hitherto believed in our society. Second, it is assumed that the innocuous garden-variety aversive events found in normal and distressed families alike are building blocks that lead to real physical violence in families. Wife beating, child beating, intense marital conflict, and extremes in children's social aggression are thought to be the outcome of relatively *normal* interactional processes that have escalated to the point where one or more members are out of control. The details of this interactional perspective as it applies to families have been outlined in Patterson (1979, 1982).

It is assumed that there is a mutuality of effects among family members. Whereas one person may be identified as the problem, the others contribute to the status of being deviant. Siblings are important contributors to this process. It is the intricate relationship between siblings and the problem child that serves as the primary focus for this article. For example, what are the variables that differentiate siblings from the identified problem child? The concept of mutuality among family members implies that, in part, the problem child's deviant behaviors may be *reactions* to sibling (and parent) initiations. Sibling reactions to the initiations by the problem child may themselves be deviant; in this sense deviancy is a shared phenomenon.

II. VIOLENCE IN THE HOME

Any illusions once held about the American home being a peaceful sanctuary were dispelled by extensive national survey studies by M. Straus and colleagues (e.g., Steinmetz & Straus, 1974; Straus, 1973). They concluded that violence seemed as characteristic of family life as did love. One survey showed over half of the sample of university students reported being recipients of actual or threatened use of physical punishment during their last year in high school (Steinmetz & Straus, 1974). In that same study, 62% reported having struck a sibling during the previous year. In another study of 150 individuals involved in divorce proceedings, 15% reported intrafamily violence (O'Brien, 1971). In Wallerstein's (1980) study of middle-class families with divorced parents, the children reported physical violence of some sort in 57% of the families. Violence is, of course, an accepted part of our culture. One-fifth of all Americans approve of slapping one's spouse; even the college educated were not exempt (Stark & McEvoy, 1970). The same study also showed that 80% of the men and 90% of the women reported having spanked a child.

In 1965, killings within the family composed 31% of all murders in this country (Field & Field, 1973). Half of these were committed by a spouse, with the other spouse as victim. It is also well known that a substantial proportion of police injuries and deaths are incurred as a result of their attempts to intervene in family quarrels (Singer, 1971). Each year thousands of children are reported to be battered by parents (Helfer & Kempe, 1968); there are even reports of siblings being murdered by siblings (Adelson, 1972).

III. COERCIVE PROCESSES

The aforementioned findings make it imperative that social scientists begin to study violence in families. One could begin such a study assuming family members involved in such violence were predisposed to do so, i.e., one or more of them possessed a *trait* to be aggressive. An alternative would be to view the occurrence of physical violence in families as the outcome of a process unfolding over time. Here, an aggressive trait may or may not be involved. For example, Straus (1971, 1973) postulated a positive feedback process that produced an upward spiral of familial aggression. I also view familial violence as the outcome of such an interactive process in which two or more members actually *train* each other to increase the rates and intensity of their attacks. These escalations are generated by the exchange of rather pedestrain aversive events among family members. It is thought that there are certain conditions under which the exchanges of these events will increase in rate and/or intensity. For example, in the Wallerstein (1980) study mentioned earlier, the children reported that, prior to the divorce, neither of the parents had been physically violent. In the present context, it would be thought that the violence that these children observed in their parents was the outcome of an escalating process.

The code system developed at the Oregon Social Learning Center measures 14 noxious events that *commonly* occur in family interactions, for example, teasing, humiliation, whining, crying, hitting, disapproval, or noncompliance, (Reid, 1978). These garden-variety aversives have been shown to occur during family interactions of normal and distressed samples alike. The mean rates across all members in normal families was shown to be .276 (SD = .191) aversive events per minute, and for families of out-of-control boys .522 (SD = .374) (Reid, 1978). Similar rates have been noted by Delfini, Bernal, and Rosen (1976) and Terdahl, Jackson, and Garner (1976).

Within the context of coercion theory, it is assumed that the parents of aggressive children are unskilled in both child management and procedures for conflict resolution. As a result of these omissions, there is for all family members a rising tide of unresolved conflicts, and a general increase in the level of coercive behavior. A series of laboratory and field studies of married couples reviewed by Patterson, Weiss, and Hops (1976) showed that in normal families major conflicts or disagreements arose on the average of one per week. Observations of problem-solving interchanges also showed that distressed couples' attempts to communicate about these problems were typically paired with aversive words, for example, "You're just like your father—you're drunk all the time." This elicited a counterattack rather than a problem-solving behavior. As a result of the well-practiced fight that ensued, an important family crisis was effectively sidetracked. Unsolved, the crisis was fated to reappear again next week. Over a period of years there was an accumulation of these unresolved issues, any one of which could produce a heated interchange. In effect, each family accumulated a collection of loaded guns, each with a hair-trigger.

It is assumed parents can be taught family management skills that will effectively control these aversive exchanges (Patterson, 1982). Not all parents have been taught these skills—they are *not* a given. In addition, the performance of even well-practiced family management skills can be disrupted by a variety of conditions such as poverty, sabotage by a spouse, prolonged illness, marital conflict, or overwhelming crises such as unemployment, psychiatric illness, and divorce. In addition, some parents may also perceive one child as special, and hold in abeyance the child management skills they have practiced effectively in the past.

It is thought that parents of children with severe conduct problems demonstrate disruption in the performance of a number of child management skills. First, they tend to track only the extremes of deviant and prosocial behaviors as being exemplars to which they might provide a consequence. They tend to not classify many protodeviant responses as being worthy of their concern, and therefore are less inclined to punish these events. In a sense, then, the timing of their punishment will be off. By punishing extremes, they ignore the higher rate preludes.

When they do punish, it tends to be less effective. Analyses of data from the Oregon Social Learning Center samples showed that parents of problem children were less effective in using punishment to suppress ongoing coercive child behaviors (Patterson, 1976, 1980a). They tended to use the same type of consequences as did parents of normal children, but when they punished, the likelihood increased that the problem behavior would continue into the next time frame, that is, parental punishment tended to make matters worse. This chain extension effect has been replicated by Snyder (1977) for parents of problem children, and by Kopfstein (1972) for institutionalized retarded children.

It is a definite clinical impression that parents of distressed children are also relatively lacking in communication (e.g., listening, paraphrasing) and problem-solving skills (neutral language, negotiating compromises, seeking alternatives). Distressed and nondistressed couples have been shown to differ significantly on these skills (Patterson *et al.*, 1976). To date, however, no data are available that compare distressed and nondistressed families on these variables.

It is thought that the inept practice of these assorted family management skills has an impact not only on the problem child but on the siblings as well. The lack of control in these families permits the problem child to be highly coercive and to be "paid off" for it. It is also likely that the siblings are allowed by parents to perform the same behavior and receive comparable payoffs. The sibling could learn how to be coercive, for example, by observing a deviant brother. Thus, the problem child may serve in the dual role of model and trainer. The siblings can see that the problem child employs whining very effectively in terminating the mother's nagging and scolding. This vicarious reinforcement could be followed by an increased likelihood the sibling(s) could try it themselves. Some of these interchanges may be directed toward the problem child, as a target, and his or her reactions will effect the likelihood of yet further depredations.

Effective performance as a coercer demands a certain amount of skill training. Not just any whine will do. It is necessary to finely tune the interchanges so that the aversive event is timed properly. For maximum effect, it should probably be accompanied by a specific facial expression, vocal inflection, and so on. Each family has its own set of implicit rules regarding what will work and what will not. Once the family has trained him or her, such a well-practiced monster can employ aversive events with all the skill of a concert master. It is a kind of two-stage process: first observe the model, then practice it on family members. One can learn about driving a car by viewing a film or a model, but, as Skinner (1969) pointed out, skilled driving *performance* requires exposure to natural contingencies.

A. Chains as Dependent Variables

It has been consistently shown that higher rates of aversive child behaviors significantly differentiate normal from distressed families (Delfini *et al.*, 1976; Johnson, Wahl, Martin, & Johanssen, 1974; Patterson, 1976; Snyder, 1977; Terdahl *et al.*, 1976). However, closer inspection of coercive behavior shows socially aggressive boys are more likely than normal boys to engage in extended coercive interchanges (Patterson, 1976, 1982). Normal boys were most likely to engage in a *single* coercive behavior lasting 6 seconds or less. For them, there was an average of 1.1 events in a chain; only 11% of the events persisted through the next 6-second time interval (Patterson, 1980). For the clinical sample, there was an average of 1.5 events in a sequence; 31% of the events persisted into the next time interval.

These extended chains of two or more coercive events in sequence have several important implications. For one thing, they provide a vehicle facilitating learning qualitative shifts in family interactions, i.e., those shifts involving increases in the intensity of the attacks and counterattacks. Presumably, these escalations in intensity over time characterize families in which physical violence occurs. According to the escalation hypothesis, violence in families is the outcome of a process; that process is most likely to occur during extended interchanges. If one person escalates in intensity, the other is likely to follow suit. Such reciprocal increases in intensity have been demonstrated by O'Leary and Dengerinck (1973) in laboratory studies. In such interchanges, one member eventually terminates the aversive exchange, that is, gives in. In so doing, that person becomes the victim. The winner is, in effect, reinforced for increasing the intensity of his or her attacks. Furthermore, when the loser stops fighting, the winner generally also stops. In this fashion the loser is reinforced for submitting. Experimental data are now available for mother–child pairs, demonstrating this reinforcement trap effect (Patterson, 1982).

The behavior of the problem child is characterized by bursts that are both more frequent and of longer duration than those for normals. If deviant chains for deviant boys are longer, then it is of some interest to discover what it is that family members do while the chain occurs. Reactions of family members during extended sequences of coercive events have been labeled *concomitants*. It is assumed they determine the length of coercive chains.

As shown in Fig. 1, the antecedent to each event in the sequence is thought of as eliciting, in a probabilistic sense, the following event, that is, its presence is associated with an increasing likelihood of the following event. A molecular analysis of mother–daughter interaction in one family showed this was indeed the case. The mother's reactions during a chain seemed to determine whether the child's coercive behavior would be brief or extended (Patterson & Moore, 1979). If the child's first complaint did not produce a prosocial reaction from the mother, then there was an increased likelihood of a second complaint by the daughter, Tina. Each child complaint in a sequence was associated with a moderate increase over the base-rate value in the likelihood of the mother reacting in a positive manner. For example, the likelihood for a prosocial reaction to the first complaint was .45, but with two complaints in sequence the likelihood of the mother being prosocial was .67, and for three it was 1.00. The data from this one family

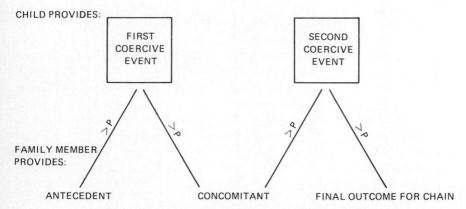

Figure 1. Components of interactive coercive chains.

suggest that, in some contexts, chain extensions may serve the useful function of producing positive payoffs. In effect, the antecedent, the response, the concomitant, and the second response represent a pattern recurring over time, and forming a type of interactional unit. E. Thomas (personal communication) has suggested these units may not be as functional as they seem: They can be predicted by simply knowing the base-rate values of the events involved. Until this issue is resolved, the functional utility of interactional units should be entertained with reservation.

B. Contexts

As pointed out by many investigators examining sequential interactions, an event can be thought of as a reaction to the events preceding it, and as a stimulus for those following. From this perspective, the behavior of the one family member may define the context for the following child reaction. The context in which events are embedded also alters the meaning attached to the functional relationship between a target event and a consequence. For example, the sequence of mother prosocial–child coerce–mother prosocial could be said to define positive reinforcement for the child's attack behavior. On the other hand, the sequence for mother scold–child coerce–mother prosocial fits the concept of negative reinforcement as defined by Hineline (1977), that is, the response is followed by termination of an aversive stimulus. The child's behavior in the second example might best be described as counterattack. In other words, context is a necessary part of the definition both for the child's behavior and for the kind of reinforcement involved.

IV. SOME HYPOTHESES ABOUT SIBLINGS

The studies reviewed earlier showed family members (other than fathers) in clinical samples were significantly more coercive than were comparable members in normal families. The question of siblings of problem children being significantly more coercive than their compatriots in normal families was explored in only one analysis of essentially a very small sample (Patterson, 1976). The analysis showed significant increases for siblings older than the problem child, but nonsignificant increases for younger siblings. In this article, these comparisons will involve larger samples and control for sex of the sibling and for sex of the target.

A. Labeling

The data show that siblings of problem children are indeed themselves coercive (Arnold, Levine, & Patterson, 1974). This raises the interesting question as to why they are not also labeled as deviant. Are the siblings different from the identified problem child? If so, what are the dimensions along which they differ?

There seems to be a modest consensus to the effect that siblings resemble each other in some general sense, and that pathology in one child is related to increased likelihood of similar problems in the other children. For example, a classroom survey of "nervous habits" showed low-level but positive correlations among siblings (Olson, 1929). The correlations between elementary school-aged brothers were .16, and between sisters, .32. Similarly, Sells and Roff (1967) found low-level positive correlations among siblings for the degree of acceptance by peers in school settings. Peer sociometric scores for Grades 3–6 were sampled across 19 cities. When the scores from members of the same family were intercorrelated, the range for siblings was .20–.38; for fraternal twins the range was .26–.40; and for identical twins .60–.77. In settings outside the home, peers and teachers perceive low-order similarities among siblings.

Lurie (1970) also investigated the relation between parent perception of impairment in siblings and in the problem child. The survey showed that 70% of the siblings of problem children were perceived as "emotionally impaired." In fact, the severity of impairment for the labeled deviant child shows a modest covariation with the severity of impairment for the sibling. These findings correspond with findings from a study of psychiatric ratings of impairment (Gersten, Langner, Eisenberg, Simcha Fagan, & McCarthy, 1976). Their ratings, based on interview data, showed a correlation of .27 between a conflict with sibling's score and magnitude of impairment for the target child. Two other longitudinal studies (Wadsworth, 1979; West & Farrington, 1973) found covariation between delinquent behavior for the target child and delinquent behavior for that child's siblings. In fact, Wadsworth showed target children with older siblings were at greater risk for delinquency than were those with younger siblings.

These findings consistently emphasize the involvement of siblings in the problem child's pathology. Certainly, conflict with siblings is one of the more frequent concerns of parents who bring their children to the Oregon Social Learning Center for treatment. It is my impression that the majority of the children referred as socially aggressive and as thieves had siblings who also presented severe conduct problems. The large-scale longitudinal study by West and Farrington (1973) provides an empirical base for these assumptions. They found a likelihood of 67.3% for delinquency in the target child given a delinquent older brother. The comparable likelihood given the younger brother was delinquent was 69.4%; the base rate for delinquency in the general population was 20%.

The Oregon Social Learning Center observation data showed that the rates of aversive behavior of the siblings were intermediate between those of normal children, on the one hand, and labeled deviant children, on the other (Arnold *et al.*, 1974; Patterson, 1976). I hypothesize that for identified conduct problem children, the siblings are "affected" by their participation in the coercive process. They have drifted some distance along a progression of steps that could eventually lead to their being labeled deviant. However, the problem child seems to perform the behaviors at a higher rate and/or intensity, and is thus more likely to be so labeled. In the Arnold *et al.* (1974) study, a mean Total Aversive Behavior (TAB) score of .75 responses per minute (rpm) for the problem child was not significantly higher than the mean-coercion mean-TAB score of .563 for siblings, $t = 1.68$ ($df = 26$; $p < .10$). The idea of siblings being fellow travelers was strongly supported by the covariation between TAB scores for siblings and problem children. The PPM correlation was .74 ($p < .001$). During treatment, 18 of the 27 parents applied the social-learning procedures to treat the siblings as well as the problem child. The termination data for 27 families showed a significant reduction in sibling coercive behaviors.

Several large-scale studies have found a relation between family size and the likelihood of antisocial behavior (Rutter, Tizard, & Whitmore, 1970; West & Farrington, 1973). To me, this suggests that in larger families *siblings exert disproportionate control.* If this were true, then family size should correlate significantly with observed rates of coercive behavior for both siblings and problem child. In keeping with this position, Burgess, Kimball, and Burgess (1978) found a correlation of .37 between family size and rates of aversive behavior for family members.

In the same vein, there are a number of studies that suggest the status of the middle child is most conducive to learning to be a social aggressor. Anderson (1969) cited her own findings as well as those from several others in support of the fact that aggressive children referred for treatment tended to be middle children, whereas neurotics tended to be firstborn children. The sample of children with conduct problems referred to the Oregon Social Learning Center also tended to be the secondborn (Patterson, 1976). Therefore, the findings for many ordinal position studies simply cannot be interpreted. The large-scale survey of the Isle of Wight by Rutter *et al.* (1970) did have base rates for various ordinal positions. Their comparisons showed that highly aggressive boys tended to be middle children significantly more often than predicted by base rates and were less often only or youngest children. This should be noted, in that base rates for different ordinal positions are not often taken into account. These findings are supportive of the position that both younger and older siblings make important contributions to the development of conduct problems. They also suggest that birth order may interact with family size in determining who will perform coercive behavior at higher rates; it is more likely if the family is large and the target individual is a male with younger *and* older siblings.

Siblings share a social environment to which they also contribute. Though this may relate to their concordance to deviancy, it is also conceivable that their shared biological processes significantly determine some of the concordance. For example, the careful study by Christiansen (1977) was based on 3586 twin pairs from the Danish Twin Register. The diagnosis of zygosity was reliably determined through blood tests. A search through the adult criminal records showed a concordance for criminality for 25% of the monozygotic male twins, and 13% for the dyzygotic male twins. The corresponding rates for females were 21 and 8%, respectively. Mednick and Christiansen (1977) present a series of papers making a reasonable, albeit not compelling, empirical case for genetic factors in antisocial behavior. Their label, *hyporeactivity*, describes the antisocial person's reaction to reduced aversive stimuli. This, in turn, they relate to a failure to learn self-control. They offer some data suggesting hyporeactivity to aversive events is partially inheritable. The *N*s are very small, and the crucial studies must be replicated before these important findings can be properly interpreted. But, as they stand, they suggest a genetic base for antisocial behavior. This may relate to the increased likelihood of siblings of aggressive children being out of control, that is, all the children in these families could be hyporeactive to punishment.

I assume that problem children display rates of coercive behavior significantly higher than those obtained for siblings. This is the primary determinant in the labeling process. The only study directly testing this hypothesis had a serious problem (Arnold *et al.*, 1974). The estimates of coercion rates for siblings and problem children were based, in part, on their reactions to each other. If one removed these bilateral effects, then it may well be that the general level of sibling coercion is indeed much lower, and, in fact, may be normal.

The alternative hypothesis, indeed the one entertained by me, is that the siblings are the key pathogens in the deviancy process. With or without the contributions of the problem child, they are more deviant than their normal compatriots (Patterson, 1982). The parents' failure to control interactions among siblings is also the key to treatment, that is, they must retain both the problem child and his or her siblings. To provide a more adequate test of the hypothesis, appropriate comparisons will be made employing larger samples, controlling for sex of siblings and for the contribution of the problem child to sibling coercive interactions.

The second major variable thought to relate to the labeling process is the role of the mother as a target for children's coercive attacks. It is assumed in normal and clinical samples that the mother is a person often selected as a target for coercive attacks. It is she, rather than the father, who is most likely to refer the child for treatment. Thus, she is thought to play the key role in determining who will be labeled as deviant. I assume she is most likely to initiate these processes for the person who hurts her the most, that is, the problem child. What hurts is her involvement in the problem child's extended coercive chains (Patterson, 1980, 1982). In addition, the data show that during these extended chains, the problem child quickly escalates in aversive intensity; siblings escalate less quickly. Incidentally, the mothers are the slowest of all to increase the intensity of attacks. Within both distressed and normal families, there are certain coercive behaviors—noncompliance, negativism, and whining—more likely associated with attacks on mothers. The kinds of children's attacks are apparently deemed appropriate as defined by the culture. It seems, then, that it may not be the kind of coercive acts, but the rate, duration, and intensity that lead to labeling as deviant.

In a later analysis, an effort was made to determine familial variables relating to status as preferred victim (Patterson, 1980). The publications of reinforcement theorists such as Catania (1966), Herrnstein (1961), and De Villiers (1977) indicated that one should not expect to find a simple covariation between response strength, on the one hand, and the likelihood of reinforcement on the other. They demonstrated in carefully controlled laboratory studies with animals that the *relative* frequency of a response covaried with the *relative* frequency of reinforcement for that response. From that framework, each subject or, in the present instance, each family may be characterized by its own internal logic.

The focus in the present context is on the process by which male and female siblings would select mothers as target for attacks. It was assumed that the relative frequency of sibling attacks on the mothers would covary with the relative frequency with which their mothers provided positive consequences for these attacks. If this correlation between relative proportions obtains, then lawful relations describing victim selection apply to problem children and siblings alike.

The fact that problem children are more likely than siblings to attack mothers may have some direct implications for the problem of labeling. It is reasonable to assume that one reason a mother labels a particular child as deviant is because the child directs *many* attacks toward her, and/or the attacks are of high *intensity*. Relatively speaking, one is likely to label that person as deviant who inflicts (relatively) the most pain. The current formulation also implies that the behavior of the victim is the prime determinant for these behaviors. This interactional stance would imply that mothers (unintentionally) behave in such a way as to increase the attacks of one or more of the children, and then refer him or her for diagnosis and labeling.

The data to be presented here do not directly address all these issues. But it does seem that mothers are the ones most likely to contact a community agency (and to involve themselves in treatment). One survey (Speer, 1917) showed that parents perceived siblings and problem children differently. Parents of problem children rated the problem child and his or her siblings on a set of four personality dimensions. Parents of nonclinic children also made similar ratings. The parents perceived the problem child to be significantly more deviant than his/her siblings, and more deviant than parents of normal children perceived their children to be.

B. Coercion Variables

As noted earlier, deviant children, in contrast to normal children, seem to be characterized by coercive chains that are of longer duration and are more frequent in occurrence (Patterson, 1976). It would be expected that interchanges with siblings would also produce coercive sequences of longer duration. As siblings acquire more coercive skills, they initiate more attacks on the problem child. His or her reactions to these increased attacks would presumably contribute to further increases in his or her coercive performance. Therefore, it would also be assumed that siblings in distressed families would provide proportionately more attack contexts than would siblings in normal families.

The mean of 50% positive outcome for coercive behavior seems to hold across age groups, clinical and normal samples, and context. This value is comparable to the mean of .42 found by Johnson *et al.* (1974). Contrary to the conventional wisdom held within social-learning theory, the final outcomes for coercive chains do not seem to differentiate distressed from nondistressed children, i.e., they do not function as determinants for individual differences in rate.[2] The earlier analysis of the familial reactions (combined data from parents and siblings) showed no significant differences in the final outcomes for coercive chains (Patterson, 1982). The nonsignificant differences for outcomes from distressed and nondistressed samples were also in accord with the comparison made by Snyder (1977). In that context, it was assumed there would be no significant differences in samples from clinical and normal families for the proportion of positive and/or negative final outcomes siblings provide the deviant, or target, child.

The key difference between problem and nonproblem children lies in the tendency of the former to engage in *extended* coercive chains. It is assumed this greater likelihood for extended chains will also characterize interchanges between problem children and their siblings. The earlier analyses had suggested it was the tendency of family members to react to coercion with countercoercion (punishment or aversive concomitant) that was a prime determinant for chain extension (Patterson, 1982).

In the current analyses, it was assumed that siblings of the problem child would be significantly more likely than siblings of normal children to provide aversive concomitants in all three contexts. The next step in the analysis will be to determine the covariation of these aversive concomitants with measures of duration of the chains. Problem children have been shown in three studies to be more likely than normal children to extend their chains if a coercive response is punished (Kopfstein, 1972; Patterson, 1976; Snyder, 1977). This response to punishment for coercion was a particular characteristic of younger socially aggressive children, and older normal boys (Patterson, 1982). The punishment extension effect occurred in both normal and distressed families if the problem or target child were punished by siblings (Patterson, 1976). In the present context, it is assumed the punishment extension phenomenon will more likely characterize punishment by siblings in dis-

[2]Prior studies showed there was no correlation between boys' rate of coercion and parent-positive consequences for these behaviors. In fact, Taplin's (1974) data showed that during treatment, when the boys' rate of coercive behavior was being reduced, the likelihood of positive consequences for these behaviors increased. See Patterson (1982) for a full discussion.

tressed families in comparison to siblings in normal families. Intuitively, one might also expect the effect to be greatest for siblings younger than the target child.

V. PROCEDURES

A. Samples

Several different analyses were carried out; each was based on sub-samples drawn from the larger population of 170 problem families and 40 nonproblem families studied at the Oregon Social Learning Center since 1968. The problem families were referred for treatment by local agencies, physicians, and counselors because one or more children were thought to have severe conduct problems. The problems ranged from stealing and fire-setting, on the one hand, to fighting, teasing, and temper tantrums on the other. About half the children had problems in school. Post hoc examination of the clinical files revealed that about one-fourth of the sample were known by agencies as abused children; about one-third had been diagnosed by professionals in the community as hyperactive and placed on medication.

The normal sample was obtained by advertising for paid volunteers who would be willing to have observers come into their home. The families were matched for age of target child and socioeconomic status (SES) level with families in the clinical sample. None of the families in the normal sample had received psychological treatment during the year prior to the study.

Fifty percent of the clinical sample were single-parent families—typically it was the father who was absent. The father was absent in 25% of the normal sample. As shown in Table I, working-class families and welfare recipients tended to be overrepresented for both samples. The classification was based on parent occupation, in turn based on the system by Hollingshead and Redlich (1956). For both samples, the median size for these families was five members. The mean age of the target sibling (the one providing the data for the functional analyses) was about 12 for the older group and about 6 for the younger group.

B. Observations

The observation coding system was designed specifically for family interaction. About half of the 29 code categories described aggressive

Table I. Demographic Data

	Social aggressive		Normal	
Variable	Younger	Older	Younger	Older
1. Mean age of target child	9.5	9.8	9.3	9.6
2. Mean occupational status[a]	5.0	4.3	4.4	4.0
3. Father present	38%	67%	85%	64%
4. Mean number of siblings	1.88	2.67	1.85	2.46
5. Mean age of target sibling	6.5	12.6	6.3	11.8
6. Mean TAB score of target child[b]	.93	.80	.21	.14

[a]From Hollingshead and Redlich (1956).

[b]The Total Aversive Behavior (TAB) score was the sum of 14 different categories that measure coercive events. The score was expressed as responses per minute.

behaviors, and the others various prosocial behaviors. The code consisted of the following categories: approval, attention, command, command negative, comply, cry, dependency, destructiveness, disapproval, high rate (hyperactive), hit, humiliate, ignore, indulge, laugh, negativism, noncomply, normative, no response, play, physical positive, receive, self-stimulation, talk, tease, touch, whine, work, and yell. A manual providing operational definitions of these categories together with the training materials was prepared by Reid (1978).

Two observers went to the home around dinner time. She or he alternately coded, in sequence, the behavior of the subject and the other person(s) with whom the subject interacted. The data were recorded continuously and provided a relatively complete, sequential account of the interaction of the target subject with all the other family members. Every 30 seconds the observer received an auditory signal from the device attached to the clipboard. At this point, the observer shifted to the next line on the protocol sheet. On the average, observers were able to code five interaction units (both members of the dyad) every 30 seconds. The data for the two observers showed an interaction unit required 5.93–6.07 seconds to record.

The data were collected by five professional observers, each of whom had had several years of prior experience using the code for family interactions. They received regular retraining sessions in order to minimize the observer drift phenomenon noted by Reid (1970).

On those evenings when reliability checks were to be obtained in the home, a single signaling device gave simultaneous auditory cues to both observers. Events had to be coded correctly by subject number and coding categories, and in the proper sequence to count as an agreement. Percentage of agreement was the proportion of the total number of events recorded by either observer for which they were in agreement divided by the sum of the total number of events noted by both observers. The sums for numerator and denominator were calculated for every 30 seconds of interaction. Five different samples of observer agreement were obtained in the present study. The mean percentages were 73.1%, 73.7%, 80.2%, 75.5%, and 74.3%. In another analysis, session frequencies were calculated for each category in 11 observer reliability checks. The reliability correlations for the categories ranged from .59 to 1.0, with a median of .91 (Reid, 1978).

A third analysis (Patterson, 1974) of observer reliability involved the units more closely analogous to present concerns: antecedents (A_1)– target response (R_j), and R_j–consequence (C_i). The protocols were examined for instances in which at least one observer noted a noxious response. The agent number and code categories were noted for the A_1s and C_is, including multiple codings of agents or categories. The A_1–R_j and R_j–C_i reliabilities were calculated separately. The total number of subjects and code events for A_1 and C_i plus the code categories listed as target response(s) were tabulated for each A_1–R_j and R_j–C_i unit. Events listed by *both* observers constituted the denominator and the events of which they agreed the numerator. The median agreement for the 14 A_1– R_j units was 56.2%, and for the R_j–C_i units was 59.9%.

C. Dependent Variables

Six to ten hours of baseline data were scored by hand to produce 34 variables thought to describe the coercive interaction of the problem or target child and the siblings. In each family, a younger or older sibling was selected as the focal point for the functional analysis. There were 11 variables describing each of three contexts, plus one variable, negative reinforcement, unique to aversive contexts. To aid the reader, the 11 variables defining interactions in aversive contexts are described in Table II.

Within each context, there were four general sets of variables. The first concerned the frequency and duration of the child's coercive chains, and the second concerned the extent to which siblings were involved. The third set defined the reactions of siblings during and following the coercive chains, and the fourth consisted of the child's tendency to accelerate beyond a single 6-second coercive response.

Table II. Description of Variables Measuring Interaction Processes

Term	Symbol	Definition
1. Chain	Ch	A chain consists of one or more coercive child behaviors carried out in sequence. A chain is said to persist until the child emits a prosocial response
	Setting variables	
2. Chain length		The mean number of coercive events in sequence; double-coded events are counted as single events
3. Percentage of chains with aversive antecedents	%AīCh	A number of aversive chains divided by the total number of chains performed by the child
4. Percentage of sibling involvement	% Sib Invol	Proportion of coercive chains in which the sibling participates. It is scored as sibling involvement if the sibling enters as an antecedent, during maintenance, and/or provides a consequence. The denominator is the number of chains in a given context
5. Proportion of positive consequences given chains with aversive antecedents	%C/AīCh	The proportion of chains with aversive antecedents that also have positive final outcomes
6. Proportion of aversive consequences given chains with aversive antecedents	%C̄/ĀCh	The proportion of chains with aversive antecedents that have an aversive consequence
7. Percentage of aversive concomitant events given chains with aversive antecedents	%Coñc/ĀCh	The proportion of chains with aversive antecedents that have one or more aversive concomitants occurring during a sequence of two coercive events. Three events in a sequence would provide two concomitants, etc. The denominator is the total number of chains in that context.
8. Percentage of negative reinforcement	%Neg Reinf	Given all coercive child behaviors, in an attack context, what proportion were characterized by positive or negative

(continued)

Table II. (*continued*)

Term	Symbol	Definition
		consequence at the end of the chain. It is really the sum of $P(C)$ plus $P(C^0)$. The denominator is the total number of chains for $\bar{A}$ context
	Child's reaction	
9. Percentage of extension for chains with aversive antecedents	%Exten/$\bar{A}$i	Given an aversive antecedent, how often did the child give more than one deviant response in sequence? The second, or nth, deviant response could consist of a repetition of the same response or any one of the 13 other coercive behaviors. The denominator consisted of the total number of chains
10. Percentage of extension given punishment for chains with aversive antecedents	%Exten/$\bar{C}$ and $\bar{A}$	Given the coercive child chains involved an aversive antecedent, and a family member provided an aversive consequence for the first and/or nth response, what was the likelihood that the child performed a second coercive response? The denominator consisted of the total number of all chains in that context in which the first (or an isolated) coercive response was punished

D. Decision Rules

Prosocial behaviors were defined by the following code categories: approval, attend, compliance, indulge, laugh, play, physical positive, receive, and talk. Coercive behaviors consisted of command negative, cry, disapproval, dependency, destructive, high rate, humiliate, ignore, noncomply, negativism, physical negative, tease, yell, and whine. The sum of these 14 coercive events is labeled Total Aversive Behavior (TAB). Neutral behaviors consisted of command, normative, no response, self-stimulation, work, and touch.

The interaction protocols had been divided into 6-second interaction units. This resulted in creating discrete 6-second units for some deviant behaviors such as cry, which were really continuous in form. A series of events sampling the same event—such as cry, cry, cry—was counted as three events defining a chain. A chain ended when the child emitted a prosocial behavior. In effect, the mean length of a chain represents a very crude estimation of duration (each event lasts roughly 6 seconds).

VI. ANALYSES

A. Who Is Deviant?

The first question concerned the assumed difference between identified problem children and normals. Are problem children more coercive? Toward whom are the coercive acts directed?

The data for this analsis were taken from various Oregon Social Learning Center samples. The samples included 20 normal, 20 abused, and 20 socially aggressive children. All children in the clinical samples were referred because of severe conduct problems. For the social aggressors, their home observation data showed their TAB scores to be greater than .45 responses per minute. The abused sample contained children identified in a retrospective analysis of community agency records as having been abused by their parents. All of the abused children had been referred because of extreme clinical problems, that is, they were socially aggressive and/or thieves.

To test whether or not the identified problem child was significantly different from children of comparable age in normal families, the mean likelihood of his or her coercive interactions was calculated for mothers, fathers, and male and female siblings as targets. In each case, the denominator consisted of the amount of social interaction with the other family member by the target child. As shown in Table III, the problem children were two or three times more likely to be coercive than were normals. In the interactions with all agents, the likelihood of attacks by identified problem children was significantly greater in the distressed than in the nondistressed families. Comparisons of within-sample differences in likelihood of selection as targets produced nonsignificant findings for all comparisons. Given that the child was interacting with a family member, he or she was about as likely to be coercive with that person as with another. The data did not address the question of which agents were most selected for interaction, but certainly these data reinforce the notion that the identified problem child "earns" his or her label. In distressed families, more than 12% of the problem child's in-

Table III. Mean Likelihood of Problem-Child Coercive Interactions with Family Members

Family agent	Abused child[a]	Normal child (N = 20)	Socially Aggressive (N = 20)	Mean	F values
		Samples			
Mother	.14 (20)	.06	.12	.11	5.45**
Father	.12 (13)	.04	.13	.09	5.42**
Male sibling	.11 (9)	.05	.14	.10	5.15**
Female sibling	.12 (15)	.04	.13	.09	8.02***
Mean	.12	.05	.13	.10	

[a]Sample size given in parentheses.
**$p < .01$.
***$p < .001$.

teractions were coercive. The target child from nondistressed families had a comparable value of around 5%.

The next question concerned the possibility that problem children came from families that were themselves extremely coercive. This time, the comparisons were made for the likelihood of a given family agent being coercive given that agent's interactions with other family members. However, some of the agent's behavior may be *reactions to* attacks initiated or perpetuated by the problem child. For this reason, family agents' interactions were analyzed that excluded interchanges involving the problem child. Given interactions without the problem child, then, as can be seen in Table IV, mothers in distressed families tended not to

Table IV. Mean Likelihood of Coercive Behaviors Excluding Those with Problem Child

Family agent	Normal (N = 20)[a]	Stealers (N = 20)	Social aggressor (N = 20)[a]	Abused[b]	F values
		Samples			
Mother	.050	.047	.051	.107 (14)	2.06
Father	.030	.023	.042 (N = 17)	.037 (8)	1.13
Male sibling	.064 (N = 6)	.045	.093 (N = 18)	.110 (8)	3.77*
Female sibling	.046 (N = 9)	.047	.077	.099 (14)	3.10*
F	1.14	1.61	3.58*	1.85	

[a]Sample sizes other than $N = 20$ are given in parentheses.
[b]Sample sizes are given in parentheses.
*$p < .05$.

differ significantly ($p < .12$) from mothers in nondistressed families. The exception was the mothers of the abused children. These mothers were twice as coercive as were mothers in the other clinical sample. There were no significant differences among fathers.

It was the data for the siblings that had surprise value. Siblings from normal and stealer samples were similar. Siblings from the abused and social aggressor samples were more coercive, contributing disproportionately to the disruption of the family. Note the mean level of 10% for boys and 8.8% for girls was only slightly less than the 12% found for the problem child. These findings were in keeping with the observations made in an earlier study of nursery school aggression (Patterson, Littman, & Bricker, 1967). In that study, children initially identified as nonaggressive received repeated attacks, to which they eventually counterattacked. Those for whom the counterattacks were reinforced eventually *intiated* attacks of their own. In like manner, siblings may model and then reinforce each other's coercive initiations. Siblings train siblings.

In families of socially aggressive children, it was the children who are out of control. The analysis of variance (ANOVA) for repeated measures showed these differences to be significant. The identified problem child was only slightly more coercive than his or her siblings. The families of stealers were not different from normals. With the exception of the father, all members of abused families tended to be out of control.

Given these findings, the problem child may serve a special function. He or she may function as a kind of psychological poltergeist, who makes an already bad situation even worse. The problem child may function as a kind of storm center that elicits coercive reactions from others, elevating their rates above their ordinary levels.

Table V summarizes the findings when interactions with the labeled deviant child were included. The analyses showed that including a non-problem target child had no effect on mean coercion levels for non-distressed families. That would be expected. What was unexpected was the fact that the problem child made only a small contribution to increased coercion likelihoods for siblings, but served as a major disruption in *parental interactions*. With one exception, the increased levels of parental coerciveness were significant.

The differences among samples were now significant for *all* family roles. Again, the normals and stealer members were consistently lower in these comparisons than members from the other distressed samples. However, the reasons for this vary. Siblings from abuse and social aggressor samples were significantly more aggressive, even with the problem child absent; his or her presence added little to their already elevated levels. With the exception of mothers of abused children, the

Table V. Mean Likelihood of Coercive Behaviors Including Those Involving Problem Child[a,b]

Family agent	Samples[c]				F values	df
	Normal	Stealers	Social aggressor	Abused		
Mother	.049	.061*	.065***	.119 (N = 14)	5.76**	3:61
Father	.033	.031**	.068*** (N = 17)	.063* (N = 8)	5.07**	3:77
Male sibling	.051 (N = 6)	.050 (N = 6)	.112 (N = 18)	.111 (N = 8)	3.91*	3:48
Female sibling	.043 (N = 9)	.049 (N = 9)	.082 (N = 9)	.103 (N = 14)	3.17*	3:59
F value	0.49	1.65	2.25	1.21		
df	3:58	3:76	3:71	3:40		

[a]From Patterson (1982).
[b]The asterisks attending the mean likelihood values signify a significant increase over the comparable value in Table IV. The differences were tested by a t test for correlated mean, one-tailed test.
[c]Sample sizes are $N = 20$ unless indicated otherwise.
*$p < .05$.
**$p < .01$.
***$p < .001$.

parents of these two samples tended to be in the normal range when left to their own devices. When the problem child was added, there was a significant increase, and these parents now differed from parents of normals (and stealers). Figure 2 summarizes these relationships.

B. Victim Selection by Siblings

The next question concerned siblings as purveyors of aversive interactions. Are male siblings more aversive than female siblings? Are siblings in distressed families more aversive than those in nondistressed families? Are siblings similar to the problem child in terms of coercing family agents at about equal rates, or do they select some as victims more than others? The data in Table VI summarize the comparisons. The dependent variable was that proportion of deviant interaction with a specific victim; the denominator was the frequency of interaction for that dyad. There was little difference among family members in the likelihoods that their interactions with the male siblings would be coercive. Being a member of a distressed sample implied a higher level of coerciveness. Given that level, then, the various family members were treated approximately in the same manner.

A second question concerned the greater likelihood of attacks by male siblings in the distressed as compared to nondistressed families. The trends for each of the 10 relevant comparisons were in keeping with the

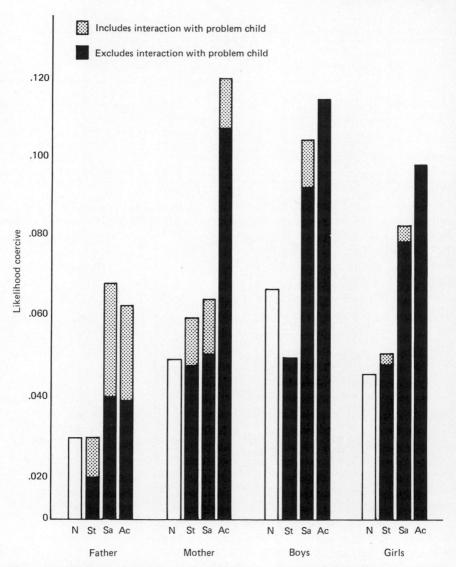

Figure 2. Likelihood of coercion by family members as a function of clinical status. N, Normal (sample size $N = 20$); ST, stealers ($N = 20$); SA, social aggressors ($N = 20$); AC, abused child ($N = 14$).

Table VI. Mean Likelihood of Coercive Behavior Given Interaction with Male Siblings

Samples	Participants[a]						
	Deviant child	Father	Mother	Brother	Sister	Mean	F value
Social aggressive	.14	.12 (14)	.08	.16 (8)	.09 (15)	.11	1.23
Normal	.05	.04 (15)	.06	.04 (8)	.05 (18)	.05	.21
Abused child	.11	.09 (6)	.13 (9)		.07 (6)	.10	.63

[a]Numbers in parentheses give sample sizes other than $N = 20$.

hypothesis; of these comparisons, 3 were significant. Male siblings from the families of socially aggressive boys were significantly more likely than their normal counterparts to have coercive interactions with the identified problem child ($t = 3.17$; $p < .05$), and with their other brothers ($t = 2.30$; $p < .05$). Male siblings from families with an abused child were significantly more likely than normals to have coercive interactions with their mothers ($t = 2.05$; $p < .05$).

The data for female siblings are summarized in Table VII. They reiterate the pattern found for male siblings. The ANOVA repeated measures showed no significant differences among agents for any of the samples. Note in Tables VI and VII the slight trend in normal samples for a cross-sex preference for sibling victims.

Between-sample comparisons produced a number of interesting findings. Given interaction with the problem child, then, sisters in distressed families were significantly more likely than their compatriots in nondistressed families to be coercive. The t was 3.00 ($p < .01$) for the comparison involving families of social aggressors, and the t was 2.50 ($p < .05$) for the comparisons involving the families of abuse children. Girls in families of abuse children were significantly more likely than girls in nondistressed families ($t = 1.87$; $p < .05$) to be coercive with their mothers. Similar comparisons for their coercive interactions with broth-

Table VII. Mean Likelihood of Coercive Behavior Given Interaction with Female Siblings

Samples	Participants[a]						
	Deviant child	Father	Mother	Brother	Sister	Mean	F value
Social aggressive	.11	.05 (18)	.07	.09 (14)	.11 (12)	.08	1.53
Normal	.03	.05	.05	.05 (17)	.02 (11)	.04	0.83
Abused child	.08 (15)	.06 (8)	.11 (15)	.09 (5)	.06 (6)	.08	0.56

[a]Numbers in parentheses give sample sizes other than $N = 20$.

ers also showed significantly greater values for girls from families of
social aggressors ($t = 3.21$; $p < .01$) and for those from families of abuse
children ($t = 2.38$; $p < .05$).

The next question examined concerned the possibility that victims
differed in the likelihood of punishment ($\bar{C}$) that they provided for coercive behavior ($\bar{R}$). Table VIII summarizes the mean likelihood data—
$p(\bar{C}/\bar{R})$—for each agent. For example, in the abuse sample, the deviant
child punished, on the average, 39% of the attacks by male siblings. In
general, other children were more likely than were parents to be punishing. Generally speaking, fathers were the least likely of all family members to punish. Male and female siblings were about equally likely to
receive punishment when they were coercive.

On the whole, sibling aggression was more likely to be punished in
socially aggressive and abused child families. By and large, they were
least likely to be punished in families of stealers and normals. This
pattern for sibling aggression matches those for comparisons involving
problem children as aggressors (Patterson, 1982).

Patterson (1976) and Kopfstein (1972) noted a greater likelihood for
children from distressed families to continue in a coercive chain when
punished for an earlier event. Would siblings from distressed families
demonstrate a similar inclination? The hypothesis was tested by tabulat-
ing the frequency with which coercive sibling behavior was punished,
and dividing this number into the frequency with which the sibling then

Table VIII. Mean Likelihood of Punishment Given Coercive Sibling Behavior

Sample	Likelihood victim will punish					
	Deviant child	Mother	Father	Brother	Sister	Mean
Male sibling						
Abuse	.39	.31	.38		.48	.39
Normal	.37	.20	.18	.39	.17	.26
Social aggressor	.37	.22	.18	.49	.34	.32
Stealer	.30	.18	.11	.25	.29	.23
Mean	.36	.23	.21	.38	.32	.30
Female sibling						
Abuse	.40	.19	.11	.29	.30	.26
Normal	.28	.20	.17	.21	.20	.21
Social aggressor	.37	.24	.22	.38	.36	.31
Stealer	.21	.14	.09	.23	.14	.16
Mean	.32	.19	.15	.28	.25	.24

went on to perform a second coercive response in the next 6 seconds. The figures in parentheses describe the corrected base-rate estimate that the coercive behavior will stop. The data are summarized in Table IX. Generally, the siblings stop after a single coercive event. The mean (of means) across samples and agents showed male siblings stopped 56.2% of the time when punished, and female siblings 54.6% of the time. There were no remarkable differences for male and female siblings in the base-rate likelihood of stop, nor did the differences by agent and sample seem to require a formal test for significance. The base rates for the stealer sample may be an exception.

Comparisons of base rate to the conditional probability values describing the impact of contingent aversives showed a surprisingly consistent effect. Whereas the magnitude varied by agent and sample, aversive consequences tended to be accompanied by increased likelihoods of continuance. This also held true for normal families. In short, aversive consequences, as they are usually employed by sisters, brothers, or mothers or fathers, tend to be followed by further coercive sibling reactions. Under the circumstances, one should probably not refer to most of the $\bar{R}$–$\bar{C}$ arrangements as *punishment*. It seems the term *nattering* would be a more descriptive term. The individual is reacting aversively as an

Table IX. Punishment Suppression for Sibling Coercion[a,b]

Sample	Mean likelihood attack will stop when punished by				
	Deviant child	Mother	Father	Brother	Sister
	Attacker: Male sibling				
Abuse	.61 (.76)	.66 (.74)	.59 (.85)		
Normal	.49 (.69)	.62 (.74)	.38 (.63)	.88 (.83)	.53 (.74)
Social aggressor	.53 (.77)	.71 (.79)	.44 (.77)	.69 (.80)	.61 (.80)
Stealer	.49 (.81)	.50 (.75)	.28 (.57)	.37 (.63)	.49 (.71)
Mean	.53	.62	.42	.65	.59
	Attacker: Female sibling				
Abuse	.62 (.88)	.77 (.70)		.42 (.77)	.98 (.89)
Normal	.67 (.81)	.67 (.74)	.49 (.70)	.63 (.85)	.58 (.76)
Social aggressor	.60 (.83)	.58 (.73)	.43 (.75)	.62 (.72)	.76 (.77)
Stealer	.40 (.71)	.38 (.62)	.18 (.44)	.32 (.63)	.45 (.69)
Mean	.57	.60	.37	.50	.69

[a]Figures in parentheses describe corrected base rate (likelihood of stop given all non-aversive consequences).

[b]Blank cells indicate insufficient data for an analysis.

expression of his or her irritation, but it is not presented as a confrontation. Nattering serves more as an elicitor for yet further unpleasant interchanges than as a punisher with a suppressing function. In that regard, the data in Table IX show one surprising consistency. Not only were fathers somewhat less likely to react aversively (see Table VIII), but when they did react in this manner they tended to be less effective. This seemed to hold in their dealings with male and female siblings across most of the samples. If fathers responded aversively to coercive child behavior, then the exchange was likely to continue.

It seems that each child must learn to make the subtle distinction between a parental nattering and those aversive reactions that indicate *stop*.

C. Mothers' Payoffs for Sibling Coercion

The next alternative to be evaluated concerned the possibility that the status as victim for sibling attacks covaries with the victim's positive payoffs for these attacks.

There were several problems to be considered; primary among them was the fact that past efforts to establish covariations of this kind were simply not successful. An observation study of nursery school children (Patterson *et al.*, 1967) showed no significant covariation between victim rankings and the likelihood of their providing a positive outcome for attacks. Furthermore, Taplin (1974) found little evidence for a covariation in rates of deviant child behavior and likelihood of parent-positive consequences. During intervention, the correlation for mothers was .28 (n.s.), and for fathers .22 (n.s.). His cross-lagged panel correlations showed that changes over time in deviant behavior "caused" changes in parent-positive consequences (rather than the converse). Finally, Taplin showed that during treatment the deviant child behavior decreased in rate whereas the likelihood of parent–positive payoffs *increased*.

The matching-law literature emphasizes the necessity of taking into account the system in which the victim is functioning, for example, to calculate relative frequency of attack within a given family, and within that context, the relative frequency of victim-provided payoffs. In the present context, the two questions of interest were (a) What proportion of sibling attacks within this family was directed to the mother? and (b) What proportion of positive payoffs for sibling attacks was provided by the mother? These two proportions were calculated separately for male sibling and female sibling attacks. The assumption made in the victim selection analyses was that the relative frequency of selection as victim would covary with the relative frequency with which the victim provided positive consequences for attacks by that particular aggressor. For example, if the male sibling directed 33% of his attacks at his mother, it was expected that about one-third of the positive payoffs he received for his attacks would also come from her.

If the relation between relative victim status and payoffs is a general law, it should hold across normal and clinical samples. To test this, data were analyzed for a small sample of social aggressors and a small sample of normals. The data for attacks on mothers by male siblings are summarized in Fig. 3. A perfect match would place the symbol for each dyad exactly on the line. As can be seen, the fit is, in fact, very close, and it held equally well for the normal as for the clinical families.

What is being done in this analysis is to parcel out the effect of individual differences among families, both in the rates of attacks on mother, and in the (absolute) likelihood of payoffs for attacks. The analysis sets aside the familial differences in level for both of these variables.[3] If one puts these individual differences "back in," then the question becomes one of why some mothers get attacked five times an hour and others only once. Do reinforcement schedules determine this? If one calculates the covariation between response strength (frequency mother victimized–frequency sibling interacts with mother) and schedule of reinforcement (frequency mother payoff–frequency sibling attack), the correlations were nonsignificant. For the social aggressor sample, the correlation was $-.48$ (n.s.), and for the normal sample $.11$ (n.s.).

Data are summarized in Figure 4 for attacks on mothers by female siblings. Again, covariations are nonsignificant for attacks by female siblings and schedule of payoffs by mothers. The probability for the social aggressor sample was $+.08$; for the normal sample $+.32$ (n.s.). On the other hand, if one parcels out the effect of differences in level of coercion and positive consequence among families, then one approaches the problem from the perspective of the attacker. From their own perspective, female siblings maximize their likelihood of payoffs by matching victim selection precisely to payoffs, just as did their male compatriots.

---

[3] I am particularly thankful to Norman Garmezy for his refusal to understand the meaning of Figure 1. The discussion with him did much to clarify some of the implicit assumptions underlying this analysis. The remaining ambiguities have been copyrighted. Later developments in my application of the Matching Law suggest Garmezy's intuition is correct. R. Vreeland pointed out a match does not obtain unless the probability of reinforcement is a constant, for example, for prosocial and deviant categories it is the same. If this is true, then a statement of matching is redundant, and one still has the problem of explaining why a mother is victimized 30% of the time. The match between relative frequency of victimization and relative frequency of payoff is a reliable effect, but exactly what it means is in doubt.

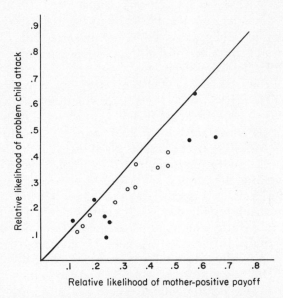

Figure 3. Relative likelihoods for attack by male siblings and positive payoffs by mothers. Normal family, ●; family of socially aggressive children, ○.

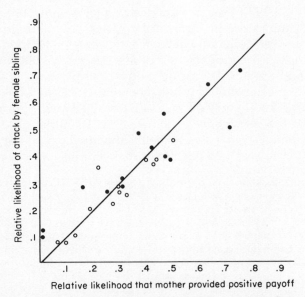

Figure 4. Relative likelihoods of attacks by female siblings vs relative likelihood of mother's positive payoff. Normal family, ●; family of socially aggressive children, ○.

VII. INTERACTION OF THE PROBLEM CHILD WITH HIS OR HER SIBLINGS

It was hypothesized that in distressed families sibling interactions made an important contribution to the coercion performance level of the problem child. The format for the investigation was a comparison design testing for differences between sibling reactions to the problem child in normal and distressed families. The format and samples were the same as the samples employed by Patterson (1982) for reactions of family members in general. The present analysis focused only on the reactions of siblings from those same families. The siblings were broken down into younger and older age groups (vis-à-vis the problem child). The 2 × 2 design (clinical and normal samples, younger and older siblings as targets) explored the context provided by siblings' behaviors and their reactions during and following the problem child's coercive chains.

A. Context

It seemed reasonable to begin with data relating to the contextual contributions provided by siblings. The earlier analyses of family members in general showed that for both normal and clinical samples the antecedent for coercive child behaviors was most likely to be positive, for example, the other person was talking or playing when the coercion was initiated.

The current analyses were based on data from the baseline protocols of two samples. The clinical sample included 34 boys referred for treatment as socially aggressive children: Their mean age was 9.5 years old. To be selected for the clinical sample, the observation in the home had to show a TAB score in excess of .45 coercive responses per minute. The normal samples included 24 normal boys matched for age, occupation level of parents, and father presence. The mean TAB score for this sample was .17 rpm. Sixteen of the boys were analyzed for their reactions to siblings younger than themselves, and 18 of the boys were studied for their reactions to siblings older than themselves. Thirteen target children were analyzed in terms of their reactions to younger siblings and 11 for their reactions to older siblings.

Table X summarizes the data separately by context, sample, and age groupings of the victim. Contexts were defined by the behavior of the sibling that occurred immediately prior to the problem child's initial coercive response. Antecedents were categorized as neutral (e.g., work), aversive (e.g., tease, hit) or positive (e.g., talk, play). The rate of episodes (per hour) describes coercive behavior in natural units, for

Table X. Antecedents for Coercive Interactions of Problem Children with Siblings

| | Mean rate coercive episodes per hour | | | | | | |
| | Social aggressive with | | Normal with | | F values by | | |
Context	Younger sibling (N = 16)	Older sibling (N = 18)	Younger sibling (N = 13)	Older sibling (N = 11)	Group	Age of sibling	Interaction
Neutral	7.30	5.13	1.77	1.53	24.99***	1.73	1.11
Aversive	5.51	4.54	2.25	0.89	14.26***	1.61	0.04
Positive	6.02	4.48	2.78	2.06	9.95**	1.60	0.20
Total	18.83	14.15	6.80	4.47	25.58***	2.69	0.31

**$p < .01$.
***$p < .001$.

example, three whines recorded in consecutive 6-second intervals would be counted as three events defining an episode. Many episodes consist of but a single 6-second event.

For all contexts, the results of the 2 × 2 ANOVA showed significant differences by sample. This was also demonstrated in the prior analysis of the reactions of all family members, including siblings. Regardless of context, there were more coercive interchanges per hour in the problem child's interchanges with siblings in the distressed than in the nondistressed families. In keeping with the prior analyses, about one-third of the coercive behaviors involved a positive context, for example, the sibling had been talking or playing immediately prior to the attack. This context tended to be selected more often in nondistressed families, whereas in distressed families the favored context tended to be neutral.

The earlier study showed that parents were involved in approximately 86% of all the problem child's coercive episodes; the differences between distressed and nondistressed samples were nonsignificant (Patterson, 1982). It was apparent when examining the protocols that many interchanges involved both a parent *and* a sibling. It was of considerable interest then to reexamine the data to determine the contributions of siblings. The analyses summarized in Table XI showed that the target siblings were enmeshed at some point in 59% of all the problem child's episodes. This figure describes only the reactions of the target child and the preselected target sibling. In that it ignored the involvement of other siblings, the figure was clearly a conservative estimate of the actual level of sibling involvement.

Table XI summarizes the appropriate comparisons using the propor-

Table XI. Proportion Target Child Episodes Involving Siblings

| Context | Social aggressor and | | Normal and | | F value by | | |
	Younger sibling[a]	Older sibling[a]	Younger sibling[a]	Older sibling[a]	Group	Age of sibling	Interaction
Prosocial	.52 (16)	.48 (18)	.66 (12)	.70 (9)	5.33*	0.00	.34
Aversive	.45 (16)	.47 (18)	.54 (11)	.38 (9)	0.00	0.68	1.14
Neutral	.81 (16)	.79 (18)	.90 (11)	.89 (8)	1.76	0.04	0.00
Total	.57 (16)	.58 (18)	.64 (12)	.62 (11)	0.81	0.02	0.06

[a]Sample sizes are given in parentheses.
*$p < .05$.

tion of sibling involvement for each context as a dependent variable. In normal families, the siblings were more likely than those in distressed families to be engaged in a prosocial behavior immediately prior to the attack. Perhaps the most interesting finding in that analysis concerned the contributions of siblings in neutral contexts. In that context, regardless of sample, the target sibling was involved in *80 to 90% of the coercive episodes.* One might think of neutral antecedents as being one operational definition for short-term boredom, that is, nothing is going on. Given such a situation, then, the target child in normal families and the problem child in distressed families may be more likely to attack a sibling. Presumably this occurs because, relative to parents, siblings are more likely to pay off attacks in a neutral context. As yet, neither of these hypotheses has been tested.

In conjunction with these speculations, a prior analysis by Patterson and Cobb (1973) and Patterson (1977) showed that siblings were the family agents most likely implicated in a certain class of coercive behaviors performed by problem children. Teasing and physically negative behaviors were shown to be members of a functionally defined response class controlled by shared networks of antecedent and accelerating events provided by siblings (Patterson, 1977). It would be of great interest to determine the impact of boredom (or noninteraction) as a controlling stimulus for events in this class. Are extended periods of noninteractions for the problem child accompanied by an increased likelihood of his or her teasing and/or hitting a sibling?

B. Final Outcomes for Coercive Episodes

For a decade, the social learning literature has emphasized the major role played by positive consequences for coercive child behavior as a major determinant for children's aggression. Several studies showed significant differences on this variable between distressed and non-distressed samples (Sallows, 1972; Snyder, 1977). A more refined analysis, using somewhat larger samples, showed that the effect may be due to a confound in the variables measuring outcomes (Patterson, 1982). In Sallow's study, the score for the percentage of positive consequences was summed across two variables—final outcome and concomitants. I assume the latter does differentiate between normal and clinical samples, whereas the former does not. When measures of concomitants were parceled out, the outcome for the problem child's coercive episodes showed no significant differences between clinical and normal samples in the likelihood of positive reactions by family members (Patterson, 1982). For both samples, the final outcome for coercive chains was positive roughly 40% of the time (cf. Table XII). In keeping with the earlier findings for family members as a whole, there were no significant differences for final outcomes provided by siblings. It seems then that siblings provide about the same final payoffs for chains as did family

Table XII. Likelihood of Various Final Outcomes Involving Siblings

| | Samples | | | | F values by | | | |
| | Social aggressor | | Normal | | | | | |
Outcomes	Younger ($N = 16$)	Older ($N = 18$)	Younger ($N = 12$)[a]	Older[b]	Mean	Group	Age	Interaction
			Prosocial context					
Positive	.43	.51	.44	.48 (09)	.46	0.03	0.79	0.12
Punishing	.32	.28	.28	.31 (09)	.30	0.01	0.03	0.25
Neutral	.25	.21	.28	.22 (09)	.24	0.09	0.51	0.02
			Aversive context					
Positive	.34	.31	.39 (11)	.37 (09)	.35	0.48	0.12	0.01
Punishing	.43	.39	.34 (11)	.45 (09)	.40	0.06	0.47	1.54
Neutral	.23	.30	.28 (11)	.18 (09)	.25	0.30	0.08	1.73
Utility	.57	.61	.67 (11)	.55 (09)	.60	0.06	0.47	1.54
Negative reinforcement	.21	.24	.23	.17 (11)	.21	0.67	0.36	2.97
			Neutral context					
Positive	.36	.34	.44	.37 (08)	.37	0.38	0.24	0.12
Punishing	.42	.38	.33	.45 (08)	.39	0.00	0.26	0.88
Neutral	.23	.28	.23	.18 (08)	.24	0.46	0.00	0.40

[a]Sample sizes other than $N = 12$ are given in parentheses.
[b]Sample sizes are given in parentheses.

members considered as a group. It is also instructive to note that in any given context there was a 30–40% likelihood for positive and for punishing consequences; either type of consequence was about *equally likely*.

C. Duration of Episodes

Analyses have shown that out-of-control boys, in general (Patterson, 1976; Snyder, 1977) younger, socially aggressive boys, were significantly likelier than normal children to engage in extended coercive interchanges.

The data in Table XIII shows that, given that the target child was interacting with siblings, then about one time in five he or she extended the event to include a second. The likelihood of chain extension was significantly higher for interactions in distressed than nondistressed families for both prosocial and aversive antecedents. Given a clinical sample, the likelihood was better than one in four that it would be extended to include a second event. These values were very close to those obtained when analyzing familial reactions to coercive child behavior.

The findings emphasize the importance of considering duration or density as *the* dependent variable for measuring aggression in children. Hartup (1979) has also made a strong argument for this perspective. Thinking in these terms raises a new set of questions, for example, what variables determine duration of aggressive behaviors? It seems to me that those variables that determine the *frequency* of coercive child behaviors may be quite different from those that determine *duration*. For exam-

Table XIII. Likelihood of Extending the Duration of a Coercive Episode

| | Samples | | | | | F values by | | |
| | Social aggressor | | Normal | | | | | |
Given context	Younger sibling (N = 16)	Older sibling (N = 18)	Younger sibling[a]	Older sibling[a]	Mean	Group	Age	Interaction
Prosocial	.26	.31	.11 (N = 12)	.08 (N = 9)	.22	20.92***	0.05	0.87
Neutral	.24	.24	.22 (N = 11)	.14 (N = 8)	.22	0.86	0.30	0.40
Aversive	.32	.28	.14 (N = 11)	.03 (N = 9)	.22	32.81***	4.16	0.79
Mean	.27	.28	.15	.07	.21	39.21***	2.15	2.18

[a]Sample sizes are given in parentheses.
***$p < .001$.

ple, it is probably the reactions of family members and/or siblings *during* series of coercive episodes that determine duration. These reactions, labeled as concomitants, were classified as neutral, positive, or aversive. The score for concomitants consisted of the frequency for that type of occurrence (positive, neutral, or aversive) divided by the number of episodes consisting of two or more adjacent coercive events. By definition, a concomitant could *not* occur *unless* an episode extension occurred. Given this situation, then one would expect to find some significant differentiations in likelihood for concomitants between clinical and normal samples because clinical samples have more chains. It is instructive to note (see Table XIV) that in all three contexts there was a significantly greater likelihood for aversive concomitants for interactions in distressed than in nondistressed families. Because of the manner in

Table XIV. Likelihood of Various Concomitants by Context

	Samples				F values by		
	Social aggressor		Normal				
Concomitants	Younger $(N = 16)$	Older $(N = 18)$	Younger $(N = 12)^a$	Older[b]	Group	Age	Interaction
Prosocial context							
Positive	.10	.10	.07	.04 (09)	2.81	0.30	0.21
Aversive	.14	.19	.04	.04 (09)	10.19**	0.31	0.36
Neutral	.02	.03	.00	.00 (09)	5.33*	0.11	0.11
Sum	.26	.31	.11	.08 (09)			
Aversive context							
Positive	.06	.02	.01	.00 (09)	8.22**	4.64*	2.04
Aversive	.22	.22	.12	.02 (09)	26.39***	2.73	2.69
Neutral	.03	.04	.01	.01 (09)	2.00	0.00	0.01
Sum	.32	.28	.14	.03 (09)			
Neutral context							
Positive	.05	.03	.12 (11)	.03 (08)	0.56	1.58	0.79
Aversive	.14	.14	.03 (11)	.00 (08)	8.84**	0.06	0.12
Neutral	.05	.07	.05 (11)	.11 (08)	0.33	1.17	0.12
Sum	.24	.24	.22 (11)	.14 (08)			

[a]Sample sizes other than $N = 12$ are given in parentheses.
[b]Sample sizes are given in parentheses.
 *$p < .05$.
 **$p < .01$.
 ***$p < .001$.

which these scores are calculated, one would expect them to be found more often in the distressed than in the nondistressed families. However, the significant differences should be equally distributed among the three types of concomitants. There is no reason to expect all of the comparisons involving the aversive concomitants to be significant.

Aversive concomitants provided by siblings may serve some unique function in maintaining coercive episodes once they were initiated. This possibility was briefly explored in a series of correlational analyses. The baseline data for the distressed and nondistressed samples were combined. Each of the six coercion variables listed in Table XV was correlated separately by context with the rate of chains (per hour) found within that context and the overall rate of chains (across contexts). As

Table XV. Correlation of Coercion Variables with Rate of Chains per Hour

Coercion variables	Chain rate within a context	Overall rate of chains
Given prosocial context		
$p(C+/Chain)$	.04	.10
$p(C-/Chain)$	.10	−.05
$p(C^0/Chain)$	−.13	−.03
$p(Conc+/\bar{R}_2)$	.16	.23
$p(Conc-/\bar{R}_2)$	.30*	.23
$p(Conc^0/\bar{R}_2)$	.13	.23
Given aversive context		
$p(C+/Chain)$	−.03	−.01
$p(C-/Chain)$	−.05	−.12
$p(C^0/Chain)$	.08	.13
$p(Conc+/\bar{R}_2)$	.28*	.34*
$p(Conc-/\bar{R}_2)$	.43**	.48***
$p(Conc^0/\bar{R}_2)$	.08	.21
Given neutral context		
$p(C+/Chain)$	−.03	.01
$p(C-/Chain)$	−.06	−.09
$p(C^0/Chain)$	.10	.09
$p(Conc+/\bar{R}_2)$	−.07	−.06
$p(Conc-/\bar{R}_2)$	.59***	.57***
$p(Conc^0/\bar{R}_2)$	−.06	.05

*$p < .05$.
**$p < .01$.
***$p < .001$.

shown there, none of the likelihoods associated with the final outcome correlated with performance rates.[4]

Because of the way in which the concomitant variable was defined (given a second coercive event in a chain), it would be expected that high chain rates would be associated with high likelihood scores for concomitants. For the 18 correlations relating to this issue, the range was −.07 to +.59; the median was +.22. However, the confound built into the two variables would *not* predict that one type of concomitant would correlate any more highly with the rate of chains than would another type. As shown in Table XV, the most significant covariations related to aversive concomitants.

This further implicates the interrelations that hold among measures of chain rate, chain extension, and aversive concomitants. It suggests that well-practiced coercers tend to continue until all aversive reactions (prior to *and* during) are terminated. On the other hand, well-practiced coercers tend to live with family members who are more likely to provide just this kind of reactions (aversive) that tend to keep things going.

VIII. DISCUSSION

The findings and the accompanying questions they raise illustrate an interactional approach to understanding the aggressive child. Clearly, the presence of a problem child affects the behavior of his or her siblings. The siblings, in turn, influence his or her behavior. Sibling behaviors define the context in which much of the problem child's coercive interchanges occur; they also serve to maintain extended sequences of coercive events. In effect, siblings are the teachers, as are the parents, for the very process that disrupts their lives. Though unlabeled, siblings are nevertheless fellow travelers in a process similar to that which led to the problem child being labeled deviant. In fact, some will progress to a point where they will be labeled deviant as well.

These findings underscore several respects in which siblings contribute to deviancy. Before summarizing the details of the current findings that relate to this issue, it should be noted that under certain conditions the presence of siblings may also make a profound contribution to more

---

[4]As might be expected, the rate of chains within contexts all correlated with the overall rate of chains. The correlations were .83 for the neutral context, .91 for aversive context, and .88 with positive context. A correlational analysis in Patterson (1979) showed the likelihood of acceleration within a context correlated moderately with the rate of chain measures.

positive features of the socializing process. Whiting and Whiting (1975) observed children in six cultures. Children in some of the primitive cultures spent extensive time each day in caring for their infant siblings. The effect of this was to significantly increase the amount of nurturant behaviors observed for both male and female caretakers. In our own Western culture, there is typically no provision made for assigning care-taking (or any other) responsibility to young children. The primitive cultures' emphasis on caretaking young siblings and other chores may have much to do with their effectiveness in training a sense of responsibility for others.

The siblings in distressed families tend to be more coercive than are siblings from nondistressed families. This difference holds even when the interactions with the problem child are parceled out. The unique effect of the problem child's interactions was to increase the coerciveness level of the parents, but added little to the already elevated levels of the male and female siblings.

Siblings were involved in about 59% of the coercive child's episodes. In all families, but particularly in distressed families, the interactions between a sibling and the problem child were more likely to occur in a neutral context, that is, while the sibling was working or watching a game, but essentially not interacting with the problem child when attacked by him or her. In any setting, given the problem child's attack on a sibling, there was about one chance in four of his or her extending the attack in distressed families, and in normal families about one chance in eight.

There was no difference in final outcomes provided for coercive chains by siblings from normal or distressed families. Furthermore, siblings from both samples were about as likely to punish as they were to give positive payoffs. There was, however, a significantly greater likelihood of siblings from distressed families providing aversive concomitant reactions *during* the problem child's commission of a coercive chain. The correlational analyses showed that these variables seemed to facilitate episode extensions.

The identified problem child coerces all family members, including the mother, at higher rates than do the siblings. In that the mother is the parent most likely to initiate referrals to professional agencies, one might conclude that in some large part deviancy labeling accurately reflects what is happening to the mother. The relative frequency of sibling and problem child attacks on the mother tended to match the relative frequency of positive payoffs for attacks provided by the mother. In effect, the mother may inadvertently contribute to attacks on herself, which leads, in turn, to the attacker being labeled as deviant. From the interactional stance taken here, it would seem that both the child *and* the mother directly determine the use of the label "deviant."

Siblings in distressed families are members of a distressed system to which all family members contribute. They are more likely than their counterparts in nondistressed families to coerce other members. There is another facet of this process that needs elaboration. Given that the other family members are behaving in a peaceful or neutral fashion, mothers and problem children in distressed families are significantly more likely than their counterparts in nondistressed families to launch unprovoked (surprise) attacks. Siblings will presumably also be shown to contribute their own measure to this general uncertainty. It seems that members of these distressed families (including siblings) may have in common a disposition that contributes to a general uncertainty in interaction.

It is our clinical impression that members of normal families either ignore a coercive (child) event, or they effectively punish it and stop it. Most of their coercive episodes consist of a single event that no one takes very seriously; the other family members ignore it and often go right on talking as if it did not happen. In a distressed family, on the other hand, a coercive event cannot be allowed to pass unnoticed. One, maybe two or three, persons leap into the fray and produce an instant explosion. Siblings and parents alike respond as if coercive events served a powerful *eliciting* function for their own coercive acts.

In keeping with this formulation, Kelly and Main (1977) taught one parent to practice benign neglect. The mother simply refused to become involved in sibling conflicts. This interesting study is certainly in keeping with the current stance at the Oregon Social Learning Center. Therapists encourage mothers and fathers who deal with sibling coercion to "Ignore it if you can. When you cannot ignore it, then use an effective punishment (e.g., time-out) to stop it."

The viewpoint taken here is that normal and distressed families can be ordered along the same dimension of coercive interaction. Similarly, problem and nonproblem children do not differ in kind so much as they do in quantity. In that regard, these data show siblings to stand at some intermediate point between normal and problem children. They tend to be slightly less coercive than the labeled problem child, but significantly more coercive than their normal counterpart.

Acknowledgments

The data analyses for this report were made possible by funding from the National Institutes of Mental Health section, Crime and Delinquency, Grant MH 29757-03. The author is grateful for financial support provided by the Spencer Foundation and NSF BNS

78-24671. Special thanks go to Kathleen Haller, Debbie Toobert, Rudy Lorber, and their platoons of work study students who painstakingly tabulated these masses of data, and then rechecked them. Finally, I wish to thank Rolf Loeber for his critique of an earlier draft of the manuscript.

References

Adelson, L. The battering child. *The Journal of the American Medical Association,* 1972, **2**(222), 159–161.

Anderson, L. M. Personality characteristics of parents of neurotic, aggressive and normal preadolescent boys. *Journal of Clinical and Consulting Psychology,* 1969, **33,** 575–581.

Arnold, J., Levine, A., & Patterson, G. R. Changes in sibling behavior following family intervention. *Journal of Clinical and Consulting Psychology,* 1974, **28,** 1–13.

Burgess, J. M., Kimball, W. H., & Burgess, R. L. Family interaction as a function of family size. Paper read at the meeting of the Southeastern Conference on Human Development, 1978.

Catania, C. A. Concurrent operants. In W. Honig (Ed.), *Operant behavior: Areas of research and application.* New York: Appleton-Century-Crofts, 1966.

Christiansen, K. O. A preliminary study of criminality among twins. In S. Mednick & K. O. Christiansen (Eds.), *Biosocial bases of criminal behavior.* New York: Gardner, 1977.

DeVilliers, P. Choice in concurrent schedules and a quantitative formulation of the law of effect. In W. K. Honig & J. E. Staddon (Eds.), *Handbook of operant behavior.* Englewood Cliffs, New Jersey: Prentice-Hall, 1977.

Delfini, L. F., Bernal, M. E., & Rosen, P. M. Comparison of deviant and normal boys in home settings. In E. J. Mash, L. A. Hamerlynck, & L. C. Handy (Eds.), *Behavior modification and families.* New York: Brunner/Mazel, 1976.

Field, M. H., & Field, H. J. Marital violence and the criminal process: Neither justice nor peace. *Social Service Review,* 1973, **47** (2), 221–240.

Gerston, J. C., Langner, T. S., Eisenberg, J. G., Simcha Fagan, O., & McCarthy, E. D. Stability and change in types of behavioral disturbance of children and adolescents. *Journal of Abnormal Child Psychology,* 1976, **4,** 111–127.

Hartup, W. W. Levels of analysis in the study of social interaction: An historical perspective. In M. E. Lamb, S. J. Suomi, & G. R. Stephenson (Eds.), *Social interaction analysis.* Madison: University of Wisconsin Press, 1979.

Helfer, R. E., & Kempe, C. H. (Eds.). *The battered child.* Chicago: University of Chicago Press, 1968.

Herrnstein, R. J. Relative and absolute strength of response as a function of frequency of development. *Journal of the Experimental Analysis of Behavior,* 1961, **4,** 267–272.

Hineline, P. Negative reinforcement and avoidance. In W. Honig & J. E. Staddon (Eds.), *Handbook of operant behavior.* Englewood Cliffs, New Jersey: Prentice-Hall, 1977.

Hollingshead, A. B., & Redlich, F. C. *A review of social class and mental illness.* New York: Wiley, 1956.

Johnson, S. M., Wahl, G., Martin, S., & Johanssen, S. How deviant is the normal child: A behavioral analysis of the preschool child and his family. In R. D. Rubin, J. P. Brady, & J. D. Henderson (Eds.). *Advances in behavior therapy* (Vol. 4). New York: Academic Press, 1974.

Kelly, F. D., & Main, F. O. Sibling conflict in a single-parent family: An empirical case history. *The American Journal of Family Therapists,* 1977, **7** (Spring), 39–47.

Kopfstein, D. The effects of accelerating and decelerating consequences on the social behavior of trainable retarded children. *Child Development,* 1972, **43,** 800–809.

Lurie, O. R. The emotional health of children in the family setting. *Community Mental Health Journal,* 1970, **6,** 229–235.

Mednick, S., & Christiansen, K. O. *Biosocial bases of criminal behavior.* New York: Gardner, 1977.

O'Brien, J. E. Violence in divorce-prone families. In S. K. Steinmetz & M. Straus (Eds.), *Violence in the family.* New York: Dodd, Mead, 1971.

O'Leary, M. R., & Dengerinck, H. A. Aggression as a function of the intensity and patterns of attack. *Journal of Research in Personality,* 1973, **7,** 482–492.

Olson, W. C. *The measurement of nervous habits in normal children.* Minneapolis: University of Minnesota Press, 1929.

Patterson, G. R. A basis for identifying stimuli which control behavior in natural settings. *Child Development,* 1974, **45,** 900–911.

Patterson, G. R. The aggressive child: Victim and architect. In E. Mash, L. A. Hamerlynck, C. Handy (Eds.), *Behavior modification and families.* New York: Brunner/Mazel, 1976.

Patterson, G. R. Accelerating stimuli for two classes of coercive behavior. *Journal of Abnormal Child Psychology,* 1977, **5** (4), 335–350.

Patterson, G. R. A performance theory for coercive family interaction. In R. B. Cairns (Ed.), *The analysis of social interactions: Methods, issues, and illustrations.* Hillsdale, New Jersey: Erlbaum, 1979.

Patterson, G. R. *Coercive family processes.* Eugene, Oregon: Castalia, 1982.

Patterson, G. R. Mothers: The unacknowledged victims. *Monographs of the Society for Research in Child Development,* 1980, **45.**

Patterson, G. R., & Cobb, J. A. Stimulus control for classes of noxious behaviors. In J. F. Knutson (Ed.), *The control of aggression: Implications from basic research.* Chicago: Aldine Press, 1973.

Patterson, G. R., Littman, R. A., & Bricker, W. Assertive behavior in children: A step toward a theory of aggression. *Monographs of the Society for Research in Child Development,* 1967, **32** (5).

Patterson, G. R., & Moore, D. R. Interactive patterns as units. In S. J. Suomi, M. E. Lamb, & G. R. Stephenson (Eds.), *The study of social interaction: Methodological issues.* Madison: University of Wisconsin Press, 1979.

Patterson, G. R., Weiss, R. L., & Hops, H. Training of marital skills: Some problems and concepts. In H. Leitenberg (Ed.), *Handbook of operant techniques.* Englewood Cliffs, New Jersey: Prentice-Hall, 1976.

Reid, J. B. Reliability assessment of observation data: A possible methodological problem. *Child Development,* 1970, **41,** 1143–1150.

Reid, J. B. *A social learning approach to family intervention: Observation in home settings* (Vol. 2). Eugene, Oregon: Castalia, 1978.

Rutter, M., Tizard, J., & Whitmore, R. *Education, health and behavior.* New York: Wiley, 1970.

Sallows, G. *Comparative responsiveness of normal and deviant children to naturally occurring consequences.* Unpublished doctoral dissertation, University of Oregon, 1972.

Sells, S. B., & Roff, M. Peer acceptance–rejection and personal development. *Final Report OE-5-0417* and *OE2-10-051,* 1967.

Singer, J. L. *The control of aggression and violence.* New York: Academic Press, 1971.

Skinner, B. F. *Contingencies of reinforcement.* New York: Appleton-Century-Crofts, 1969.

Snyder, J. J. A reinforcement analysis of interaction in problem and nonproblem children. *Journal of Abnormal Psychology,* 1977, **86** (5), 528–535.

Speer, D. Behavior problem checklist (Peterson Quay). *Journal of Consulting and Clinical Psychology,* 1971, **36,** 221–228.

Stark, R., & McEvoy, J. Middleclass violence. *Psychology Today,* 1970, **4** (6), 107–112.

Steinmetz, S. K., & Straus, M. H. (Eds.). *Violence in the family.* New York: Dodd, Mead, 1974.

Straus, M. A. Some social antecedents of physical punishment: A linkage theory interpretation. *Journal of Marriage and the Family,* 1971, **33** (4), 658–663.

Straus, M. A. A general systems theory approach to a theory of violence between family members. *Social Science Information,* 1973, **12** (3) 105–125.

Taplin, P. *Changes in parental consequation as a function of intervention.* Unpublished doctoral thesis, University of Wisconsin, 1974.

Terdahl, L., Jackson, R. J., & Garner, A. M. Mother–child interactions: A comparison between normal and developmentally delayed groups. In E. J. Mash, L. Hamerlynck, & L. C. Handy (Eds.), *Behavior modification and families.* New York: Brunner/Mazel, 1976.

Wadsworth, M. E. J. Delinquency predictions and its uses: The experience of a 21-year follow-up study. *International Journal of Mental Health,* 1979, **7** (3–4), 43–62.

Wallerstein, J. Children and divorce. *Pediatrics in Review,* 1980.

West, D. J., & Farrington, D. T. *Who becomes delinquent: Second Report of the Cambridge Study in Delinquent Development.* New York: Crane, Russak, 1973.

Whiting, B. B., & Whiting, J. M. *Children of six cultures.* Cambridge, Massachusetts: Harvard University Press, 1975.

Advances in Aggression Research: The Future

Bowling Green State University, Bowling Green, Ohio, and Tufts University, Medford, Massachusetts

I shall review the articles in this volume from the viewpoint of poly-systemic theory. Briefly summarized, living material is organized into a

Advances in the
Study of Aggression, Volume 1

set of systems and subsystems with feedback relationships not only within systems but between them; thus interrelationships occur both on the same levels of organization and on different levels. It follows that any complete picture of the causes of aggressive behavior must take into consideration all of these different varieties of systems organization (Scott, 1975).

The word *aggression* has acquired so many secondary meanings that it has become almost useless from an analytic viewpoint, although it still has some value in relating basic research to practical problems, which are usually labeled aggression. In this article I shall use chiefly the term *agonistic behavior,* defined as behavior that is adaptive in situations of conflict between members of the same species. It includes a broad spectrum of behavior patterns ranging from attack and defense to flight to passivity.

Research workers in the past have tended to concentrate their work on a single level of systems organization, often leading to false claims of universality of particular phenomena. Also, many experimenters have employed mechanistic causal models that assume one-way causation. This can be a useful formulation and has led to much interesting research. From the viewpoint of systems theory, however, such analyses are always incomplete. In the future, such research should be confined to situations where one-way causation actually exists, as in the transmission of the heredity of one generation to the next. There is no way that offspring can affect the heredity of parents. Behaviorally, on the other hand, offspring and parents show complex feedback interactions with two-way causation.

From an evolutionary viewpoint, the function of agonistic behavior should always change in the direction of preservation of living systems at all levels. In the past, most research has dealt not with the positive functions of agonistic behavior but its dysfunction, which is not only more dramatic, but is also directly related to many practical human problems, particularly those dealing with harmful violence.

At the present time, we have information from basic research that is sufficient to greatly reduce the incidence of harmful violence, but most of this knowledge still remains unused. Therefore, the two major aspects of research on aggression are the furtherance of basic knowledge and developmental research on the employment of such knowledge. In either case, one way of evaluating research is to examine it in respect to its potential for practical utilization, and in this review I shall examine each of the articles, in turn, in that context. I shall also point out areas where new research is urgently needed.

I. THE EFFECTS OF GENETIC SYSTEMS ON AGONISTIC BEHAVIOR

A. Results of Research on Nonhuman Animals

From the very first there has been strong evidence of the importance of genetic variation on agonistic behavior, derived from a variety of species of mammals and birds but also to some extent in all other classes of vertebrates. These variations include the results of sex differences, which are, in part, based on the effects of genes carried by a chromosome peculiar to one sex (the Y chromosome in male mammals, and the W chromosome of female birds). More importantly, major differences result from the action of the sex hormones, which affect both anatomy and behavior. In the large majority of mammals, males are anatomically and physiologically specialized for agonistic behavior, in contrast to the females, and the same thing is true of many avian species.

In the very first years of this research (Ginsburg & Allee 1942; Scott, 1942) important strain differences in house mice were discovered, and major breed differences in agonistic behavior were described in dogs (Scott & Fuller, 1965). In the case of the dogs, important individual differences may occur within breeds, which are closed genetic populations but within which genetic variation still occurs. Similar breed differences were found in chickens (Potter, 1949) and have been repeatedly confirmed.

All levels of organization are affected by genetic variation. In the first place, genes must act through physiological processes. Primary gene action is, of course, the formation of enzymes that modify biochemical reactions, and the interaction between enzymes acting on nutrient materials eventually results in the organization of an organism. Genetic modifications of development can affect the structure and function of the sense organs, motor organs, and the nervous system itself. As an example, the wirehaired fox terrier dog is a breed that has been selected for its ability to fight. The sense organs are affected in that fox terriers have a very high pain threshold. Further, such dogs appear to be easily excited to attack. The skin around the neck and shoulders, which is the point most often bitten in combats between dogs, is unusually tough. The teeth are large and strong, relative to the size of the animal. Contrasted with this breed is the beagle, a breed that is selected for its ability to live in packs without fighting. Whereas beagles show all of the behavior patterns associated with agonistic behavior in dogs, they rarely carry these to the point of actual combat. The pain threshold is relatively low, and the skin is thin. The long floppy ears are easily damaged in a fight, and the loose, baggy lips are such that in a fight a beagle is as likely to bite himself as he is another dog. Thus, the anatomy and physiology of these two breeds have been modified in many different ways that contribute to the contrasting form and degree of aggressive behavior— differences that can be measured objectively.

Behavior is an attribute of the organism as a whole and is manifested on the level of organismic systems. Behavior patterns, as indicated, can be modified by genetic variation. In the case of dogs, barking has been modified in beagles into a prolonged baying sound, and in the African basenji barking occurs only rarely, producing an almost barkless dog. The end result is that this behavior pattern is frequently utilized in one breed and not in the other (Scott, 1976).

Finally, genetics will affect the nature of the social relationships that are developed from agonistic behavior. Fox terriers quickly form rigid dominance hierarchies whereas beagles form only loose hierarchies in which dominance and subordination are often not apparent (Pawlowski & Scott, 1956).

The study of the effects of genetic variation on human agonistic behavior has rarely been attempted, for various reasons. The sex-related differences between boys and girls and between men and women are obvious, but they are also affected by the cultural norms for agonistic behavior, making it very difficult to determine how much of this divergence is due to genetics. What is more important, there is obvious individual variation within each of the two sexes, so that one sees some very aggressive girls and some very mild and peaceful boys. Within each sex there are obvious individual differences in physique that may lead to success or lack of success in any kind of physical combat. But other differences such as pain thresholds, thresholds of excitation, and ease of arousal of various emotions, including fear and anger, are difficult to study and measure. With modern techniques, especially radiotelemetry, it should be possible to measure emotional and physiological responses in active human beings. Research along these lines is badly needed. Because of the rarity of information regarding human genetic variation in aggressiveness, the article by Olweus is especially important.

B. A Study in Developmental Genetics

Studying the development of individual differences is one of the basic techniques of genetics. From the behavioral viewpoint, such a longitudinal study is especially important because it involves repeated measurements and allows one to see whether or not individual differences are consistent and stable. Olweus finds that differences in aggressiveness in boys detected early in life do persist over long periods and that the behavior is indeed stable. This not only applies to his own work but also to that of others which he reviews. The study is limited only by the fact that it was done on boys, omitting girls. This eliminates half the human race, but Olweus points out that in six other studies that have been done on girls, aggressiveness is also stable. While Olweus did not intend to emphasize genetics in his study, it is, nevertheless, a contribution in that area.

From the systems viewpoint, the stability of the behavior might have been even more obvious if Olweus had defined the social relationships in which the behavior occurred. The ratings were made by both peers and teachers in classroom and school situations, in which the same boys stayed together year after year. One would expect under such circumstances that stable relationships would be found between pairs of individuals, and, if the behavior had been measured with respect to each pair rather than with respect to all possible pairs, stability might have been even greater. The existence of what Olweus calls "bullies" and "whipping boys" implies the existence of a dominance order, the bully being alpha and the whipping boy omega in any particular group. A question arises as to whether the intermediate boys also fell into ranks. As Omark and co-workers have found in American school boys (Omark, Strayer, & Freedman, 1980), the formation of dominance orders is quite obvious.

The article by Olweus is also interesting in that he attempts a path analysis of his data. As he points out, this technique, which was originally developed by Wright for analyzing the effects of heredity, is only applicable in situations where one can assume one-way causation. Whereas one-way causation may occur in some respects, it can never result in any complete accounting for variation in a social situation involving feedback. In Olweus' data the path analysis accounted for approximately one-third of the variance among boys in Grade 6 and only one-fifth in Grade 9. The factors used by Olweus were ranked in importance as follows: (1) mother's permissiveness, (2) mother's negativism, (3) boy's temperament, and (4) the mother's and father's use of power assertion models (i.e. the use of violent punishment).

Of these factors, only the boy's temperament could directly reflect heredity. The other three factors reflect behavior of the parents. The path diagram indicates that the boy's temperament affects the mother's permissiveness, but no other effects of the boy's behavior on that of the parents are shown. As stated above, such an analysis based on one-way causation must always be incomplete; an analysis of relationships should account for a greater proportion of variance.

One also wonders about the effect of the peers on the behavior of the children. After all, the agonistic behavior measured is largely the interaction between peers, and they must have an effect on each other. This implies the study of dominance relationships. As with dogs, it is very unlikely that a so-called bully in a particular class will be a small and undersized individual. Also, one of the techniques for controlling bullies by peers is the ganging up of several smaller boys on such an individual. In American schools a bully is frequently a boy who has been kept back in school for one reason or another and is consequently larger. Therefore, another factor that should be studied in such situations is relative age, although Olweus states that boys in Sweden are infrequently held back, and that the chief difference between bullies and whipping boys is physical strength rather than size or age (personal communication, 1982).

The Olweus study is a sound basis for further research. The major question that it poses is that of the genetic basis of variation in agonistic behavior, studied within a single culture, that of Sweden. But if we are to make comparative studies, the factor of variation associated with culture must be explored also. We also need better measures of aggressiveness, particularly on the physiological level.

Basic research on genetic variation in human agonistic behavior is thus far from complete. The nonhuman studies have established the nature of the variables, but they have still to be verified in our own species, along with modes of inheritance, including the results of interaction between genes and between genotypes. This is a task for the human behavioral geneticist.

Development of applied research must await the gathering of basic information. But one can anticipate that it will recognize that individual variation is inevitable, and that it should be respected rather than neglected.

II. RESEARCH ON PHYSIOLOGICAL SYSTEMS

Such research has a long history in both humans and other animals, beginning with Cannon's *Bodily Changes in Hunger, Pain, Fear and Rage* (1929). Great advances have been made, albeit in a small number of animal species. Other than humans, most of this research has been done with cats, monkeys, rats, and mice. The chapter by Brain presents a

comprehensive account of current research on the physiology of agonistic behavior, and he points out that modern opinion is in favor of a
complex interaction between many parts of the neuroendocrine system.
Most researchers have abandoned the hope of finding a single control
center in some part of the brain.

Because the physiology is so well understood in many ways, current
research tends to be concentrated on problems of therapy, or applied
research of various sorts. Most investigators have found that at least half
of the violent individuals confined to institutions show some form of
neurological damage. In most studies, however, there are no comparable figures for control populations of individuals outside institutions. It
can still be argued that much of the neurological damage is coincidental.
Whatever the cause of their violence, such individuals impose a tremendous drain on the resources of our society. Three general sorts of al-
leviating physiological treatment have been advocated and to some extent have been put into practice.

A. Hormonal Treatments

The obvious hormone that is related to violent behavior is testosterone
because this is present in males. Castration has been used for centuries
to control violence in domestic animals, particularly in horses and cattle.
As Brain points out, castration has actually been used on human subjects, but the preferred method today would be the use of various antiandrogenic drugs because the effects are reversible. A general problem
relating to such treatment is that of controlling the level of the hormone.
Most of the animal research indicates that there is a threshold effect of
testosterone. Below the threshold nothing occurs, and an additional
amount of the hormone above the threshold produces no additional
effect. Also, other variable factors may be as important as the hormonal
levels. In one of the original research papers on this subject, Beeman
(1947) found that if fighting male mice were castrated and given a rest
period of several days they stopped fighting, but if they were given daily
fighting immediately after the castration procedure they continued to
fight as usual. This indicates that training has a very strong effect on
fighting behavior. Also, there are wide genetic differences in agonistic
behavior that are independent of hormones. The conclusion is that hormonal treatments can be highly variable in their effects. Research in the
future would be most productive if done from the systems theory viewpoint (for example, employing combinations of hormones and looking at
the response of the entire neuroendocrine system to changes that have
been made).

B. Psychosurgery

This treatment is perhaps the most controversial of all. As it is applied in human cases, it has usually been used to correct a behavioral problem rather than to alter a known physiological lesion. Because of their irreversible effects, and because they have many effects on other aspects of behavior than the violence that is to be corrected, such operations should be used in only a limited number of cases. Brain reviews the literature on the subject, from which it is fair to conclude that we need to know a great deal more about the function of the brain as a system before psychosurgery can be used intelligently.

C. Pharmacological Research

There is no reason to expect that a specific antiaggression drug will be discovered, any more than one could expect to find a drug that would specifically increase aggression. Almost any psychotropic drug will have some effect on fighting behavior, if for no other reason than it may make the animal feel sick. Drugs alter physiological states, and the animal or human will react to them in the context of how this altered state feels and the circumstances in which the animal finds himself. Drug research can, however, throw much light on the biochemistry of agonistic behavior. In order to get a complete picture of a drug effect, one needs to look at all of the different behavior patterns that the animal exhibits, and also to look at drug effects in different kinds of social relationships. For example, much of the work that has been done with fighting mice in the past has been done with naive subjects. We also need to know what the drug will do to a trained fighter or a trained loser, and how drugs affect particular behavior patterns. Brain's review indicates that there is a trend in this direction. Workers in this field also need to remember that they are working not only with a biochemical system but a system that involves interactions on behavioral and social levels as well.

D. Conclusion

The emphasis on curing the ills resulting from violent behavior that comes out of this research should not blind us to the fact that fear and anger, flight, defense, and attack all have their useful effects as well as being capable of harmful distortion. Research should therefore be directed toward the positive direction of improving the useful performance of individuals with respect to agonistic behavior.

III. THE ORGANISMIC LEVEL

Most psychologists have been indoctrinated with the concept of the independently behaving individual, and this concept is reinforced by statistical methods that assume that each measure is independent. Further, most psychologists (at the least the older ones) have been reared in the tradition of the stimulus–response theory, which is essentially a mechanistic concept based on one-way causation. Social psychologists are no exception, and some still hope for simple mechanistic explanations of social behavior.

Mechanistic assumptions lead experimenters to believe that if all external conditions were controlled, behavior would be entirely predictable. Such control can only be achieved in the laboratory situation, with the result that as more and more variables are controlled the experiments themselves become more and more trivial. More seriously, the assumption of independence leads them to do research only on the organismic level, even though the subject matter of the research is obviously social.

However well conducted such research may be, it neglects the social system as a major overriding variable. Because agonistic behavior is the interaction between two or more individuals, it necessarily involves the next highest level, that of social systems. I have repeatedly found in my own work that the major determinant of agonistic behavior is the nature and presence or absence of a social system, usually expressed as a social relationship within which the behavior takes place.

At the very least, the experimenters need to specify the social relationship, or relationships, in which the behavior that they are studying occurs. Relationships fall into two types, *specific* and *generalized*. A specific relationship is that between two individuals and those two only, whereas a generalized relationship is one that relates a specific individual to a class of other individuals. Thus a child may have a specific relationship with its mother, and the same child may have a generalized relationship with a whole class of individuals, as in the relationship of the child with all older people. Finally, both specific and generalized relationships can be grouped into categories, such as a group of specific child + parent relationships, and another category of generalized child + elders relationships. Such categories are an important part of human culture, and form the principle basis of the concept of "role." Thus a "parental role," which implies the existence of a child, is one part of a culturally defined parent + child relationship. The role concept itself illustrates our cultural tendency (even in science) to emphasize individuality, even to the point of artifically dividing relationships.

Applying the relationship concept to experimental research on human aggression, most of this research is done with college sophomores. The specific relationships involved are those between an experimenter or experimenters and each particular student. The experimenter also has a generalized relationship with all students, and each student a generalized relationship with all teachers. These, in turn, can be grouped into categories. Assuming that both experimenters and students are working chiefly under the influence of generalized relationships, the overall relationship is one of teacher + students. Actually, the design of the experiment is usually such that a population of one or two generalized teacher + students relationships is balanced against a larger population of generalized student + teachers relationships.

Are such relationships important? Tests for the importance of teacher + students relationships can be embodied in experimental design by utilizing at least two experimenters and analyzing the results from each on a population of student + teachers relationships. A further element in the design should be the inclusion of both male and female experimenters.

Considered as a population of student + teacher relationships, the assumption of independence is appropriate, as long as it is remembered that all of these relationships have been subjected to a common cultural experience. They cannot be completely independent, as they are all subject to a common factor acting on a higher level of organization.

Much more serious is the degree of generality of the results. The usual assumption is that the college sophomores are a sample of the whole human race, which indeed they are, but hardly a random one. Such a sample comes from a particular human culture, a particular age group, a particular educational institution, and is usually biased toward the upper brackets of socioeconomic status. Some samples may be limited to one sex. Finally, members of such a sample have had some 14 years of training in generalized student + teachers relationships. Can the results be extended to other relationships within the culture? Would the results from college sophomores apply to the relationships between husbands and wives? Or, to take a more extreme example, between criminals and police? Or, to elders and youths in a tribal society where teacher + students relationships do not exist?

Two courses of action are open. One is to gather experimental data on a variety of relationships in a variety of cultures. The other, and perhaps more valuable one, is to gather observational and descriptive data on the occurrence of agonistic behavior in a variety of relationships and cultures. This latter is the only way to avoid restricting the observed phenomenon to harmless and usually artificial manifestations of aggression.

Valuable applied research has already emerged from other aspects of laboratory studies. It has been established beyond question that the development and expression of violent behavior are strongly affected by the violence that people see, hear, and experience in the family and in the world of entertainment. Also, the "weapons effect" (Berkowitz and Donnerstein, 1982) is a powerful argument in favor of gun control.

I shall now review the article on the control of aggressive behavior in the context of relationship theory. This article, by Eron and Huesmann, is a major contribution to research on aggression. Basically developmental in design, the study has been carried out over an unusually long time period (ages 8–30) and includes samples of hundreds of individuals. The original group of subjects included 875 children, of which 409 were restudied at age 30. Subsequently, the authors conducted an intensive developmental project on 672 children from a socially heterogeneous suburb of Chicago plus 86 from two inner city parochial schools in that city. This latter study concentrated on children around the ages of 6 and 8, when differences in aggressive behavior begin to emerge, and has since been repeated in 5 other countries in widely distributed geographical regions, but all having cultures in or derived from Western Europe. Further, the authors measured aggression in a variety of social relationships and situations.

The results of these studies and the conclusions derived from them must therefore be taken seriously. As with all the numerous studies (except possibly one) on the effects of television viewing, Eron and Huesmann have found a correlation between the viewing of violence on television and violence expressed against others. The important new finding is that the authors have discovered a developmental and experiential explanation of these findings.

They report that there is a sensitive or critical period around the age of 8 years (third grade) in United States children during which they are establishing role models for social interaction. If they observe role models depicting violence with successful outcomes, they are more likely to adopt violence as part of their own personal repertoires of behavior. Testing this hypothesis, the authors taught children of this age (a) that television is not a realistic picture of the real world, (b) that the violence depicted there is not acceptable in real situations, and (c) that it is not good to act like television characters. The children were seen three times in the first year and twice in the second, and experimentals were significantly less aggressive than controls at the end of the 2 years.

From the viewpoint of relationship theory, an interesting theoretical point emerges from these studies. The authors conclude that aggressiveness is a stable personality trait which is generalized to many forms of behavior. In addition to genetic variation there are several learning processes which promote it: (1) Exposure to persons who gain attractive goals and peer adulation by physical violence (television is a primary model of this sort for at least some children); (2) aggression is normative for boys (a cultural factor); and (3) nurturing and monitoring by family members may modify aggressiveness, usually in the negative direction.

Relationship theory, on the other hand, provides a somewhat different model of the development of personality. Based on genetic variation, social behavior (including the expression of aggression) should be modified by learning and experience differentially in each social relationship as it develops, with the result that a given individual may express aggressiveness in different ways and to different degrees in different relationships. Alternatively, an individual might develop a generalized relationship toward all individuals (the general trait hypothesis), but this is less likely.

Relationship theory would predict stability in a given relationship, i.e., the more often a given behavioral interaction is repeated, the more firmly fixed the habits of the two parties should become. It would also predict that the time of onset of development of a particular relationship such as that of the peer relationship among American boys would be a critical one for determining the nature of that relationship. Incidentally, this timing does not appear to be uniform in all cultures; again relationship theory would predict cultural differences based on different belief systems and different forms of social relationships.

Eron and Huesmann report that peer-nominated aggression in boys at age 8 (aggressiveness in the peer relationship) is correlated with violence expressed in a variety of ways at age 30. These correlations are low, on the order of .25, but highly significant. It is possible that these correlations might be higher if they were sorted out according to the relationships in which they are expressed (violence against peers at age 30 should be correlated with violence against peers at the early age).

Girls, on the other hand, show only one such correlation at age 30, that of severity of punishment of children of the subject. Eron and Huesmann attribute this difference to the success of socialization training regarding the expression of aggression in girls, and they suggest that another method for controlling injurious violence would be to institute a cultural change in the form of socializing boys in the same way that we do girls. I suspect that there is already considerable variation among families in this regard, and it could be investigated.

In short, Eron and Huesmann demonstrate that the control of harmful violence and the concomitant promotion of prosocial behavior are attainable goals, at least on the levels of individuals and their primary social relationships.

IV. THE SOCIAL LEVEL

All agonistic behavior is social in the general sense of the term; expressed interaction in a situation of conflict between two or more individuals. Whether it is prosocial, antisocial, or some of each, depends on its consequences.

More importantly, agonistic behavior is expressed within social systems, and the nature of these systems is always an important determinant of its expression. Further, agonistic behavior becomes a part of the social system itself, demonstrating the reciprocal causal relationships that exist in systems.

On the principle of adaptation, social systems should develop organization in ways that promote the continuation and maintenance of each system with a minimum of effort. This principle should apply to both evolutionary processes and to those of social development. How then do we explain the existence of social systems that seemingly maximize effort and minimize the probability that the system will be maintained, as happens in systems where injurious and destructive violence occurs? Unless such a system reorganizes, we can predict that it will function in a maladaptive fashion, ranging from inefficiency, through harm to the individuals concerned, to self-destruction.

At the same time, we should not neglect the possibility that the destruction of a system may itself be adaptive, depending on the species concerned. For example, a mother raccoon and her litter form a tightly knit social unit as long as the young are immature, but when they reach sexual maturity they become mutually aggressive, the system is destroyed, and the young adults take on the solitary existence that is characteristic of individuals in this species except during the breeding season and in interactions with the ensuing litters that are born.

Some of this self-destructive quality appears in human families in our culture, where adults are expected to leave their primary families and go on to form other independent family units. Even so, much of the fighting and quarreling that goes on is maladaptive. The human family as it appears in our culture is one of the oldest forms of systems organization, one of the least complex, and one in which the greatest amount of overt violence is expressed (Strauss, Gelles, & Steinmetz, 1980). What is going on in the family? Patterson has approached this problem directly by observing family systems and using the observational techniques of human ethology.

In many ways, this article is the most interesting one of this series, in that it breaks the most new ground. It is often alleged that the human species is highly aggressive, implying that other species are not, but the data are usually indirect or lacking. This is an attempt to find out what people actually do in terms of expressed violence and to measure this in rates per hour. The method is that of human ethology: to observe, describe, count, and classify behaviors.

As with all new pieces of research, this one lacks generality. The author has chosen two populations—170 problem families and 40 non-problem volunteer control families, both working with the Oregon Social Learning Center. This is not a random sample, and it was obtained in one geographical area within one culture. Furthermore, it is a relatively small sample not involving socioeconomic variables, such as might be important in various subcultures. But a beginning must be made somewhere, and this is a sound one.

The data were collected at dinner time, probably because this was the easiest point at which all members of the family could be observed together. Casual observation of the American home would indicate, I am sure, that this before-mealtime period is also one in which a maximum amount of aggression is likely to occur. The rates therefore, cannot be generalized to all hours of the day. This raises the question of how many contact hours the children actually have and also what about behavior at other contact hours?

The principal conclusion from these data was that the whole family, and particularly the siblings, is involved in aggression, and this is especially marked when a problem child is involved. The implication is that the family system, rather than one individual (which is what is reported to the authorities), is out of control. As a remedy, Patterson recommends the technique usually followed in normal families, namely ignoring coercive behavior unless it becomes serious, when the parents step in and effectively stop it by punishment.

From a theoretical viewpoint, one can raise questions regarding the use of punishment to control aggression. Punishment, and especially painful physical punishment, is one of the most effective ways of eliciting agonistic behavior. Likewise, ignoring aggression is only effective to the extent that aggression is unrewarded. A more effective method is to

stimulate some alternate form of behavior of a constructive and rewarding sort. If force must be used—and sometimes it is the only alternative—restraint is much more desirable than punishment (Scott, 1975).

Systems analysis could be applied in much more depth to the data.
Analyzing the behavior in terms of relationships should be rewarding.
One would expect that dominance–subordination relationships would
exist and that these would be related to relative age and sex. Also, one
would anticipate that there would be a tendency to form alliances, especially with a parent against a child. Though the author is dealing with
a system as a whole, he has often analyzed it as a mechanism with one-
way causation probably because the readily available statistical techniques are of this sort. A more detailed analysis should include social
relationships.

Patterson shows that fathers are involved differently than are mothers, but one would also expect that fathers would act differently toward
daughters than sons, and that the opposite might be true in a case of
mothers. Also, we have the cultural variable that in our society males are
expected to dominate females, but in a family a mother is expected to
dominate her children, including the males. This confusion of rules is
bound to lead to difficulties and perhaps explains Patterson's finding
that mothers are more often involved in violent behavior than are
fathers.

The title "Fellow Travelers" implies that siblings are passive participants, whereas Patterson's data indicate that they are active members of
a system, and where there is a problem child they all contribute to his or
her aggressiveness. But despite all the ways in which one might hope
that future work will be done, this is a sound beginning, if in no other
way than that meaningful data had been collected that can be compared
with those obtained from other family systems in different cultures and
subcultures.

V. THE ORGANIZATION
OF AGONISTIC BEHAVIOR

In their article, the Blanchards have addressed the general problem of
the organization of aggression. In the past, I have held that behavior
adapted to conflict between species mates forms a single behavioral
system, the agonistic. I and most authors agree that this system is distinct from behavior involved in predator–prey relationships between
members of different species. I have further argued that agonistic behavior is most likely to have evolved from a generalized defensive system

against injury that would be equally adaptive against other species or against conspecifics (Scott, 1981).

At first glance, the view presented by the Blanchards appears contrary to the concept of a single behavioral system. On the basis of one of the most detailed analyses of agonistic behavior ever undertaken, including detailed descriptions of behavior patterns, effects on interacting animals, and the effects of neurological lesions, they conclude that the agonistic system can be separated into two distinct parts or systems: offensive aggression and defensive aggression, not only behaviorally but neurophysiologically. They further imply that a given animal will not combine the two but employ them as alternatives.

Which of the two systems is employed usually depends on the situation, but when cues are ambiguous, the choice of the animal may depend on its emotional response, anger leading to offensive and fear to defensive aggression. The Blanchards thus postulate for these systems a new function of emotion in addition to the four general ones that I have described (social signaling, the maintenance of behavior, the reinforcement of behavior, and the maintenance of homeostasis; Scott, 1981). The new function is that of a discriminator between two options of adaptive behavior.

Agonistic behavior is also organized through learning. In this context they state that the form of the patterns of behavior is established with little prior experience and hence may be called innate. (I may point out here that one of the principal activities of young rats is playful fighting, and this experience may also contribute to the development of these patterns). Given, however, that the *form* of behavior patterns is relatively little modified by experience, these patterns of course can become associated with given situations and with given individuals and so become organized with respect to the external environment through learning processes.

Emotional responses are even less modifiable than are behavior patterns. Yet the Blanchards imply that it is the emotions that become associated with a particular situation rather than the behavior patterns. From a theoretical viewpoint, either overt behavior or internal physiological responses are subject to conditioning, as Pavlov long ago demonstrated. Perhaps the point is, whereas behavior patterns act as operants, emotions in the sense of feelings do not, and hence may be more influenced by classical associative learning. (An emotion expressed as an external signal can easily become an operant, however.) At any rate, no one can deny the effects of learning (in the broad sense) on agonistic behavior.

The authors point out that the form of the behavior patterns in rats has the net effect of minimizing although not eliminating the chance of serious injury by the participants. Offensive bites are delivered to the back instead of the more vulnerable feet and belly. Defensive biting, though directed at vulnerable parts, is less likely to be used. All this suggests an evolutionary tendency for agonistic behavior to become optimally functional for the species.

Finally, the authors hypothesize that a similar two-system organization exists in other species, particularly mice, cats, and man. This should be a fruitful hypothesis, stimulating analysis in these and other species. For example, whereas the behavior patterns of domestic mice have been thoroughly described, they need to be reexamined in terms of targets of attack in the way that the Blanchards have done for rats. Their preliminary work indicates some species differences.

With respect to man, this extension of findings is more difficult. Behavior patterns are far less specific; from very early childhood children are taught techniques of hurting others and communicate these to each other. Some observations of fighting in young children suggest that the primary behavior pattern of offensive attack is to raise the hands high and bring them down openhanded on the head of the other individual, certainly a relatively harmless form of behavior, but children are soon taught to use their fists and even to use weapons. From the emotional viewpoint, subjective human experience suggests a split between offensive and defensive behavior, anger being associated with attack and fear with escape.

In one way rats and mice are very different from humans; they lack the capacity to form complex dominance–subordination relationships. In a group of male mice there is usually one dominant animal, all the rest being subordinate to him. The dominant animal never seems to reduce his attacks to harmless threats or signals. The losing mice also are never able to develop dominance relationships between themselves as are chickens, dogs, and people.

There may be more flexibility and hence more possibility of overlap between offensive and defensive systems in humans than is the case in rats. Further, in mammalian species that are capable of forming complex dominant orders, the animals are also capable of combining the behavior patterns available to them in complex social relationships. For example, the subordinate animal in a pair of goats may employ the pattern of offensive attitude, butting, but only in response to an attack by the dominant. Thus the same behavior pattern can function either aggressively or defensively.

With respect to the original problem of a unitary versus a double system, I do not see that there is any essential disagreement. I long ago concluded on the basis of genetic evidence that offensive and defensive behavior varied independently, and concluded that it was not possible to arrange the two on a linear continuum. I also concluded that, at least in the rat, there is an overall agonistic system subdivided into two largely separable subsystems, offensive and defensive. The two subsystems are united by a common function, that of adaptation to conflict between species mates, by the fact that they present alternate methods of adaptation to similar situations, and by the fact that they are closely related to each other in animals interacting in a social relationship. This is especially true in dominance–subordination relationships, where the dominant animal always exhibits offensive attack or threat, and the subordinate animal always shows defensive behavior or escape.

Still unanswered are the following questions:

1. Are the different patterns of defensive behavior, such as upright posture and running away, similarly separable neurologically?
2. Is the condition found in the rat a general one in other species of mammals and, indeed, in other vertebrates?
3. Is defensive behavior against other species identical to defensive behavior against conspecifics? If so, it would bolster the evolutionary hypothesis that the latter was derived from the former.

Though the evidence still rests on a very small number of species, the Blanchards raise provocative and stimulating questions that should produce further research.

VI. FUTURE RESEARCH ON AGGRESSION

Reviewing the research in this volume on the basis of polysystemic theory I find that four levels of organization are represented: genetic, physiological, organismic, and social. An outstanding omission is the level of the ecosystems: the effects of climate, temperature, availability of food, and interactions with nonspecies mates such as in the human + pet relationship. People with pets survive longer than individuals living alone; are they also more peaceful?

Except in Olweus' article, which relates genetics to human agonistic behavior, interaction between systems levels is omitted. Yet, a fundamental tenet of systems theory is feedback relationships between levels as well as among systems on the same level. Another obvious omission is the effect of cultural variation, especially that in culturally organized institutions, on human agonistic behavior.

Some of the omissions may be remedied in future volumes of this series, but many represent large fields where too little research is being done. Even in the fields represented here, there are obvious areas of ignorance. We need more basic information on the effects of genetic variation on human agonistic behavior, and the most fruitful field for future research should be that of the emotions. We shall never be able to make precise generalizations regarding cognition and emotions until we know the physiological nature and genetic variation of the emotions to which an individual is responding. Furthermore, the nature of emotional reactions is the weakest point in the physiological research reviewed by Brain.

Because research on the effects of human culture and subcultures has been neglected, it is impossible realistically to compare human behavior with that of the nonlingual animals, as the Blanchards have attempted to do in the case of the rat. Part of the cognitive organization of aggressive behavior arises from verbal codes regulating such behavior. Can these codes modify the fundamental organization of behavior that the Blanchards have described? On the animal side, interspecies comparisons (which involve differences as well as resemblances) would be immeasurably strengthened by their extension to a wider variety of species than those of the half dozen or so mammals that have been studied in detail.

Academic researchers on aggression need to venture outside the one social relationship within which most of their work has been done: the teacher + students relationship. Work with other species indicates that the nature of the social relationship is a major variable, and there is no reason why this concept cannot be explored in precisely controlled experiments among humans. One of the best designs would be to explore the agonistic behavior of an individual as it is organized and expressed in any two or more of the major relationships in which he or she is involved. Is his or her behavior toward peers in the school setting the same as toward siblings and either parent in family relationships? And how about behavior in a work relationship? The research reported by Patterson is a promising beginning, but only a beginning.

Another technique that has been seldom used in human research is that of using the relationship itself as the dependent variable, as is the case of the studies of the dominance–subordination relationships studied in nonhuman animals. Finally, we need to assess the relative needs for basic and applied research. Whereas much important basic research remains to be done, a great deal of what goes on merely gives support to that which is already known. If we could persuade people to apply what has been firmly established, and this is the province of developmental research, we could make an immense improvement in the quality of human life.

If we really want a nonviolent existence, the basic information is there. The sticking point is getting people to use it, which involves bringing about changes in stable social systems. Therefore, we need research on how to bring about social change, a problem that I addressed in an earlier volume (Scott & Scott, 1971).

In some ways, our culture readily accepts changes. As family relationships are founded on an assumption of biological heredity, we are ready to accept genetic explanations of differences in aggressive behavior. Unfortunately, genetic change, which is essentially evolutionary change, has very little practical use, involving as it does dozens and often hundreds of generations.

Similarly, our culture permits us to readily accept change related to health and medicine. If a wondrous "peace drug" were developed, it would probably be adopted immediately. Unfortunately, the physiological and medical approach to the modification of violent behavior is largely limited to individuals who are physiologically malfunctioning, and these individuals form only a relatively small part of the practical problem of dealing with violence.

As our knowledge stands today, our best and most enduring procedure for dealing with violent behavior in normal individuals is to induce positive, pleasurable, and constructive behavior in as many social relationships as possible. This is well done in nursery school and is usually continued effectively in further education. It is also practiced in many families, but certainly not in all. Outside family and educational institutions, the equivalent technique is to give an individual a satisfactory, constructive, and adequately paid job. As the person works, he or she is forming strong habits of being peaceful. If we really want a nonviolent culture, we must pay the price of providing full employment.

References

Beeman, E. A. The effect of male hormone on aggressive behavior in mice. *Physiological Zoology*, 1947, **20,** 373–405.

Berkowitz, L., & Donnerstein, E. External validity is more than skin deep: some answers to criticisms of laboratory experiments. *American Psychologist*, 1982, **37,** 245–257.

Cannon, W. B. *Bodily changes in hunger, pain, fear and rage.* Boston: Branford, 1929.

Ginsburg, B., & Allee, W. C. Some effects of conditioning on social dominance and subordination in inbred strains of mice. *Physiological Zoology*, 1942, **15,** 485–506.

Omark, D. R., Strayer, S. S., & Freedman, D. G. (Eds.). *Dominance relations: an ethological view of human conflict and social interaction.* New York: Garland, 1980.

Pawlowski, A. A., & Scott, J. P. Hereditary differences in the development of dominance in litters of puppies. *Journal of Comparative and Physiological Psychology*, 1956, **49,** 353–358.

Potter, J. H. Dominance relations between different breeds of domestic hens. *Physiological Zoology*, 1949, **22,** 261–280.

Scott, J. P. Genetic differences in the social behavior of inbred strains of mice. *Journal of Heredity*, 1942, **33,** 11–15.

Scott, J. P. *Aggression* (2nd ed.). Chicago: University of Chicago Press, 1975.

Scott, J. P. Genetic variation and the evolution of communication. In M. Hahn and E. Simmel (Eds.), *Communicative behavior and evolution*. New York: Academic Press, 1976.

Scott, J. P. The evolution of function in agonistic behavior. In P. F. Brain & D. Benton (Eds.), *Multidisciplinary approaches to aggression research*. Amsterdam: Elsevier/North Holland, 1981. Pp. 129–157.

Scott, J. P. A systems approach to research on aggressive behavior. In E. C. Simmel, M. E. Hahn, & J. K. Walters (Eds.), *Aggressive behavior: genetic and neural aspects*. Hillsdale, N.J.: Erlbaum, 1983.

Scott, J. P., & Fuller, J. L. *Genetics and the social behavior of the dog*. Chicago: University of Chicago Press, 1965.

Scott, J. P., & Scott, S. F. (Eds.) *Social control and social change*. Chicago: University of Chicago Press, 1971.

Strauss, M. A., Gelles, R. J., & Steinmetz, S. K. *Behind closed doors: Violence in the American family*. Garden City, N.Y.: Anchor/Doubleday, 1980.

Index

A

Age and size, as factors in dominance
  relationship, 222
Aggression
  and birth order, 183
  cognitions as causes, 48–52, 115
  correlations among different indices,
    112–113, 117–118
  defined in terms of human behavior,
    65
  elicited by aversive events, 15–17, 46–
    47
  elicited by physical pain, 15–17, 46–47
  and employment, 236
  evolutionary perspectives, 28–36
  and family problem-solving skills, 177,
    185
  and flight or defense behavior, 8–17
  goals of, 11–12, 15–17
  due to interaction of biological and ex-
    periential factors, 54–56, 65–66
  modeling of, 55, 129, 178
  as a negative attribute, 65
  peer rating scales, 109–110
  sibling influences, 173–214
  stability of direct observation data, 112
  systems organization, 217–218
  as a unitary concept, 4, 64
Aggression research
  analytic approaches to, 4
  applicability of, 2–4
  future of, 234–236
Aggression within families, 229–230

Aggressive reaction patterns, in males
  development of, 117–134
    genetic factors, 128–129
    effects of peers, 129–130
    role of television, 130–131
    role of testosterone, 131–134
  stability of, 104–117
Agonistic behavior, 218
  alcohol and, 79–80, 86
  amphetamines and, 79
  barbiturates and, 79
  breed differences in, 219–220
  genetic effects on, 219–222
  lithium and, 79–80
  offensive and defensive components,
    233
  organization of, 231–234
  useful aspects of, 224
Alcohol and agonistic behavior, 79–80, 86
Aldosterone and manic-depressive psy-
    chosis, 84
Amphetamines and agonistic behavior, 79
Amygdala, functions in aggression, 36–
    37, 75–78
Androgen insensitivity syndrome, 81–82
Androgenital syndrome, 81
Anger, 17–22, 47–52
Anger control mechanisms, 52–54
Angry aggression
  behaviors (human) 45–46
  causes, 47–52, 58
    challenging conspecific, 30–31, 50, 57
    in children, 51
    prerogative challenge, 50–52, 57